When sh
Where do I
What's the best

MW01099124

frommers.travelocity.com

Frommer's, the travel guide leader, has teamed up with **Travelocity.com**, the leader in online travel, to bring you an in-depth, easy-to-use resource designed to help you plan and book your trip online.

At **frommers.travelocity.com**, you'll find free online updates about your destination from the experts at Frommer's plus the outstanding travel planning and purchasing features of Travelocity.com. Travelocity.com provides reservations capabilities for 95 percent of all airline seats sold, more than 47,000 hotels, and over 50 car rental companies. In addition, Travelocity.com offers more than 2,000 exciting vacation and cruise packages. Travelocity.com puts you in complete control of your travel planning with these and other great features:

Expert travel guidance from Frommer's – over 150 writers reporting from around the world!

Best Fare Finder – an interactive calendar tells you when to travel to get the best airfare

Fare Watcher – we'll track airfare changes to your favorite destinations

Dream Maps – a mapping feature that suggests travel opportunities based on your budget

Shop Safe Guarantee – 24 hours a day / 7 days a week live customer service, and more!

Whether traveling on a tight budget, looking for a quick weekend getaway, or planning the trip of a lifetime, Frommer's guides and Travelocity.com will make your travel dreams a reality. You've bought the book, now book the trip!

Travelocity.com
A Sabre Company

Frommer's®

A New Star-Rating System & Other Exciting News from Frommer's!

In our continuing effort to publish the savviest, most up-to-date, and most appealing travel guides available, we've added some great new features.

Frommer's guides now include a new **star-rating system**. Every hotel, restaurant, and attraction is rated from 0 to 3 stars to help you set priorities and organize your time.

We've also added **seven brand-new features** that point you to the great deals, in-the-know advice, and unique experiences that separate travelers from tourists. Throughout the guide look for:

Finds	Special finds—those places only insiders know about
Fun Fact	Fun facts—details that make travelers more informed and their trips more fun
Kids	Best bets for kids—advice for the whole family
Moments	Special moments—those experiences that memories are made of
Overrated	Places or experiences not worth your time or money
Tips	Insider tips—some great ways to save time and money
Value	Great values—where to get the best deals

We've also added a **"What's New"** section in every guide—a timely crash course in what's hot and what's not in every destination we cover.

Other Great Guides for Your Trip:

Frommer's Canada

Frommer's Montreal and Quebec City

Frommer's Toronto with Kids

Frommer's Vancouver with Kids

Ottawa
with Kids
1st Edition

by Louise Dearden

Here's what the critics say about Frommer's:

"Amazingly easy to use. Very portable, very complete."

—*Booklist*

"The only mainstream guide to list specific prices. The Walter Cronkite of guidebooks—with all that implies."

—*Travel & Leisure*

"Complete, concise, and filled with useful information."

—*New York Daily News*

"Detailed, accurate and easy-to-read information for all price ranges."

—*Glamour Magazine*

CDG Books Canada
Toronto, ON

About the Author

Canadian writer **Louise Dearden** was bitten by the travel bug on her first trip to Europe as a child. At the age of 17 she left Canada to pursue adventure in the U.K., where she lived and worked for fifteen years, visiting mainland Western Europe, particularly France, as often as possible. She has resided in Ontario for the past ten years with her husband and two children. When she is not pounding away at her keyboard, Louise can be found working in her garden or traveling throughout Ontario and Quebec.

Published by:

CDG Books Canada, Inc.

99 Yorkville Avenue, Suite 400
Toronto, ON M5R 3K5

National Library of Canada Cataloguing in Publication Data

Dearden, Louise
    Ottawa

(Frommer's with kids)

Includes index.

ISBN 1–894413–33–4
ISSN: 1499–1594

1. Children—Travel—Ontario—Ottawa—Guidebooks.
2. Family recreation—Ontario—Ottawa—Guidebooks.
3. Ottawa (Ont.)—Guidebooks. I. Title. II. Series.

FC3096.18.D42 2001   917.13'84044'083   C2001–901474–0
F1059.5.O9D42 2001

Editorial Director: Joan Whitman	Map Editor: Allyson Latta
Editor: Jennifer Lambert	Cover design by Kyle Gell
Director of Production: Donna Brown	Cover illustration by Kathryn Adams
Production Editor: Rebecca Conolly	Text layout: IBEX Graphic Communications
Copy Editor: Marcia Miron	Special Help: Susan Johnson
Cartographer: Mapping Specialists, Ltd.	

Special Sales

This book is available at special discounts for bulk purchases by your group or organization for sales promotions, premiums, fundraising and seminars. For details, contact: CDG Books Canada Inc., 99 Yorkville Avenue, Suite 400, Toronto, ON, M5R 3K5. Tel: 416-963-8830. Toll Free: 1-877-963-8830. Fax: 416-923-4821. Web site: cdgbooks.com.

1 2 3 4 5 TRANS 05 04 03 02 01

Manufactured in Canada

Contents

List of Maps   vii

1 Introducing Ottawa for Families   1

1 The Best Ottawa Family
   Experiences 2
2 The Best of Ottawa for Grandparents . . .4
3 The Best Hotel Bets for Families 6

4 The Best Dining Bets for Families 8
   *A History Lesson on Canada's
   Capital* 10

2 Planning a Family Trip to Ottawa   12

1 Visitor Information & Entry
   Requirements 12
2 Money 14
   *The Canadian Dollar, the
   U.S. Dollar & the British Pound* 15
   What Things Cost in Ottawa 16
3 When to Go 16
   Kids' Guide to Ottawa Events 17
4 Getting the Kids Interested 23

   *Hey, I Didn't Know That about
   Ottawa!* 23
5 Health & Safety 24
6 Tips for Travelers with Disabilities . . .26
7 Getting There 26
   Travel-Planning Websites 27
   *Survival Tips for Traveling
   with Kids* .30

3 Getting to Know Ottawa   31

1 Orientation 31
   Neighborhoods in Brief 33
2 Getting Around 37

   The View from Here 39
   Fast Facts: Ottawa 41

4 Family-Friendly Accommodations   46

1 Downtown (West of the Canal) 48
2 Downtown (East of the Canal) 56
3 The Glebe & South Central 59

4 Ottawa East 61
5 Ottawa West 62
6 The Airport 63

5 Family-Friendly Dining   65

1 Restaurants by Cuisine 66
2 Downtown (West of the Canal) 67
3 Downtown (East of the Canal) 69
   Chow Down on Chains 70
4 The Glebe .77

5 Wellington Street West 79
6 Chinatown 79
7 Little Italy .80
8 Further Out 81

6 What Kids Like to See & Do 83

*Suggested Itineraries by
Age Group* 84

1 Top 10 Attractions for Kids 87

Canada's Government: The Basics . . .87

All About the Mounties 106

2 Museums & Galleries 107

3 Heritage Attractions 111

4 Kid-Friendly Tours 114

*Terry Fox: A Symbol of Hope &
Courage* 117

5 For Kids with Special Interests 118

7 For the Active Family 121

Maps for Active Families 121

1 Green Ottawa 122

2 Playing Indoors 128

3 Sports & Games 129

Sunday Bikedays 132

The Trans Canada Trail 134

4 Classes & Workshops 136

8 Entertainment for the Whole Family 137

1 The Big Venues 138

2 Seasonal Events 139

3 Theater 140

4 Dance 142

5 Music 143

6 Films 144

7 Puppet Shows 145

8 Story Hours 145

9 Spectator Sports 146

9 Shopping for the Whole Family 148

1 The Shopping Scene 148

2 Shopping A to Z 151

10 Exploring the Region 162

1 Hull, Gatineau & the Outaouais
Hills 162

Special Events in Gatineau Park . . .169

2 The Rideau Valley 170

3 Family Adventures 172

Index 178

List of Maps

Ottawa-Hull   34
Family-Friendly Ottawa Accommodations   54
Family-Friendly Ottawa Dining   72
What Kids Like to See & Do   90
For the Active Family   124
Exploring the Region   163

Acknowledgments

To my friends and colleagues who are members of the Periodical Writers Association of Canada, thank you for your support and friendship throughout my years as a writer. Thanks to Mark Kearney for encouraging me to pursue a writing career when I was his student. Thanks to Doug English, past travel editor at the *London Free Press*, where many of my early travel articles appeared. Thanks to my children for their patience and understanding during this project. And finally, deepest gratitude to my husband, Steve, whose generosity of spirit has given me the freedom to pursue my dream of becoming an author.

—Louise Dearden

An Invitation to the Reader

In researching this book, we discovered many wonderful places—hotels, restaurants, shops, and more. We're sure you'll find others. Please tell us about them, so we can share the information with your fellow travelers in upcoming editions. If you were disappointed with a recommendation, we'd love to know that too. Please write to:

Frommer's Ottawa with Kids, 1st Edition
CDG Books Canada • 99 Yorkville Ave., Suite 400 • Toronto, ON M5R 3K5

An Additional Note

Please be advised that travel information is subject to change at any time—and this is especially true of prices. We therefore suggest that you write or call ahead for confirmation when making your travel plans. The authors, editors, and publishers cannot be held responsible for the experiences of readers while traveling. Your safety is important to us, however, so we encourage you to stay alert and be aware of your surroundings. Keep a close eye on cameras, purses, and wallets, all favorite targets of thieves and pickpockets.

New! Frommer's Star Ratings & Icons

Every hotel, restaurant and attraction listing in this guide has been ranked for quality, value, service, amenities, and special features using a star-rating scale. In country, state, and regional guides, we also rate towns and regions to help you narrow down your choices and budget your time accordingly. Hotels and restaurants in the Very Expensive and Expensive categories are rated on a scale of one (highly recommended) to three stars (exceptional). Those in the Moderate and Inexpensive categories rate from zero (recommended) to two stars (very highly recommended). Attractions, towns, and regions are rated according to the following scale: zero stars (recommended), one star (highly recommended), two stars (very highly recommended), and three stars (must-see).

In addition to the rating system, we also use seven icons to highlight insider information, useful tips, special bargains, hidden gems, memorable experiences, kid-friendly venues, places to avoid, and other useful information:

(Finds   (Fun Fact   (Kids   (Moments   (Overrated   (Tips   (Value

The following abbreviations are used for credit cards:

AE	American Express	DISC	Discover	V	Visa
DC	Diners Club	MC	MasterCard		

FROMMERS.COM

Now that you have the guidebook to a great trip, visit our website at **www.frommers.com** for travel information on nearly 2,000 destinations. With features updated regularly, we give you instant access to the most current trip-planning information available. At Frommers.com, you'll also find the best prices on air fares, accommodations, and car rentals—you can even book travel online though our travel booking partners. At Frommers.com you'll find the following:

- Daily Newsletter highlighting the best travel deals
- Hot Spot of the Month/Vacation Sweepstakes & Travel Photo Contest
- More than 200 Travel Message Boards
- Outspoken Newsletters and Feature Articles on travel bargains, vacation ideas, tips & resources, and more!

Introducing Ottawa for Families

My first visit to Ottawa was as a guest at the biggest birthday party I'd ever attended. There were thousands of party-goers decked out in red and white, but the atmosphere in the huge crowd was benevolent and relaxed. As we threaded our way along the downtown streets, we exchanged smiles and greetings with strangers, bound by our nationality. I remember the day as a blur of pageantry, ceremony, music, and dancing, with a grand finale of fireworks exploding in the sky. Celebrating Canada Day in the nation's capital turned out to be one of the best family vacations I have ever taken and sparked an affection for Ottawa that has continued to grow over the past 6 years.

Since the trip involved three generations of our family and since Ottawa offers such a wide choice of suite accommodations, for the first time we booked into a two-bedroom hotel suite with a kitchenette. With our group including two small children and two pairs of adults whose taste in food sat at opposite ends of the spectrum, having our own kitchen made meal times a breeze. Two bedrooms, a living/dining room, and a balcony gave us enough room to spread out and let everyone have their own space. We could tuck the kids in at their normal bedtime, then put our feet up and enjoy a glass of wine while we planned the next day's fun in peace. Suddenly a vacation with children seemed like a good idea instead of an exercise in temper control. We were sold on suites for family vacation accommodation on that trip, and we've used them ever since.

During the Canada Day celebrations, we took shelter from a sudden brief rain shower in the alcove of a downtown building, along with a string quartet made up of bilingual teenagers. The music entertained us, but they won our hearts while chattering away to one another between pieces. Their easy blend of French and English innocently swept separatism aside.

But Ottawa wasn't finished with charming us yet. One sultry summer evening, leaving the kids with their grandparents, my spouse and I strolled down to the ByWard Market. We discovered a tiny restaurant hidden in a cobblestone courtyard off George Street, in an area of carefully preserved stone buildings that provided a welcome escape from the 20th century. Sheltered from the noise and light of the city, and enclosed by history, we sipped a cool drink on the terrace and watched the stars come out in the evening sky.

More pleasant surprises were in store when we ventured into museums and other attractions in the city. The exhibits were first class but admission fees were decidedly lower end. Once the excitement of Canada Day had subsided, the city settled back into its regular routine and the lack of crowds was refreshing. As a bonus for stroller-pushing parents, 8-year-old legs, and middle-aged feet, most of the tourist destinations were conveniently located within easy walking distance of each other in the downtown core.

Our next visit was in the wintertime. We dealt with mountains of snow, bitter winds, and expanses of ice. But the weather didn't slow us down. We took a daytrip to ski at Mont Ste-Marie, driving along a scenic roadway past snowy hills, rocky outcrops, and frozen lakes in the Outaouais Hills. We trudged through drifts to visit the farm animals at the Agriculture Museum. We *almost* went skating on the canal but a recent warm spell had weakened the ice, so we had to tuck that experience away for a future visit.

A year ago our family moved within easy driving distance of Ottawa, and suddenly we felt more like residents than tourists. We began to shop, eat, and play in Ottawa regularly and grew to appreciate the city more and more as we discovered its many treasures.

Now, having experienced Ottawa's national museums, comfortable accommodations, heritage attractions, world-class entertainment, excellent cuisine, and satisfying shopping, and having traveled the city's vast green spaces, networks of pathways, beautiful parks, waterways, and safe streets as both a researcher and a tourist, I can enthusiastically recommend Ottawa for a family vacation. I'm not a native, so I may still be looking at the city through tourist–tinted glasses, but I find Ottawa to be bursting with attractions and activities for families. Every time I visit I discover something new and exciting. I hope that you do too.

1 The Best Ottawa Family Experiences

Here are some of the best activities to do with your kids in and around Ottawa. Tailor each one to suit the ages and abilities in your family. See chapter 6, "What Kids Like to See & Do," p. 84 for specific age recommendations.

- **Celebrating Canada's Birthday:** Spend Canada Day in the nation's capital—there's no experience quite like it. Head downtown and prepare for a full day of uniquely Canadian celebrations. Start the day with the ceremony of the changing of the guard. Watch the Canadian flag rise above the Peace Tower on Parliament Hill, chat with one of the Mounties mingling with the crowds, and take in a free concert. Have your face painted or tattooed (temporarily) in red and white, wave a paper flag, and buy a hat or T-shirt with a Canadian symbol to blend in with the throngs of people wandering the streets. Watch the Snowbirds' airshow overhead at midday, and in the evening, cast your eyes skyward again for the best fireworks display of the year. See chapter 2, p. 20.

- **Skating on the Rideau Canal:** Skating in your home town most likely takes place at an indoor community rink, where you end up skating around … and around … and around. An hour or two of that is enough to make anyone hang up their blades for good. But in Ottawa, you can experience the world's ultimate skating rink—the Rideau Canal—which offers almost 8 kilometres (5 miles) of wide-open space, ever-changing scenery, warm-up huts stationed along the way, places to sip a hot chocolate or munch a Beaver Tail, and lots and lots of ice. Skate and sled rentals are available. See chapter 7, p. 134.

- **Enjoying the Waterways:** Ottawa's history is deeply tied to the waterways in the region, and the scenic Ottawa River, Rideau River, and Rideau Canal make a major contribution to the beauty of the city today. You can take a boat tour of the Ottawa River or the Canal, rent a paddleboat, canoe, or kayak on Dow's Lake, picnic on the city's riverbanks, sizzle on a sandy beach, or ride the white water of the Ottawa River northwest of the city. See chapter 6, p. 96.

- **Spending a Day at the Canadian Museum of Civilization:** This stunning, award-winning building holds some of the most impressive museum exhibits I've seen. Life-size renderings of the social, cultural, and material history of Canada since the landing of the first Europeans in A.D. 1000 will captivate even the most reluctant museum-goer. The majestic Grand Hall displays more than 40 gigantic totem poles from the Pacific Northwest. The Children's Museum, which the kids will stay in all day if you let them, is housed within the building, as is the Postal Museum. An IMAX theater, two restaurants, two boutiques, and an extensive outdoor children's playground round off the attractions. Spend a day here? You might want to spend two. See chapter 6, p. 98.

- **Sinking Your Teeth into a Beaver Tail:** Visit the original stand in the ByWard Market of this now famous fast-food treat, which was first served in 1978 and now enjoys a huge following. But don't worry—there are no real furry creatures involved. Beaver Tails are flat, deep-fried pastries shaped like a beaver tail. But with toppings like drizzled chocolate, cinnamon and sugar, garlic, and cheese, they certainly taste better. See chapter 5, p. 75.

- **Viewing the Parliament Buildings and the Ottawa Skyline:** From the Alexandra Bridge, Jacques-Cartier Park in Hull, and the pathways along the north shore of the Ottawa River, you'll get a breathtaking view of the Parliament Buildings and the Ottawa skyline. The view from the Capital Infocentre on Wellington Street facing toward the front of Parliament Hill is also a Kodak moment. See chapter 3, p. 31.

- **Riding to the Top of the Peace Tower:** When you've taken in the grace and majesty of the exterior of the Parliament Buildings, hop in the elevator and ride up to the observation deck at the top of the Peace Tower. Built between 1919 and 1927, the 92-meter (302 ft.) tower is a memorial to the more than 60,000 Canadian soldiers who lost their lives during World War I. The glass-enclosed observation deck offers magnificent views in all directions. See chapter 6, p. 89.

- **Strolling the ByWard Market:** The ByWard Market district has something for everyone, from funky shops to swank restaurants, outdoor cafes, and an authentic farmer's market with excellent quality fresh produce and flowers. The place bustles with activity and bubbles with a lively personality. See chapter 6, p. 112.

- **Tiptoeing through the Tulips:** Visit Ottawa in mid-May and you'll be dazzled by literally millions of tulips blooming throughout the capital region. Commissioner's Park, alongside Dow's Lake, features an orchestrated display of tulip beds with over 300,000 blooms. Many of the events of the 10-day Canadian Tulip Festival take place in Major Hill's Park, northeast of the Parliament Buildings and behind the Fairmont Château Laurier Hotel.

Ottawa's festival of tulips began with a gift of 100,000 bulbs from the Dutch royal family after World War II. Since then, the tulips of Ottawa have grown to represent international friendship and the arrival of spring in Canada. See chapter 2, p. 19.

2 The Best of Ottawa for Grandparents

There are as many different kinds of grandparents as there are grandchildren. Some grandparents like to keep active with walking, cycling, and skating, some like to sit quietly and read together, and others like to while away an afternoon window shopping. But whatever their style, all grandparents like to share their special interests with their grandkids and treat them to something special when they get the chance to spend some time together. Here are a few suggestions for vacation treats the older generation can enjoy with the youngsters.

- **Best Attractions:** Ottawa has so many top attractions appealing to all age groups that it's difficult and perhaps a little unfair to single out a few. Browse the animal barns, demonstrations, and special events at the **Agriculture Museum,** and take in the dinosaurs, rocks and minerals, and creepy critters at the **Museum of Nature.** At the **RCMP Musical Ride Centre,** tour the stables and watch the Mounties rehearse their routines free of charge. Visit the **Aviation Museum,** with its large collection of authentic aircraft, and the exceptional **Canadian Museum of Civilization,** with its world-class exhibits, IMAX films, and Children's Museum. See chapter 6.

- **Best Outdoors:** Head for **Gatineau Park** across the river in Quebec in any season and enjoy the hiking trails. Drop into the visitor center before you hike and buy a trail map showing the topography in detail so you can select hiking trails to suit your fitness level and ability. See chapter 7, p. 127.

- **Best Fancy Dining:** There is nothing more civilized than afternoon tea, and **Zoe's** at the **Fairmont Château Laurier** (1 Rideau St. ✆ **613/241-1414**) does it very well. Waiters in waistcoats and bow ties serve afternoon tea, complete with white linen and a silver tea service, in the glass-enclosed terrace of **Zoe's** restaurant (to the right of the main hotel lobby), Monday to Friday from 3 to 5:30pm. Reservations are recommended. Make sure your grandchildren bring their best table manners with them, as well as an appetite for fresh fruit, seasonal fruit tartlets, tea cakes, Victorian scones with Devonshire cream and strawberry jam, and dainty finger sandwiches, all served with tea, coffee, or juice. See chapter 5, p. 71.

- **Best Casual Dining:** The **Elgin Street Diner** (374 Elgin St. ✆ **613/237-9700**) is a comfy, neighborhood kind of place where you can saunter in, flop into a chair, and hang out with a coffee while the kids slurp milkshakes and chomp peanut butter and jam sandwiches. There are plenty of old-fashioned dinners on the menu, including meatloaf, shepherd's pie, and liver and onions. See chapter 5, p. 69.

- **Best Shopping:** Cuddling up in a cozy armchair to read a book together is a favorite pastime of grandparents and grandchildren. **Chapters** has become a familiar name with Canadian shoppers over the past few years, and with five locations to choose from in the Ottawa area, you're never far from their extensive selection of books, magazines, computer software, and music. The children's section is large, with a reading area, a CD-ROM station, and books for every age group. Some stores hold children's story times as often as twice daily—call ahead to find out about scheduled events. Branches are located at 47 Rideau St. (© **613/241-0073**), 2735 Iris St. (© **613/596-3003**), 2210 Bank St. (© **613/521-9199**), 2401 City Park Dr. (© **613/744-5175**), and 400 Earl Grey Dr. (© **613/271-7553**). **Collected Works,** at 1242 Wellington St. (© **613/722-1265**), is an independent bookstore carrying general fiction and nonfiction, with an emphasis on literary fiction and children's books. A drop-in children's story time is held on Mondays and Fridays between 10:30 and 11am. Specializing in British authors and publishers, **Nicholas Hoare** (419 Sussex Dr. © **613/562-2665**) offers a delightful experience for young and old bibliophiles. At the back of the shop is a comprehensive children's section, with child-size comfortable chairs that invite curling up with a good book. The atmosphere is calm and the background music soothing. Bookshelves line the walls from floor to ceiling, with elegant library ladders that glide on a guide rail allowing access to the top shelves.

Treating the grandchildren to a new outfit is lots of fun at these children's clothing stores, which offer a refreshing change from mall wear. **Kid's Cosy Cottons,** at 517 Sussex Dr. (© **800/267-2679** or 613/562-2679) is best known for its practical cotton basics in sizes ranging from 3 months to adults. Besides clothing in polar fleece and microfiber textiles, you'll find socks, pyjamas, and underwear—all Canadian made. Excellent quality British clothing for little girls is available at **Laura Ashley Shops Ltd.** (136 Bank St. © **613/238-4882**). **R.W. Kids** is Ottawa's Osh Kosh store. The store is well laid out with cascading hangers lining the walls so that styles and sizes are easy to find. A C$10 (US$7) annual membership entitles you to 15% discount on all regular-price items. R.W. Kids is in Hampton Park Plaza, at Carling and Kirkwood avenues (© **613/724-4576**). If you're looking for top-quality upscale clothing for infants to teens, visit **West End Kids** at 373 Richmond Rd. (© **613/722-8947**). Labels include Mexx, Columbia, Tommy Hilfiger, Deux Par Deux, and Fresh Produce.

Once you've bought some new togs and grabbed something to eat, check out some of these stores for pure fun and enjoyment. **Lilliput** (9 Murray St. © **613/241-1183**) has a delightful collection of domestic miniatures. Dollhouse furniture, fixtures, and accessories are beautifully displayed. Dollhouse kits in several styles are available, and some completed models are on show. For family members who want to try their hand at catching the big one, drop by **Brightwater Fly Fishing** (336 Cumberland St. © **613/241-6798**) to pick up everything a fishing fanatic could ever want. Rentals and fly-tying instruction are available. Fishing is permitted in designated areas of **Gatineau Park**—don't forget to purchase a provincial license before casting your line. **The Sassy Bead Co.,** with two locations at 757 Bank St. (℗ **613/567-7886**) and 11 William St. (℗ **613/562-2812**), is a girly sort of place. Females of all ages love to wander among the colorful jars, trays, and boxes filled with beads of every description. Tables are waiting for you and granddaughter to sit down and create your own one-of-a-kind jewelry right in the shop. **Dynamic Hobbies** are radio-control model specialists. You'll find cars, airplanes, helicopters, and boats running on indoor and outdoor tracks, plus a 45-meter (150 ft.) slot car track. They're located at 21 Concourse Gate, Unit 6 (℗ **613/225-9634**).

The ByWard Farmer's Market is a thriving outdoor market heaped with outstanding produce. In spring and early summer, flower stalls abound. The market is open every day in and around 55 ByWard Market Square. Situated where else but at the geographical centre of Ottawa, **A World of Maps** (1235 Wellington St.W. ℗ **800/214-8524** or 613/724-6776) is both a retailer and mail-order company. Topographical, aeronautical, nautical, international, and world maps, atlases, globes, travel books, and other map-related items are available here.

If you like the great outdoors, hike over to **Irving Rivers** (24 ByWard Market Sq. ℗ **613/241-1415),** an outdoor emporium stuffed with rain gear, camping clothing, travel appliances, backpacks, heavy-duty footwear, and everything else for a back-to-nature vacation. **Birder's Corner,** at 2 Beechwood Ave. (℗ **613/741-0945),** has everything for the care and feeding of wild birds, from bird baths to feeders, seed, books, videos, and a small selection of nature- and environment-themed educational toys.

Finally, when you really want to spoil your grandkids, head for the **Disney Store** or **Mrs. Tiggy-winkles.** The Disney Store has all kinds of Disney-themed products, ranging from videos to dress-up costumes, baby and preschool clothing, beach towels, and stuffed toys. You'll find them in the Rideau Centre, 50 Rideau Street, and Bayshore Shopping Centre, 100 Bayshore Drive. Mrs. T's stocks a wide variety of educational and high-quality toys and games for infants to teens. There's a two-floor emporium in the Glebe at 809 Bank Street, and you'll find branches in Bayshore Shopping Centre; the Rideau Centre; and Place d'Orléans Shopping Centre. See chapter 9.

3 The Best Hotel Bets for Families

See chapter 4, "Family-Friendly Accommodations" for full reviews.

- **Best Luxury Hotel:** If you're looking for tradition, luxury, and attentive service, the **Fairmont Château Laurier** (1 Rideau St. ℗ **800/441-1414** or 613/562-7001) is the place to stay—royalty and celebrities have always been attracted to the hotel's grace and

beauty. You'll pay for the pleasure, but the surroundings are exceptional. At the check-in desk, there's a cute set of steps so that little guests can see over the counter and collect a special welcome kit, with puzzles, games, and coloring books. In the health club complex, a children's play-room offers toys and games for younger children.

- **Best B&B:** As with most B&Bs, the owners of **A Mid-Towne Heritage B&B** (220 Lyon St. ℂ **888/669-8888** or 613/236-1169) accept children at their discretion, and suggest that ages 8 and up are best suited to the tranquil charm of this home. This is one of the few B&Bs with suite accommodations. The second floor offers two suites—one with two bedrooms (twin beds in one), a private bathroom, and balcony, and the other with twin beds (plus the option of having two cots in the sitting room) and a private bathroom. Families will enjoy the shade trees in the private garden. Parliament Hill is only a 10-minute stroll along Wellington Street.

- **Best Cool Place for Kids:** Want to spend a night behind bars? Before becoming a hostel, the **Ottawa International Hostel** (75 Nicholas St. ℂ **613/235-2595**) was the Carleton County Gaol (1862 to 1972). The former cells have been renovated and enlarged, enabling guests to enjoy a quiet night's sleep in the clink—if the ghost of the unfortunate criminal to be executed at Canada's last public hanging doesn't disturb you. Accommodations and facilities are basic, clean, and inexpensive.

- **Best Suites:** Families are guaranteed comfort at the all-suite **Marriott Residence Inn Ottawa** (161 Laurier Ave. W. ℂ **877/478-4838** or 613/231-2020), where the units are at least 50% larger than those in standard hotels. A two-bedroom suite boasts a well-equipped kitchen, two full bathrooms, and three TVs. The kids' welcome pack, with small toys,

snacks, and coloring books, and the indoor pool will keep your little ones busy.

- **Best Guest Services:** The **Westin Ottawa** (11 Colonel By Dr. ℂ **613/560-7000**) offers all kinds of helpful items and services for people traveling with kids, including safety kits, cribs, highchairs, and jogging strollers. Rooms for families are set up prior to check-in so there's no need to call down to the front desk to arrange those little extras after arrival. A free kids' movie, child-care services, special laundry pricing, express meal service, and a kids' menu with free drink refills are some of the advantages of Westin's Kids Club, designed for infants to 12-year-olds.

- **Best for Families with Tots and Teens:** The **Best Western Victoria Park Suites** (377 O'Connor St. ℂ **800/465-7275** or 613/567-7275) is located right around the corner from the Canadian Museum of Nature, with its huge dinosaurs, creepy insects, beautiful birds, life-size woolly mammoth family, and green space for running around or enjoying a picnic. All units are wired with Web TV and in-room Nintendo, to keep your preteens and teens entertained. Best Western Victoria guests have free access to the kids' club (ages 3 to 12) that runs daily in July and August at the Albert at Bay Suite Hotel, right around the corner at 435 Albert St. (ℂ **800/267-6644** or 613/238-8858).

- **Best for Younger Children:** The **Cartier Place and Towers Suite Hotels** (180 Cooper St. ℂ **800/236-8399** or 613/236-5000) is a high-end hotel with wonderful amenities for children. Besides the indoor pool, with glass doors leading onto a sundeck, there is a play structure for preschoolers in the pool area and a well-equipped children's playroom. In the summer, kids can explore the climbing structure and children's play equipment in the outdoor courtyard, and in winter, they'll have the unforgettable experience of skating on the rooftop ice rink. All units are suites with full kitchens.

- **Best Downtown Hotel: Minto Place Suite Hotel** (433 Laurier Ave. W. ℂ **800/267-3377** or 613/782-2350) is one of the top choices in the city for family accommodation. The suites are spacious and stylish and offer kitchenettes or full kitchens, and the hotel provides direct access to the indoor shopping concourse. The skylit pool, 20 meters (65 ft.) long and with a uniform depth of 1.2 meters (4 ft.), is sparkling clean. A sun deck leads off the pool area. In the summer, your kids can sign up for the fun and games at the kids' club. Staff are pleasant and experienced in helping families to make the most of their stay in Ottawa.

- **Best East-End Hotel:** Comfortable surroundings in a brand-new building, a spotless indoor pool, and competitive pricing give the **Hampton Inn** (100 Coventry Rd. ℂ **877/701-1281** or 613/741-2300) an edge over other hotels in the area. The large guest rooms have high-quality furnishings and oversized bathrooms. Each room has a kitchenette with a microwave, sink, and small fridge.

- **Best West-End Hotel:** If you have a car and don't mind a bit of a drive (15 minutes on the Queensway/Hwy. 417 outside of rush hours), the **Best Western Barons Hotel** (3700 Richmond Rd. ℂ **800/528-1234** or 613/828-2741) offers a family-friendly atmosphere and attractive prices. A large regional shopping mall, the Bayshore, is 5 minutes away by car, and the Corel Centre is only 10 minutes west on the Queensway. Family packages are offered in the summer months, with deals on rates and freebies such as comics, museum passes, and a disposable camera.

4 The Best Dining Bets for Families

See chapter 5, "Family-Friendly Dining" for full reviews.

- **Best Asian:** The small Vietnamese restaurant **New Mee Fung** (350 Booth St. ℂ **613/567-8228**) is clean, simply furnished, and casual. With lots of finger foods, dishes that require assembly, and chopsticks to master, this is a fun place for kids. Grilled chicken, beef, and pork feature in many of the dishes, and soups, spring rolls, salads, and noodles abound. The service is also charming.

- **Best Bagels:** You could also call **Kettleman's Bagels** (912 Bank St. ℂ **613/567-7100**) the best show and probably the best breakfast (if you're a bagel person). You must bring your kids here to watch the bagel bakers at work. With deft hands, they cut strips from huge mounds of dough, shape them into circles, line them up on long wooden planks, and slide them into the open wood-burning oven. The end result is delicious. There are two other locations at 2177 Carling Avenue (ℂ **613/722-4357**) in the west end and 1222 Place D'Orléans Drive (ℂ **613/841-4409**) in the east end.

- **Best Cafe:** At the north end of the ByWard Market building you'll find **Le Moulin de Provence** (55 Byward Market ℂ 613/241-9152), a lively mix of bakery, cafe, patisserie, and light fare. The French pastries are irresistible. Huge picture windows are perfect for people-watching, an essential ingredient of any good cafe. Cup your hands around a bowl of café au lait (order hot chocolate for the kids) and sip as you watch the world go by.

- **Best Casual Italian:** Housed in a heritage stone building, **Mamma Grazzi's Kitchen** (25 George St. ℂ 613/241-8656) is especially pleasant in the summer, when you can eat alfresco in the cobblestone courtyard at the rear. The quaint courtyard is flanked by the terraces of several other eateries, lending a European atmosphere. Whether you like your pasta dressed with tomato, cream, or olive oil, you'll have several combinations of ingredients to choose from. Because they make everything to order, you may have to wait a little, but it's worth it.

- **Best Croissants:** Reputed to have the flakiest, richest, most buttery croissants in the city, the **French Baker/Le Boulanger Français** (119 Murray St. ℂ 613/789-7941) also has authentic baguettes and other breads and pastries.

- **Best Fun:** If you've never experienced Mövenpick's **Marchélino,** you must pay a visit to this unique market-style restaurant, located just inside the east entrance of the Rideau Centre (50 Rideau St. ℂ 613/569-4934). This is gourmet fast food and it's lots of fun. The market bustles with activity as staff at various food stations energetically roll out dough, bake bread, slide pizzas in and out of the stone hearth oven, assemble Japanese sushi delicacies, and squeeze fresh juice.

- **Best Gourmet Takeout:** The gourmet food shop **L'Amuse Gueule** (915 Bank St. ℂ 613/234-9400) is a little slice of France. The weekly dinner entree menu offers a different dish every day. Feast on boeuf bourguignon, herb-roasted grain-fed chicken, lobster-filled crepes, or filet of sole. Taste local and imported cheeses and pick up a baguette or two. There are a few tables and chairs inside, but this is primarily a takeout and catering operation. For a special family treat, order a gourmet picnic basket filled with a selection of tasty dishes and head down to the banks of the canal or one of the nearby parks.

- **Best Ice Cream:** I always say you can never have too much ice cream, and it's impossible for me to drive past **Pure Gelato** (350 Elgin St. ℂ 613/237-3799) without stopping in for a dish of their delicious gelato. We like the fruit ones best—pear, raspberry, lemon, lime, strawberry, mandarin, kiwi, and lots more. For chocoholics, I counted more than nine chocolate concoctions; some unusual flavors like ginger, Toblerone, and chestnut are also on offer.

- **Best Pasta:** We make regular visits to **Luciano's,** a take-home-only pasta shop at 106 Preston St. (ℂ 613/236-7545) to stock our freezer with ravioli, agnolotti, and tortellini stuffed with yummy fillings like sundried tomato, spinach and ricotta, and butternut squash. Choose spaghetti, fettucine, linguine, or rigatoni and top it with one of their homemade sauces—Bolognese, clam, tomato, putanesca, mushroom, or pepper. Lasagna and cannelloni are packed in oven-ready portions. Add pesto, Parmesan cheese, baguettes, olive oil, and tubs of gelato to your shopping bag—everything is of consistently high quality.

- **Best Pizza:** Pizzas almost fly from the oven onto tables and out the door at **Café Colonnade** (280 Metcalfe St. ℂ **613/237-3179**). Their famous pizza has a thick crust with a sprinkling of cheese around the edge, a generous smear of tangy tomato sauce, and gooey mozzarella to hold the toppings in place. On warm summer days and evenings you can hang out on the outdoor terrace that stretches along one side of the building. Takeout is also available.
- **Best Seafood: The Fish Market** (54 York St. ℂ **613/2413474**), established in 1979, is Ottawa's original fresh fish restaurant. The menu is refreshed twice daily as supplies of an astounding array of fish and seafood from around the world ebb and flow in the kitchen. My daughter, who has eaten her fair share of fish and chips in England, declares the battered cod and chips the best she's tasted this side of the Atlantic. Upstairs is the more casual Coasters Seafood Grill, featuring a central fireplace and open kitchen.
- **Best Sunday Brunch:** One of the best places to eat in the ByWard Market area, the **Black Tomato** (11 George St. ℂ **613/789-8123**)

gets top marks for the food and the surroundings. The kitchen has heaps of culinary talent, so prepare yourself for a hedonistic meal. It's not a place for toddlers, but bring along kids from about age 5 and up (although parents will appreciate this place more than the kids). Make the scrumptious Sunday brunch a family event—three courses are yours for C$14 (US$9.25). My daughter polished off a wedge of French toast (cut from a round loaf) with strawberries and mango whipped cream, sautéed potatoes, and bacon, while I savored every spoonful of my black bean and corn chowder. Arrive early because the place gets extremely busy.

- **Best View:** Having the distinct advantage of a converted boat-house setting, the **Canal Ritz** (375 Queen Elizabeth Dr. ℂ **613/238-8998**) boasts an outstanding view of the Rideau Canal. The constantly changing panorama means your kids will never be bored here. In summer, boats glide right past the tables on the huge terrace. In the winter, when the canal freezes and transforms itself into the world's longest skating rink, you can play "I spy" games with the myriad of skaters slipping and sliding along the ice. The parking lot is on the south side of Fifth Avenue, directly opposite the restaurant.

 A History Lesson on Canada's Capital

Here are some interesting facts about Ottawa to share with your kids:

Early Days   Ottawa's history can be traced to the region's development as a trading site by the **Algonquins,** although other Native peoples had used the mighty Ottawa River as a transportation route for thousands of years.

1613   The French explorer **Samuel de Champlain** is the first European to arrive in the region.

1800   Philemon Wright, a United Empire Loyalist, arrives from Massachusetts with settlers and lumberjacks to establish the first non-Native settlement on the north side of the Ottawa River. Wrightsville, now known as Hull, Quebec, grows and prospers along with the expanding lumber trade in the area.

1850–1855   The Chaudière Falls on the Ottawa River are harnessed as a source of mechanical power and the region becomes a major lumber producer, with the largest concentration of milling operations in the world. Stores, banks, newspapers, and schools serve Bytown's population which has risen to 10,000. The city is renamed **Ottawa,** to commemorate the 200th anniversary of the first descent of the Outaouak Native people down the river.

1857   Queen Victoria chooses Ottawa as the capital of the British Provinces of Upper and Lower Canada, despite protests from Kingston and Toronto.

1866   The **Parliament Buildings,** modeled on the British Houses of Parliament, are completed.

1867   With **Confederation,** Ottawa becomes the capital of the new Dominion of Canada.

1916   A devastating fire sweeps the Parliament Buildings—only the Parliamentary Library is saved. The Parliament Buildings must be almost completely rebuilt.

Post–World War II   French planner **Jacques Gréber** is commissioned by Prime Minister William Lyon Mackenzie King to lay out a new plan for the growing city. Gréber's design is largely responsible for the protected parkland surrounding much of the city.

2001   Ottawa's new city motto "Technically Beautiful" undoubtedly meant to play on Ottawa's growing reputation as Silicon Valley north, is met with much popular disapproval and dropped by the city's tourism authority.

2

Planning a Family Trip to Ottawa

Whether you're a careful plan-ahead type of person or a spur-of-the-moment decision maker, if kids are in the picture, you'd be well advised to take some time planning your trip. You've already made the right decision in choosing Ottawa as your vacation destination—the city is bursting with attractions and activities that the whole family will enjoy.

1 Visitor Information & Entry Requirements

VISITOR INFORMATION

FROM NORTH AMERICA Your starting point is the **Capital Infocentre,** 90 Wellington St., Ottawa, ON K1P 1C7 (✆ **800/465-1867** or 613/239-5000; www.capcan.ca), which provides information on Ottawa and the surrounding region and is administered by the National Capital Commission. The call center provides visitor information 8:30am to 9pm daily from mid-May to Labour Day, and 9am to 5pm during the rest of the year. To receive written material on the National Capital Region, write to the Capital Infocentre at 40 Elgin St., Room 202, Ottawa, ON K1P 1C7.

The **Ottawa Tourism and Convention Authority Inc. (OTCA),** 130 Albert St., Suite 1800, Ottawa, ON K1P 5G4, publishes a comprehensive annual visitor's guide, which includes maps and listings of cultural sites, things to see and do, accommodations, places to dine and shop, and services. You can obtain a free copy of the guide by phoning ✆ **800/465-1867.** Allow up to 2 weeks for delivery. You can also pick up a copy at the Capital Infocentre when you arrive in the city. Most of the information contained in the guide is posted on the website **www.ottawa.com.** Other websites with visitor information include **www.ottawakiosk.com** and **www.festivalseeker.com**.

For information about Ontario, contact **Tourism Ontario,** P.O. Box 104, Toronto, ON M5B 2H1, or by phone or web through the **Ontario Tourism Marketing Partnership** (Ontario Ministry of Tourism), at ✆ **800/ONTARIO** or www.ontariotravel.net.

The Canadian consulates in the United States do not provide tourist information. They will refer you to the offices above. Consular offices in Buffalo, Detroit, Los Angeles, New York, Seattle, and Washington, D.C., deal with visas and other political and immigration issues.

FROM ABROAD The following consulates can provide information or refer you to the appropriate offices.

U.K. and Ireland: The **Canadian High Commission,** MacDonald House, 1 Grosvenor Sq., London W1X 0AB (✆ **0171/258-6600;** fax 0171/258-6384).

Australia: The **Canadian High Commission,** Commonwealth Avenue, Canberra, ACT 2600 (✆ 02/6273-3844), or the **Consulate-General of Canada,** Level 5, Quay West Building, 111 Harrington St., Sydney, NSW 2000 (✆ 02/9364-3000). The consulate-general also has offices in Melbourne and Perth.

New Zealand: The **Canadian High Commission,** 3rd Floor, 61 Molesworth St., Thomdon, Wellington (✆ 04/473-9577), or the **Consulate of Canada,** Level 9, Jetset Centre, 44–48 Emily Place, Auckland (✆ 09/309-3690).

South Africa: The **Canadian High Commission,** 1103 Arcadia St., Hatfield 0083, Pretoria (✆ 012/342-6923). The commission also has offices in Cape Town and Johannesburg.

ENTRY REQUIREMENTS
DOCUMENTS

Entry requirements for entering Canada have tightened in recent years. All visitors to Canada must show proof of citizenship. U.S. citizens and permanent U.S. residents do not need a passport to enter Canada, though it is the easiest and most convenient method of proving citizenship. If you don't have a passport, you'll need to carry a certificate of naturalization, a citizenship certificate, a birth certificate with photo ID, a voter's registration card with photo ID, or a social security card. Although border officers are allowed to ask for these forms of identification, in most cases all they will ask to see is a U.S. driver's license. Permanent U.S. residents who are not U.S. citizens must carry their Alien Registration Cards (green cards). If you plan to drive into Canada, be sure to bring your car's registration papers. If you are traveling with children under the age of 19 who are not your own, make sure they carry identification papers as well as a written statement from their parents or guardians granting permission to travel to Canada.

Citizens of most European countries and former British colonies, as well as certain other countries (such as Israel, Korea, and Japan), do not need visas but must carry passports. Entry visas are required for citizens of more than 130 countries. You must apply for and recieve your entry visa from the Canadian embassy in your home country. For detailed information, call your local Canadian consulate or embassy.

CUSTOMS
What You Can Bring In

Generally, you are allowed to bring goods for personal use during your trip into Canada, although there are restrictions on plants, meats, and pets. Fishing tackle poses no problems, but the bearer must possess a nonresident license for the province where he or she plans to use it. There are severe restrictions on firearms and weapons. All guns must be declared—otherwise, they may be seized by customs officers. Handguns require a special permit and may be imported only under specific conditions. Long guns can be brought into Canada only under special circumstances, such as for use in competitions or for hunting in season. Provided you are 19 or over, you can bring with you up to 200 cigarettes, 50 cigars or cigarillos, 200 tobacco sticks, and 200 grams (7 oz.) of manufactured tobacco without having to pay duty. In Ontario, if you are 19 years or older you can bring in no more than 1.14 liters (40 fl. oz.) of liquor, or 1.5 liters (52 fl. oz.) of wine or wine coolers, or 24 containers of beer (355ml, or 12 fl. oz., each) duty-free. Dogs, cats, and most pets can enter Canada with their owners, but you should bring a valid rabies vaccination certificate with you.

For more details concerning customs regulations, call **Canada Customs and Revenue Agency,** at ✆ **800/ 461-9999** (Canada only) or ✆ 613/ 993-0534. Detailed information for Canadian residents and visitors to Canada can be found at the CCRA website, at www.ccra-adrc.gc.ca.

What You Can Bring Home
- **U.S. citizens** should contact the **U.S. Customs Service,** 1301 Constitution Ave., P.O. Box 7407, Washington, D.C. 20044 (✆ **202/ 927-6724**) and request the free pamphlet *Know Before You Go.* Information is also available at www.customs.ustreas.gov. *Be warned:* Cuban tobacco products purchased in Canada cannot be brought back to the United States

- **U.K. citizens** can contact **HM Customs and Excise, Passenger Enquiry Point,** 2nd Floor, Wayfarer House, Great South West Rd., Feltham, Middlesex TW14 8NP (✆ **020/8910-3744**; www. open.gov.uk).
- **Australian citizens** should contact the **Australian Customs Services,** G.P.O. Box 8, Sydney, NSW 2001 (✆ **02/9213-2000**), to obtain a *Know Before You Go* brochure.
- **New Zealand Citizens** may contact **New Zealand Customs,** 50 Anzac Ave., P.O. Box 29, Auckland (✆ **09/359-6655**), to request the *New Zealand Customs Guide for Travellers, Notice No. 4.*

2 Money

CURRENCY

The currency of Canada is the Canadian dollar, made up of 100 cents. U.S. visitors enjoy a distinct advantage—the Canadian dollar has been fluctuating at around 66 cents in U.S. money, give or take a couple of points' variation, for the past few years. What this means is that your American money gets you about 34% more the moment you exchange it for local currency. Since the cost of many goods is roughly on par with U.S. prices, the difference is real, not imaginary. The British pound has been hovering at around C$2.16. Be aware that sales taxes are high in Canada, although you may be able to claim a tax refund for some purchases (see "Taxes" under "Fast Facts" in chapter 3, "Getting to Know Ottawa").

Paper currency comes in $5, $10, $20, $50, and $100 denominations. Coins come in 1-, 5-, 10-, and 25-cent (penny, nickel, dime, and quarter) and 1- and 2-dollar denominations. The common name for the brass 1-dollar

coin is a "loonie" because of the loon on its "tails" side. The more recently released 2-dollar coin has been dubbed the "toonie."

You can bring any amount of money either way across the border between Canada and the United States, but if you are carrying $5,000 or more you must file a report of the transaction with the appropriate customs authority. Most tourist establishments in Canada will accept U.S. cash, but to get the best rate, change your funds into Canadian currency upon arrival.

If you do spend American money at Canadian establishments, you should understand how the conversion is calculated. Often there is a sign at the cash register stating "U.S. Currency 50%." This 50% is the "premium," which means that for every U.S. greenback you hand over, the cashier will consider it $1.50 Canadian. For example, to pay a $15 tab you'll need only $10 in U.S. currency.

The Canadian Dollar, the U.S. Dollar & the British Pound

The prices in this guide are given first in Canadian dollars, then in U.S. dollars. Amounts over $5 have been rounded to the nearest dollar. Note that the Canadian dollar is worth about 30% less than the American dollar but buys nearly as much. At the time of writing, C$1 was worth about US$0.66 and that was the equivalency used to figure the prices in this guide. The British pound is included here for your reference with C$1 worth about £0.47. Note that exchange rates are subject to fluctuation, and you should always check the most recent currency rates when preparing for your trip. Here's a quick table of equivalents:

C $	U.S. $	UK £	U.S. $	C $	UK £
1	0.66	0.48	1	1.51	0.73
5	3.30	2.40	5	7.58	3.65
10	6.60	4.80	10	15.15	7.30
20	13.20	9.60	20	30.30	14.60
50	33.00	24.00	50	75.75	36.50
80	52.80	36.00	80	121.21	58.40
100	66.00	48.00	100	151.52	73.00

You'll usually get the best rate of exchange through an **ATM,** and it's handy not to have to carry cash and traveler's checks around. Always bring sufficient Canadian funds to take you through your first day or so, when you'll likely need cash for cab or bus fare and a snack. Try to limit your ATM transactions because you will pay a fee for each withdrawal. You can find ATMs at most banks. Both the **Cirrus** (© 800/424-7787; www.mastercard.com/atm) and the **Plus** (© 800/843-7587; www.visa.com/atms) networks have automated ATM locators listing the banks in Canada that will accept your card. You can also get cash advances against your Master-Card or Visa, but you'll need a personal identification number (PIN) to access this service. Note that the credit card company will begin charging interest on the cash advance immediately and may charge a fee for this service.

If you prefer the extra security of **traveler's checks,** almost all hotels, restaurants, shops, and attractions accept U.S.-dollar traveler's checks, and you can exchange them for cash at banks if you show ID. There may be a charge for this service. Be sure to keep a record of the serial numbers of your traveler's checks (separately from the checks, of course), so you're ensured a refund if they're lost or stolen.

American Express (© 800/221-7282) is the most widely recognized traveler's check; depending on where you purchase them, expect to pay a 1% to 4% commission. Checks are free to members of the **American Automobile Association (AAA).**

Citicorp (© 800/645-6556 in the U.S. or 813/623-1709 collect in Canada) issues checks in U.S. dollars or British pounds.

MasterCard International (© 800/223-9920 in the U.S.) issues checks in about a dozen currencies.

Thomas Cook (© 800/223-7373 in the U.S.) issues checks in a variety of currencies.

Credit cards are invaluable when traveling—they provide a safe way to carry money and a convenient record of all your expenses. Almost every credit card company has an emergency toll-free number to call if your credit card is stolen. They may be able to wire you a cash advance from your credit card immediately, and in many places they can deliver an emergency card in a day or two. A toll-free information directory at ☎ 800/555-1212 will provide the number for you. Citi- corp Visa's U.S. emergency number is ☎ 800/336-8472. **American Express** cardholders and traveler's check holders should call ☎ **800/221-7282,** and **MasterCard** holders should call ☎ **800/307-7309.** The best and fastest way to get assistance when you are in your home country is to call your card issuer.

What Things Cost in Ottawa	C$	US$	UK£
Shuttle fare from airport to downtown hotel, family of four	14.00	9.00	6.72
Newspaper	0.50	0.33	0.24
Local telephone call	0.25	0.17	0.12
Movie tickets, family of four	38.00	25.00	18.24
Taxi from downtown hotel to Museum of Civilization	12.00	8.00	5.76
Bus ticket (adult single)	2.25	1.50	1.08
Bus ticket (child single 6–11)	1.25	0.80	0.60
Bus day pass (unlimited travel)	5.00	3.00	2.40
Parking meter, downtown per hour	1.50	1.00	0.72
All-day parking lot, downtown	9.00	6.00	4.32
Museum entrance fee, family of four	12.00	7.92	5.64
Roll of Kodak film, 24-exposure print	6.00	4.00	2.88
Cup of coffee	1.50	1.00	0.72
Bottle of juice	2.00	1.30	0.96
Hot dog from corner umbrella cart	2.00	1.30	0.96
Ice-cream cone	1.00	0.65	0.48
Large takeout pizza	20.00	13.00	9.60
Diapers, 48 disposable medium	16.00	10.00	7.68
Baby formula, 12 ready-to-use 235mL (8 oz.) cans	26.00	17.00	12.48

3 When to Go

Most families plan vacations for the school holidays, and Ottawa's tourism industry accordingly plans family accommodation packages, events, and festivals for the peak periods of June, July, August, and the March break. The city is most crowded with visitors at these times, though, and there are other wonderful times of year to enjoy the region. The spring weather in May, when the tulips are in bloom, is often bright and refreshing; the sunshine is warm but you'll need light jackets for cooler days. If you visit in the fall, you can bike or hike through the beautiful Gatineau Hills and enjoy nature's art show. January and February are the months to enjoy skating on the Rideau Canal, and the first three weekends in February bring Winterlude, Ottawa's annual winter festival. During the March break, many of Ottawa's museums and attractions offer special workshops and programs for children and families. Unfortunately, the canal skating season is usually over by March break, but if it's been a long, cold winter, you may get lucky—contact the tourist information center (© **613/239-5234**) for up-to-the-minute conditions on the canal. March is also maple syrup season, so head out to a farm to see some tree tapping and sample this Canadian treat. For an exuberant birthday celebration, visit the nation's capital over Canada Day, on July 1. Hotel rooms fill up quickly for the Canada Day weekend, so book well ahead.

THE CLIMATE

Spring runs from late March to mid-May (although sometimes there's a late snowfall in April); **summer,** mid-May to mid-September; **fall,** mid-September to mid-November; **winter,** mid-November to late March. The average annual high is 10°C (50°F) and the average annual low is 0°C (32°F). In winter, fluctuations in temperature sometimes cause freezing rain, a serious hazard for drivers.

Ottawa's Average Temperatures (°C/°F)

	Jan	Feb	Mar	Apr	May	June	July	Aug	Sept	Oct	Nov	Dec
High	−4/25	−6/22	3/37	9/48	17/63	20/69	23/74	22/72	18/64	12/54	5/42	−3/27
Low	−18/0	−18/0	−13/9	−1/31	8/47	14/58	17/62	15/59	11/52	2/36	−6/21	−15/5

HOLIDAYS

On most public holidays, banks, government offices, schools, and post offices are closed. Museums, stores, and restaurants vary widely in their policies for holiday openings and closings, so to avoid disappointment, call before you go.

Ottawa celebrates the following holidays: New Year's Day (January 1), Good Friday and/or Easter Monday (March or April), Victoria Day (Monday following the third weekend in May), Canada Day (July 1), Civic Holiday (first Monday in August), Labour Day (first Monday in September), Thanksgiving (second Monday in October), Remembrance Day (November 11), Christmas Day (December 25), and Boxing Day (December 26).

KIDS' GUIDE TO OTTAWA EVENTS

The following list of events will help you to plan your visit to Ottawa. Contact the **Capital Infocentre** (© **800/465-1867**) to confirm details if a particular event is a major reason for your vacation. Even the largest, most successful events sometimes retire, a few events are biennial, and dates may change from those listed here. In addition to the following events, numerous smaller community and cultural events take place throughout the year. **Lansdowne Park** hosts many trade and consumer shows catering to special interests—contact **Lansdowne Park** at © **613/580-2429**. Various websites list upcoming events, such as www.tourottawa.org, www.ottawa.com, www.capcan.ca, www.ottawakiosk.com, and www.festivalseeker.com.

January

The Governor General's New Year's Day Levee at Rideau Hall, the official residence of the governor general. Members of the public are invited to meet the governor general, visit the historic residence's public rooms, and enjoy entertainment and light refreshments. © **800/465-6890** or 613/991-4422.

The Ottawa-Hull International Auto Show at the Ottawa Congress Centre (adjoining the Rideau Centre) brings you up-to-date with what's happening in the world of cars, minivans, pickups, and SUVs. ✆ 613/563-1983.

February

Winterlude. Every year, the first three weekends of February are filled with snow, ice, and loads of family fun as the city celebrates its chilliest season. Downtown Ottawa and Hull are transformed into winter wonderlands filled with gigantic snow sculptures, glittering ice sculptures, and a Snowflake Kingdom especially for kids. Children's entertainment, craft workshops, horse-drawn sleigh rides, snowboarding demonstrations, dogsled rides, and more are on offer for little ones. Activities are based at Parliament Hill, New Ottawa City Hall and Festival Plaza, Confederation Park, Rideau Canal Skateway at Fifth Avenue, Dow's Lake, and Jacques-Cartier Park in Hull. A free shuttle bus operates between sites. ✆ 800/465-1867.

Canadian Ski Marathon. The world's longest cross-country ski tour is a skier's paradise and offers some of the best wilderness trails anywhere. You can ski as little as 15 kilometers (9 miles) or as much as 160 kilometers (99 miles)—you set the pace. The marathon attracts 1,500 to 2,000 novice and veteran skiers from ages 3 to 85. ✆ 819/770-6556.

Keskinada Loppet. Close to 3,000 skiers from more than a dozen countries gather to participate in Canada's biggest cross-country ski event, held annually in Gatineau Park. There's a 5-kilometer (3 mile) and a 10-kilometer (6 mile) family race. Kids under 13 can ski, snow-shoe, or walk the 2-kilometer (1.25 mile) Mini-Keski. ✆ 800/465-1867 or 819/827-2020.

Ottawa Boat, Sportsmen's & Cottage Show. Revel in the outdoors at this show for fishers, hunters, and weekend cottagers, held in Lansdowne Park. Dozens of demos feature everything from tying a fly to paddling a canoe. ✆ 613/580-2429.

Ottawa Spring RV and Camping Show. Mobile homes, travel and tent trailers, vans, and sport utility and all-terrain vehicles motor into Lansdowne Park for this trade show. ✆ 613/580-2429.

March

Ottawa Spring Home Show. More than 300 exhibitors gather to showcase furnishings, swimming pools, landscaping, plumbing, kitchens, and baths at Lansdowne Park. Seminars on renovating, gardening, interior design, and do-it-yourself will also be featured. ✆ 613/580-2429.

Ottawa Paddlesport & Outdoor Adventure Show. The show highlights the latest in camping, canoe, and kayak gear, as well as adventure sport activities such as white-water rafting, rock climbing, mountain biking, scuba diving, parachuting, and backpacking. ✆ 613/580-2429.

April

Kiwanis Music Festival. This annual competitive music festival, held in local venues, brings together close to 4,000 competitors of all ages and at all levels of training and ability. Teachers and performers of the highest professional standing come from across North America to act as adjudicators.

The Ottawa Lynx. Ottawa's premier baseball team, the Triple-A affiliate of the Montreal Expos, provides fun and affordable family entertainment at JetForm Park. The Lynx play 72 home games between April and September. The 10,332-seat stadium boasts a full-service restaurant, luxury suites, and a picnic area. © **800/663-0985** or 613/747-LYNX (5969).

May

Canadian Tulip Festival. A visit to this spring festival in mid-May will dazzle you with the blooming of over three million tulips in a rainbow of colors. The 10-day tulip festival includes concerts, an arts and crafts market, fireworks displays, and the colorful Tulip Flotilla, a floating parade on the Rideau Canal. Stroll along the banks of the canal and through the gardens at Dow's Lake to catch the full effect of the carpet of flowers. © **800/668-TULIP** (668-8547) or 613/567-5757.

National Capital Race Weekend. Thousands of runners, volunteers, spectators, and visitors gather for this world-class 10-kilometer (6 mile) race. A 5-kilometer (3 mile) and 2-kilometer (1 mile) family walk/run and in-line skating are also part of the fun. © **613/234-2221.**

Wind Odyssey: Sound and Light on Parliament Hill. This free, dynamic show illuminates Parliament Hill on summer evenings. © **800/465-1867.**

Mother's Day Celebration. The ByWard Market is the place to be on Mother's Day. Over 75 ByWard Market restaurants roll out the red carpet for mom and the family, and many offer special menus. © **613/562-3325.**

Classic Cars. Owners and enthusiasts are invited to Place d'Orléans Wednesday evenings from 6 to 9pm, May to September, to view 350 classic cars during this outdoor, family event. © **613/824-9050.**

Sheep Shearing Festival. The Canadian Agriculture Museum presents its annual sheep-shearing extravaganza with shearing demonstrations, displays of sheep-herding by border collies, rare breed exhibits, wool crafts, children's activities, and much more. © **613/991-3044.**

Odawa Spring Pow Wow. Held at Nepean Tent and Trailer Park, this energetic and colorful event is designed to bring First Nations culture to Native and non-Native audiences through the sharing of music, dance, art, and food. © **613/722-3811.**

RCMP Musical Ride. From May to October, the world-famous Royal Canadian Mounted Police and their majestic horses perform a musical show for appreciative audiences throughout Canada, with some dates in Ottawa. Tours of the stables are offered year-round. © **613/993-3751** or 613/998-8199.

June

Festival 4–15 (Ottawa Festival of the Arts for Young Audiences). Formerly known as the Children's Festival, this event brings the best of live theatrical arts to children at sites in and around the Canada Science and Technology Museum. Families will enjoy music, theater, crafts, and other kids' entertainment. © **613/241-0999.**

Gloucester Fair. This old-fashioned fair offers agricultural displays, gymkhana and western horse shows, a demolition derby, a lumberjack show, midway rides, bubblegum-blowing contests, pony rides, face painting, and more. © **613/744-2671.**

Festival Franco-Ontarien. One of the most important French celebrations in North America is held in the ByWard Market area, with a variety of musical and theatrical performances to entertain all ages. © **613/741-1225.**

National Capital Dragon Boat Festival. Held at the Rideau Canoe Club at Mooney's Bay, this festival features dragon boat races, multicultural stage performers, exhibitors, and activities for children. Admission is free. © **613/238-7711.**

Changing of the Guard. This half-hour ceremony is one of Ottawa's most outstanding attractions. From late June to late August, the Ceremonial Guard parades daily from the Cartier Square Drill Hall to Parliament Hill between 9:30 and 10am. The ceremony begins at 10am, weather permitting. © **800/ 465-1867.**

ByWard Market Auto Classic. On the first Sunday in June the ByWard Market hosts the Auto Classic, a showcase of automotive history with over 150 vintage, classic, and high-performance cars on display for fun and prizes. The event is free to the public and classic car owners alike. © **613/562-3325.**

Italian Week. Corso Italia (Preston Street), the commercial heart of Ottawa's Little Italy, is the place to be in mid-June to celebrate the food, music, pageantry, and art that is Italy. The year 2002 will mark the 28th anniversary of the festival. © **613/726-0920.**

Carnival of Cultures. The picturesque, outdoor Astrolabe Theatre is the setting for a summer kaleidoscope of cultures, with music, food, treasures, and dance from around the world. The dynamic entertainment includes international artists and Ottawa's top folk dancers,

singers, and musicians. © **800/ 465-1867.**

UniSong. Over 400 members of youth and children's choirs from across Canada perform 4 days of concerts at the National Arts Centre and other locations. Enjoy a full program of Canadian music and celebrations on Canada Day at the Festival Plaza, on Laurier Avenue near Elgin Street, 4:30pm, free. © **800/267-8526** or 613/234-3360.

Garden Party at Rideau Hall. The governor general hosts the annual garden party at Rideau Hall on the last Saturday afternoon in June. Her Excellency greets visitors on the upper terrace of the gardens. The first Changing of the Guard ceremony of the summer is held before the party. Guests can explore the residence's public rooms, gardens, and greenhouses, and children can enjoy many special activities on the grounds, including entertainment and crafts. Light refreshments are served. © **800/ 465-6890** or 613/991-4422.

Canada Dance Festival. Next scheduled for 2002, this biennial festival showcases the finest in new Canadian contemporary choreography. Performances fill the stages, streets, and parks of Ottawa and feature emerging independent artists and established companies. © **613/ 947-7000.**

July

Canada Day. Hundreds of thousands of Canadians gather in Ottawa to celebrate the Canada's birthday. Activities center around Parliament Hill, Major's Hill Park, and Jacques-Cartier Park in Hull. Shows, street performers, and concerts mark the event. Don't miss the spectacular fireworks display over the Ottawa River. © **800/465-1867.**

Helping Other People Everywhere (HOPE). HOPE, a nonprofit charitable organization, holds the largest beach volleyball tournament in the world, with 1,000 teams playing on 79 courts. The tournament attracts over 30,000 participants and spectators, who flock to Mooney's Bay in support of HOPE. ℭ 613/237-1433.

International Youth Orchestra Festival. The festival offers joint shared concerts, broadcasts, demonstrations, and a gala massed concert. Call the Capital Infocentre ℭ 800/465-1867.

The Ottawa Chamber Music Festival. North America's largest chamber music festival and one of Canada's most respected cultural events features the finest musicians from across Canada, the United States, and Europe. Some of the most beautiful churches in downtown Ottawa host 78 concerts over 2 weeks. ℭ 613/234-8008.

Ottawa International Jazz Festival. For 10 days in July, the finest jazz musicians in the world perform in intimate studio spaces and open-air venues for thousands of fans. ℭ 613/241-2633.

Cisco Systems Bluesfest. Canada's biggest blues festival presents an outstanding array of blues musicians over 4 days at Lebreton Flats, a spectacular outdoor setting in downtown Ottawa. ℭ 613/247-1188.

Capital Classic Show Jumping Tournament. Canada's top equestrians compete at this annual event. Held at the National Capital Equestrian Park, the tournament draws lots of family spectators. Call the Capital Infocentre ℭ 800/465-1867.

Children's Hospital of Eastern Ontario Teddy Bear Picnic. Bring your kids and their bears to this annual picnic, held in the beautiful grounds of Rideau Hall on the second Saturday of July. Meet a Mountie, enjoy a pancake breakfast, visit the petting zoo, and watch live entertainment. ℭ 800/465-6890 or 613/991-4422.

August

The Canadian Agriculture Museum. This festival celebrates creamy, dreamy ice cream. From milking cows to mixing the ingredients, discover the process of making ice cream and other frozen treats. ℭ 613/991-3044.

CKCU Ottawa Folk Festival. This gathering celebrates Canada's rich folk traditions with music, dance, storytelling, and crafts. Some of Canada's finest acoustic musicians perform evening concerts on the main stage, and afternoon musical stages feature such themes as song writing, Ottawa Valley fiddling and step dancing, Celtic music, and vocal harmonics. A fun-filled area offers crafts, activities, costumes, and children's performers. ℭ 613/230-8234.

Central Canada Exhibition. This is wholesome family entertainment at a great price. The Ex combines interactive theme exhibits, agricultural programs, entertainment, and a large midway with over 60 rides, including a roller coaster. ℭ 613/237-7222.

Greek Summer Festival. Ottawa's Greek-Canadian community celebrates all things Greek at this annual festival. ℭ 613/225-8016.

The Sparks Street Mall International Busker Festival. The second-largest busker festival in Canada presents jugglers, comedians, storytellers, fire-eaters, mimes, musicians, and magicians to entertain audiences of all ages. ✆ **613/230-0984.**

September

Gatineau Hot Air Balloon Festival. Around 150 balloons take to the skies at Canada's largest balloon festival, held on Labour Day weekend. There are plenty of shows and activities, fairground rides, and a dazzling fireworks display to thrill the kids. ✆ **800/668-8383** or 819/243-2331.

Bytown Days. Step into 19th-century Bytown on the third weekend in September. Enjoy the fall harvest, watch demonstrations of 19th-century workmanship and handicrafts, take a horse-drawn hay ride, and munch your way through the corn roast. ✆ **613/562-3325.**

Ottawa 67's. Watch OHL action at the Civic Centre, Lansdowne Park. The regular season runs from September to April. ✆ **613/232-6767.**

Ottawa Senators. The Sens take on the NHL's best at the Corel Centre. The regular season runs from September to April. ✆ **613/599-0123.**

Fall Rhapsody. Workshops, guided tours, nature interpretation programs, and other outdoor activities take place in Gatineau Park against a spectacular backdrop of fall leaves. Kids can watch exciting shows and participate in games and crafts. The towns and villages surrounding Gatineau Park celebrate autumn with exhibits of arts and crafts and activities for the whole family. ✆ **819/827-2020.**

National Capital Air Show. Held at Ottawa International Airport on the second weekend in September, the air show features 2 full days of static and flying demonstrations, including exhibits of military and civilian aircraft and performances

by the Canadian Forces Snowbirds and Parachute Team and the Sky Hawks. There are interactive displays and activities for children of all ages. ✆ **613/526-1030.**

Ottawa International Animation Festival. Film industry people from around the world gather in Ottawa for this biennial event (alternating with the Student Animation Festival). Programs include competitions, retrospectives, workshops, children's days, and more. ✆ **613/232-8769.**

Fall Home Show. You'll find everything for the home at this Lansdowne Park event, from wood-burning stoves to windows, roofing, and hot tubs, along with seminars and demonstrations. ✆ **613/580-2429.**

October

International Student Animation Festival of Ottawa. This biennial animation event, which alternates with the Ottawa International Animation Festival (see above), is devoted to students and first-time animators. Competitions, workshops, recruiting, and a trade fair are part of the event. ✆ **613/232-8769.**

Great Pumpkin Weigh-Off. At the ByWard Market on the first Saturday in October, growers from Ontario, Quebec, and the northeastern United States compete for the title of the Great Pumpkin. Some of the monsters weigh in at 450 kilograms (1,000 lbs.). Expert carvers are on hand to produce jack o'lanterns. ✆ **613/562-3325.**

Ski and Snowboard Show. Head to Lansdowne Park to check out the latest, fastest, and most technologically advanced skis and snowboards. ✆ **613/580-2429.**

November

Help Santa Toy Parade. On the third Saturday in November, the annual Santa Claus Parade winds its way through downtown Ottawa. Floats, bands, and clowns entertain the crowds lining the streets. The Fire Fighter's Association collects toys along the parade route and distributes them to less fortunate children in the Ottawa area. ℂ **613/ 526-2706.**

Canada Music Week. As part of Canada Music Week, Ottawa hosts the Contemporary Showcase, a 3-day festival of Canadian music written in the past 50 years and performed by students of all ages. Leading artists in the field judge participants in a master-class competition.

December

Christmas Lights Across Canada. In the heart of the capital, more than 200,000 colorful lights glow to celebrate the beginning of the Canadian winter and to welcome the New Year. ℂ **800/465-1867.**

Christmas Carollers. Leading up to Christmas, local choirs sing Christmas carols while riding around the historic ByWard Market district in a horse-drawn carriage with sleigh bells. ℂ **613/562-3325.**

Ottawa Rebel. The National Lacrosse League team plays at the Corel Centre. The regular season runs from December to April. ℂ **613/599-0123.**

4 Getting the Kids Interested

The best way to get your kids interested in visiting Ottawa is to include them in your planning sessions. Start by gathering information. Contact tourist offices well in advance of your trip and ask them to send you a visitor's package. Visit your local library and bookstores to browse the books on Canada's capital city—picture books are particularly appealing to young children. Once you've collected some material, sit down together and talk about the things you'll see when you go.

Read the chapters of this book that cover attractions, active pursuits, and entertainment. What fascinates *your* child? Is she a hockey fan? A swimmer? A dinosaur, airplane, or art lover? Does he like boat rides or arcades? Help your children put together their own "Top Ten Things I Want to See and Do in Ottawa" list. Their answers might surprise you.

 Hey, I Didn't Know That about Ottawa!

- The name Ottawa is adapted from *Outaouak,* the name of the Algonquin people who settled and traded furs in the area.
- The world's largest gold depository is found in the Bank of Canada gold vaults, which lie under Wellington Street, one of Ottawa's main streets.
- Ottawa's official relationship with tulips began in 1945 when Queen Juliana of the Netherlands presented 100,000 bulbs to the city as a gift. They were given in appreciation of Canada's granting of a safe haven to the Dutch Royal Family during World War II and in recognition of the role that Canadian troops played in liberating the Netherlands.

Half a century later, three million tulips bloom in the city's parklands in May.

- The sport of basketball was invented by Dr. James Naismith, who hailed from Almonte, a small town just west of Ottawa.
- Canada's last public hanging took place at Ottawa's first jail. The building is now operated by Hostelling International, and guests can actually sleep behind bars in the cells.
- The Governor General's New Year's Day Levee at Rideau Hall originated from the French governors' practice of shaking hands and wishing a happy New Year to the citizens of Quebec City, a tradition begun in 1646.
- The grounds of Parliament Hill were laid out in 1873 by Calvert Vaux, the same landscape architect who designed New York's Central Park.
- The 7.8 kilometer (4.5 mile) Rideau Canal Skateway, the world's longest skating rink, is used by approximately 750,000 skaters each winter and has an average skating season of 64 days.
- The world's first international telephone call was made from Ottawa in 1927, when Canadian prime minister Mackenzie King called the British prime minister.
- North American entertainment stars Paul Anka and Rich Little were born in Ottawa and have streets named after them in the city's south end.
- Actor Dan Ackroyd was born in the region and attended Carleton University. Singer Alanis Morissette was also born here, and rock star Bryan Adams went to school in Ottawa.
- The Ottawa Senators was originally the name of a local football club in the 1920s. In 1992, the name was reclaimed for Ottawa's first National Hockey League team.
- The Stanley Cup was born in Ottawa. In 1892, Governor General Lord Stanley Preston commissioned a silversmith in England to make a gold-lined silver bowl on an ebony base, which became the premier trophy of professional hockey in North America.

5 Health & Safety

MEDICAL

Medical care in Ontario is provided to all residents through the Ontario Health Insurance Plan (OHIP), administered by the provincial government. Visitors from abroad are ineligible for OHIP coverage and should arrange for **health insurance** coverage before entering Canada. For more information, contact a private insurance company directly, or call the **Canadian Life and Health Insurance Association** at ℭ 800/268-8099. Canadian travelers are protected by their home province's health insurance plan for a limited time period. Check with your province's health insurance agency before traveling.

Ottawa has a pediatric teaching hospital with emergency care services, the **Children's Hospital of Eastern Ontario,** located at 401 Smyth Road. For details on this hospital and hospitals for adults, see Chapter 3, "Getting to Know Ottawa."

For non-life-threatening emergencies that require a physician consultation, go to a **walk-in clinic**. These clinics operate just as the name implies—you walk in and wait your turn to see a physician. Look in the Yellow Pages or ask your hotel to recommend one. Payment procedures vary between clinics, so call ahead and ask about their billing policy for non-residents of Ontario or Canada. Most clinics will accept health cards from other provinces, although Quebec residents may be required to pay cash and obtain reimbursement from their provincial government. Out-of-country patients may be required to pay cash—checks or credit cards may not be accepted. Some doctors will make house calls to your hotel. Telehealth Ontario offers free telephone access to registered nurses, 24 hours, 7 days a week (© **866/797-0000**).

For minor health problems, consult with a **pharmacist.** These professionals are trained in health consultation and will recommend whether you should see a doctor about your particular condition. Many pharmacies are open evenings and weekends and advertise their hours in the Yellow Pages. **Shopper's Drug Mart** has two **24-hour** locations: 1460 Merivale Rd. (at Baseline Rd.) (© **613/224-7270**), and Southgate Shopping Centre, 2515 Bank St. (at Hunt Club Rd.) (© **613/523-9999**).

TRAVEL INSURANCE

Before you decide to purchase travel insurance, check your existing policies to see whether they'll cover you while you're traveling. Some credit cards offer automatic **flight insurance** when you buy an airline ticket with the card. These policies provide insurance coverage for death or dismemberment in the event of a plane crash.

If you plan to rent a car, check with your credit cards to see if any of them pick up the **collision damage waiver (CDW)** in Canada. The CDW can run as much as C$16 (US$11) per day, adding as much as 50% to the cost of car rental. Check your automobile policy, too—it might cover the CDW. If you own a home or have renter's insurance, see if that policy covers off-premises **theft and loss** wherever it occurs. Find out what procedures you need to follow to make a claim. If you're traveling on a tour or package deal and have prepaid a large chunk of your travel expenses, you might want to consider buying **trip cancellation insurance.**

If, after checking all your existing insurance policies, you decide you need additional insurance, ask your travel agent for assistance.

SAFETY

As large cities go, Ottawa is generally **safe**, but be alert and use common sense, particularly at night. Remind the kids of your family's safety rules before you leave home, and discuss what they should do if they become separated from you. Make sure they know the name of your hotel. Dressing the kids in bright colors will make them easy to spot if they stray from your side, but **preschoolers**, in particular, should always hold your hand or the side of younger sibling's stroller as you walk along. When you're visiting a crowded place, consider giving each child a security whistle to use in an emergency. Set strict rules about whom they should approach if they're lost (such as a police officer, a female cashier in a store or museum, or a mother with small children) and whom they should avoid (just about everyone else).

6 Tips for Travelers with Disabilities

To find out which attractions, accommodations, and restaurants in Ottawa are accessible to people with disabilities, refer to the Ottawa visitor's guide, available from the **Capital Infocentre** (② **800/465-1867**). The guide includes symbols next to each listing to indicate whether the entry and/or washrooms are accessible. **Full accessibility** is defined as being independently accessible to people using wheelchairs or with limited upper body strength. Services should include automatic front doors, ramps, sufficient turning space for a wheelchair in the rooms or bathrooms, and wider doorways (84cm or 33 in.). **Basic accessibility** indicates that people using wheelchairs may require assistance to use the services within the establishment. The owners and managers of each establishment determine whether their property is accessible. For more information, call **Disabled Persons Community Resources** (② **613/724-5886**). If you are purchasing tickets to an entertainment event, indicate that you require special seating when you make your reservation.

OC Transpo, which provides **public transit** in Ottawa, is increasing the number of fully accessible buses, with a target set at 25% of the fleet by the end of 2001. Fully accessible buses have low floors and no stairs to climb, providing easier access for seniors, passengers with limited mobility, people using wheelchairs, and parents with small children or strollers. These buses lower to the curb and have an extendable ramp for wheelchair users. You can spot low-floor buses by the blue and white wheelchair symbol on the upper corner on the front of the bus.

For persons with permanent or short-term disabilities who are unable to walk to or board regular transit, **Para Transpo** is available. Both visitors and residents can use this service, but you must register and book a reservation a day in advance. You must also have the application form signed by an appropriate health professional. Call ② **613/244-1289** for information and registration, or ② **613/244-7272** for reservations.

7 Getting There

BY PLANE

Wherever you're traveling from, always shop the airlines and ask for the lowest fare. You'll have a better chance of landing a deal if you're willing to be flexible about when you arrive and leave.

You may be able to fly for less than the standard advance (APEX) fare by contacting a ticket broker or consolidator. These companies, which buy tickets in bulk and sell them at a discount, advertise in the Sunday travel sections of major city newspapers. You may not be able to get the lowest price

they advertise, but you're likely to pay less than the price quoted by the major airlines. Bear in mind that tickets purchased through a consolidator are often nonrefundable. If you change your itinerary after purchase, chances are you'll pay a stiff penalty.

When booking your flight, ask your air carrier about child safety restraint, transport of strollers, times of meal service, availability of children's meals, and bulkhead seating (which has extra room to stretch out). Mention any food allergies or other medical concerns.

Travel-Planning Websites

If you're a Net surfer, it's possible to get some great cyber deals on airfare, hotels, and car rentals.

www.frommers.com   Arthur Frommer's Budget Travel Online is a good place to start. You'll find indispensable travel tips, reviews, monthly vacation giveaways, and online booking services. One of the most popular features of this site is the regular "Ask the Expert" bulletin board, where you can post questions and have them answered online by Frommer's authors. You can also sign up for an electronic newsletter to receive the latest travel bargains and insider travel secrets in your e-mailbox every day. The Destinations Archive lists more than 200 domestic and international destinations, with information on great places to stay, traveling tips, and things to do while you're there.

www.travelocity.com; www.previewtravel.com; www.frommers. travelocity.com   Travelocity is Frommer's online travel-planning and booking partner. Travelocity uses the SABRE system to offer reservations and tickets for more than 400 airlines, plus reservations and booking services for more than 45,000 hotels and 50 car-rental companies.

expedia.com   Expedia is Travelocity's major competitor. It offers several ways to obtain the best possible fares. Expedia focuses on the major airlines and hotel chains, so don't expect to find many budget airlines or one-of-a-kind B&Bs here.

www.trip.com   TRIP.com began as a site geared toward business travelers, but its innovative features and highly personalized approach have broadened its appeal to leisure travelers as well. It is the leading travel site for those using mobile devices to access Internet travel information.

www.travel.yahoo.com   Yahoo! is currently the most popular of the Internet information portals, and its travel site is a comprehensive mix of online booking, daily travel news, and destination information.

WITHIN CANADA Air Canada, which also operates Air Nova, Canadian Regional, and Air Ontario, offers direct flights from the following Canadian cities: Calgary, Fredericton, Halifax, Montreal (Dorval), Quebec City, Toronto (Pearson and City Centre), Vancouver, Winnipeg. and London, Ontario. In 2000, Air Canada took over Canadian Airlines International, making the former Canada's only national airline. The central reservation number for all Air Canada–operated airlines is (C) **888/247-2262.** Bearskin Airlines (C) **800/465-5039)** serves Northern Ontario, operating direct flights from North Bay, Sudbury, and Thunder Bay. Canada 3000 (C) **888/226-3000)** flies direct from Vancouver. Canjet (C) **800/809-7777)** operates direct flights from Toronto and Halifax. Montreal and northern Canada, including Cambridge Bay, Iqaluit, Kuujjuaq, Nanisivik, Resolute, and Yellowknife, are served by First Air (C) **800/267-1247).** Royal Airlines (C) **888/828-9797)** operates between Ottawa, Montreal, and Toronto. Trillium Air (C) **877-263-0333),** primarily serving the high-tech business sector, flies between Silicon Valley North (aka Ottawa) and Kitchener-Waterloo. For a direct flight from Hamilton, contact WestJet (© 877/956-6982 or 800/ 538-5696).

FROM THE U.S. Direct flights from Boston, Chicago, New York (LaGuardia and Newark), Washington (Dulles and Reagan National), and Raleigh-Durham, North Carolina, are operated by Air Canada (© 888/247-2262). American Airlines (© 800/ 433-7300) flies direct to Ottawa from Chicago and St. Louis. Business Express (American Eagle) (© 800/345-3400) operates direct flights from Boston and New York (LaGuardia). From Newark, Continental Express (© 800/ 525-0280) flies direct to Ottawa. Travelers in the Detroit area can fly with Northwest Airlink (Mesaba Airlines) (© 800/225-2525). US Airways (US Airways Express) (© 800/ 428-4322) operates direct flights from Philadelphia and Pittsburgh.

FROM ABROAD Air Canada flies direct to Ottawa from London (Heathrow) and Canada 3000 operates between London (Gatwick) and Ottawa. From the rest of the world, there's frequent service (direct or indirect) to Toronto. A 1-hour connector flight from Toronto will land you in Ottawa.

ARRIVING IN OTTAWA

From the Ottawa International Airport, in the south end of the city, you have several options for traveling to the city. The Ottawa Airport Shuttle (© 888/862-7433 or 613/736-9993) runs between the airport and several downtown locations. The cost is C$9 (US$6) per adult one-way, and C$14 (US$9) round-trip. Two adults traveling together get a C$2 (US$1.30) reduction on each fare. Children 11 and younger travel free with their family. The shuttle operates daily with departures every 30 minutes, starting

at 5am. The following hotels have scheduled stops: Novotel, Les Suites Hotel, the Westin, the Fairmont Château Laurier, the Lord Elgin, the Sheraton, Marriott Residence Inn, the Delta Ottawa, the Crowne Plaza, and Minto Place. The shuttle will drop off and pick up at the following hotels on request: Quality Hotel, Capital Hill Hotel, Cartier Place & Towers, the Aristocrat, the Business Inn, Embassy Hotel and Suites, Marriott Residence Inn, the Roxborough, Ramada Hotel & Suites, Howard Johnson Hotel, Travelodge Hotel, Albert at Bay Suite Hotel, Best Western Victoria Park Suites, and Ramada Inn 417.

If you wish to take public transit, OC Transpo provides high-frequency rapid service along the scenic Transitway, a roadway built specifically for buses. Route 97 will whisk you downtown in less than 25 minutes. You can also hop in a taxi; the fare will be around C$22 (US$15). A 20-minute drive along the Airport Parkway will take you to the heart of downtown.

BY TRAIN

VIA Rail trains to Ottawa operate as part of the Windsor–Quebec City corridor. The **Ottawa station** (© 613/ 244-8289) is located at 200 Tremblay Rd., near the Riverside Drive exit from Highway 417, just east of downtown. VIA Rail often has special fares, and booking in advance may also get you a substantial discount. For rail information, contact **VIA Rail Canada** at © 888/VIA-RAIL (888/842-7245), www.viarail.ca. If you're traveling from the United States, call **Amtrak** at © 800/USA-RAIL (800/872-7245).

BY BUS

Ottawa Bus Central Station (© 613/238-5900) is located at 265 Catherine St., near the Kent Street exit from Highway 417, on the edge of the downtown core. **Greyhound Canada**

(✆ **800/661-TRIP,** or 800/661-8747) provides coast-to-coast bus service with connections to Ottawa. **Greyhound/Trailways** (✆ **800/231-2222**) is the only bus company that crosses the U.S. border. You can travel almost anywhere in the United States, changing buses along the way.

The bus may be faster and cheaper than the train, and its routes may be more flexible if you want to stop along the way. But there's also less space to stretch out, toilet facilities are meager, and meals are taken at roadside rest stops, so consider carefully if you're planning to take children on a long trip.

Depending on where you're coming from, check into Greyhound/Trailways special unlimited-travel passes and any discount fares that might be offered. It's hard to quote a typical fare because bus companies, like airlines, are adopting yield-management strategies, causing prices to change from one day to the next depending on demand.

BY CAR

With the completion in 2001 of Highway 416 as the link between Highway 401 and Ottawa, the approach from south and west of Canada's capital is a smooth and easy drive. Be alert to the possibility of deer suddenly appearing in the roadway in rural forested areas, particularly on Highway 416 and most often at night. Unless you're headed for the west end of the city, take exit 57 from Highway 416—look for the sign that reads BANKFIELD ROAD (COUNTY ROAD 8)/ AIRPORT/SCENIC ROUTE. Follow County Road 8 east to Highway 73 north through the countryside until you reach Hunt Club Road on the southern edge of the city. From here, you can take one of several routes downtown—Prince of Wales Drive and Riverside Drive are the most pleasant. The Airport Parkway/Bronson Avenue is the most direct, and Bank Street will take you past the most shops. From Montreal and eastern Canada, travel west along Highway 417 and enter the city via Montreal Road.

If you're arriving from south of the border, there are several convenient crossing points. From Vermont, enter Canada via Interstate 89 or 91, travel toward Montreal, and pick up the westerly route (Hwy. 417). In New York State, Interstate 81 crosses at Hill Island to Highway 401; you can also take Route 37 and enter at Ogdensburg–Johnstown or Rooseveltown–Cornwall. On Interstate 87 in New York State, cross into Quebec, travel toward Montreal, and keep to the west of the city, taking Highway 417. If you're driving from Michigan, you'll enter Ontario at Detroit–Windsor (via I–75 and the Ambassador Bridge) or Port Huron–Sarnia (via I–94 and the Bluewater Bridge).

Here are approximate driving distances in miles to Ottawa: from Boston, 465; Buffalo, 335; Chicago, 800; Detroit, 525; New York, 465; Washington, D.C., 580.

Be sure to carry your driver's license and car registration if you plan to drive your own vehicle into Canada. You should carry proof of automobile liability insurance as well.

If you are a member of the American Automobile Association (AAA), the **Canadian Automobile Association (CAA)** North and East Ontario branch provides emergency road assistance (✆ **613/820-1400**). For touring information, call ✆ **613/820-1880.**

Survival Tips for Traveling with Kids

- Don't try to see and do as much as you would if you were traveling without your children.
- Make a list of everything you want to do on vacation, then cut it in half.
- Choose accommodations close to a park or playground.
- Alternate sightseeing or travel days with unstructured play days.
- Bring medication, paper towels, and plastic bags in case of travel sickness.
- Plan meal times in advance and *always* carry snacks to appease hungry tummies.
- If you're traveling to a different time zone, schedule meals and bedtime for the new time a few days before leaving to adjust more quickly.
- Bring a few favorite bedtime stories.
- Bring toys, but avoid ones with lots of small parts that can get scattered or lost.
- Bring an umbrella stroller—it's lightweight, it folds easily, and it can be used as a feeding chair or napping place when necessary.
- Let kids pack their own entertainment backpacks.
- Buy each child a portable cassette player with earphones. You can get stories on tape as well as children's music. The trip will be *so* quiet!
- If you have a long trip, splurge at the dollar store on a few simple toys and treats. Pack them in a bag, and each time you have a rest stop, let the kids take a "lucky dip."
- Give older children their own budget to spend on souvenirs.
- Call your hotel to find out what items they have on hand for infants and small children. You may be able to leave half the kitchen sink at home.
- Finally, if you can swing it, try to schedule some vacation time away from your children.

3

Getting to Know Ottawa

Ottawa's personality is both refreshing and eclectic. The nation's top historical landmark, Parliament Hill, stands in Canada's most wired city, where 8 out of 10 households have a computer. The pomp and ceremony of the parade of the Ceremonial Guard contrasts with the relaxed attitude of the young high-tech community. And through it all run ribbons of green and blue—the region's green space, parks, and waterways.

But Ottawa is not what it used to be. On January 1, 2001, a new capital city was created for Canada as 12 local municipal governments were amalgamated to create one new municipality of Ottawa. The region was more than ready for municipal reform. Social and economic development had been hindered by the existence of 12 municipalities, each representing local interests and each with its own bureaucratic administration. In fact, three decades of political indecision preceded the launch of the new city.

The new Ottawa, now the fourth-largest city in Canada, spans 2,760 square kilometers (1711 sq. miles) and includes more than 150 communities.

The population at the time of amalgamation was 800,000, and the number of residents is expected to top one million by 2003.

With its proximity to Quebec and its high concentration of federal government employees, Ottawa is a bilingual city, offering a stimulating blend of English and French culture. As you stroll around the city, you are just as likely to hear French spoken as English. But don't worry if you don't speak French. The people you will meet as a visitor—hotel staff, restaurant servers, museum and attractions employees—are usually fluent in both official languages. Added to this mix is an increasing ethnic population. One in five Ottawa residents is an immigrant, contributing to the city's rich ethnic diversity of German, Lebanese, Italian, Polish, Dutch, Portuguese, Asian, and Greek populations, among others.

Ottawa is a wonderful city to explore with your kids. Experience one of the lively festivals, visit a couple of national museums, and be sure to leave plenty of time to play and relax. Enjoy!

1 Orientation

VISITOR INFORMATION

Across the street from the Parliament Buildings and within easy walking distance of many major tourist attractions is the **Capital Infocentre,** at 90 Wellington Street. The building has a windowed gallery facing Parliament Hill, offering a dramatic photo opportunity. The Terry Fox Memorial is situated in the square out front.

The Capital Infocentre is packed with brochures and dynamic exhibits. As you enter the building, you'll see a huge three-dimensional map of the central region. This is a great orientation tool. For a dazzling overview of Canada's capital and what's on offer for visitors, attend a presentation at the multimedia theater. Also check out the souvenir shop, which offers maps, guidebooks, clothing, and a few items for children.

To customize your itinerary in the capital, visit a "passport kiosk" in the Infocentre. Using the touch-sensitive screens, you can ask the computer for information on sites and attractions that suit your tastes and interests. The system then prints out a personalized passport with your chosen itinerary. If you prefer more personal interaction, orientation counselors are available to answer questions on Ottawa and the surrounding region and to help you plan your visit. For phone inquiries, contact the **Capital Call Centre** at ℂ **800/465-1867** or 613/239-5000, open daily 8:30am to 9pm from mid-May to Labour Day, and 9am to 5pm the rest of the year. The call center is closed Christmas Day, Boxing Day, and New Year's Day. If you're online, visit the Capital Infocentre website at **www.capcan.ca.** Other websites with visitor information include **www.ottawa.com, www.ottawakiosk.com,** and **www.festivalseeker.com.**

The **Ottawa Tourism and Convention Authority (OTCA)** publishes an annual visitor's guide, with maps and descriptions of cultural sites, things to see and do, accommodations, places to dine and shop, and services. The guide is available at the Capital Infocentre and at other locations around the city. The OCTA can be reached via the toll-free number for the Capital Call Centre listed above, or at ℂ **613/237-5150.**

For listings of upcoming events, pick up a copy of *Where,* a free monthly guide to entertainment, shopping, and dining, available at hotels and stores throughout the city. *Capital Parent,* a free monthly newspaper, and *Ottawa Families,* a free bimonthly newspaper, also contain articles of interest to parents and often advertise family-friendly events. *Ottawa City Magazine* and *Ottawa Life* magazine are city monthlies. The daily newspapers are the *Ottawa Citizen,* the *Ottawa Sun,* and *Le Droit,* Ottawa's French-language newspaper. The *Ottawa Citizen* includes a comprehensive Arts section on Fridays, with film listings and reviews, and a special Going Out section on Saturdays, with listings of upcoming live entertainment events. The back page of Sunday's A section details family events in the community for the coming week. For news and information about regional arts events and activities, drop in to **Arts Court,** 2 Daly Ave. (ℂ **613/564-7240**), or call the **Council for the Arts in Ottawa (CAO)** (ℂ **613/569-1387**).

CITY LAYOUT

The Ottawa River—Canada's second longest, at over 1,100 kilometers (700 miles)—curves around the northern edge of the city. The compact downtown area, where most major attractions are clustered within walking distance, is south of the river.

The **Rideau Canal,** sweeping past the National Arts Centre, divides the downtown area in two—**west of the Canal** (often called Centre Town) and **east of the Canal** (often called Lower Town). In the downtown area west of the canal are Parliament Hill, the Supreme Court, and the Canadian Museum of Nature. In the downtown area east of the canal are the National Gallery of Canada and the ByWard Market (a vibrant center for restaurants, boutiques, and nightlife). Further along Sussex Drive (which follows the south bank of the Ottawa River), you'll find the Canadian War Museum, the Royal Canadian Mint, and eventually the prime minister's residence, diplomat's row, Rideau Hall, and Rockcliffe Park.

The area south of the Queensway, west to Bronson Avenue and east to the canal, is known as the **Glebe** and offers wonderful shopping and trendy cafes along Bank Street. North across the river, in Quebec, lies the city of **Hull,** connected to the east end of Ottawa by the Macdonald-Cartier and Alexandra bridges and to the west by the Portage and Chaudière bridges. At the end of the Alexandra Bridge stands the architecturally stunning Museum of Civilization. North and west of Hull stretches breathtaking **Gatineau Park,** 361 square kilometers (141 sq. miles) of wilderness managed by the National Capital Commission.

Finding your way around town is occasionally bewildering, since streets have a habit of halting abruptly and then reappearing a few blocks further on, and some streets change names several times. Ottawa's main street, for example, starts as Scott Street, changes to Wellington Street as it passes through downtown in front of the Parliament Buildings, switches to Rideau Street in downtown east, and finally becomes Montreal Road on the eastern fringes of town. Take my advice: Carry a map.

⌐Tips The Main Streets

The main streets running east-west through downtown are **Wellington, Laurier,** and **Somerset;** the **Rideau Canal** separates east from west (Lower Town and Centre Town); and the main north-south streets are **Bronson, Bank,** and **Elgin.**

NEIGHBORHOODS IN BRIEF

The architecture and layout of the city of Ottawa has been said to reflect Canada's bilingual heritage. Many residents speak or understand both French and English, and a number of ethnic groups have also brought their cultures to the city. Nowhere is this diversity more apparent than in Ottawa's distinct neighborhoods. The various business and residential areas each have their own mix of shops, cuisine, architecture, and sights and sounds, representing different cultures and traditions from around the globe. Strolling through the various neighborhoods will give you an appreciation of the city's heart and soul—its people.

ByWard Market & Downtown, East of the Canal   Situated northeast of the Parliament Buildings, on the east side of the Rideau Canal and bordered by the Rideau River to the west, this historic neighborhood is the oldest section of Ottawa. Originally, **downtown, east of the Canal** (also known as **Lower Town**) was an uninhabitable cedar swamp. During the construction of the Rideau Canal, the land was drained and a mix of settlers soon moved in, including canal workers, shantymen, rivermen, and their families. The area was populated by poor Irish immigrants and French Canadians, and a reputation for general rowdiness and unlawfulness soon took hold. The building of the farmer's market in the mid-19th century helped to boost the local economy. The **ByWard Market** district, with its eclectic mix of boutiques, cafes, and bars, is now a prosperous, attractive city neighborhood with a vibrant personality.

Sussex Drive   Winding along the south shore of the Ottawa River, historic Sussex Drive is a grand boulevard featuring many well-known landmarks. The National Gallery of Canada, Royal Canadian Mint, Canadian War Museum, Notre Dame Basilica, U.S. embassy, French embassy, residence of the

Ottawa–Hull

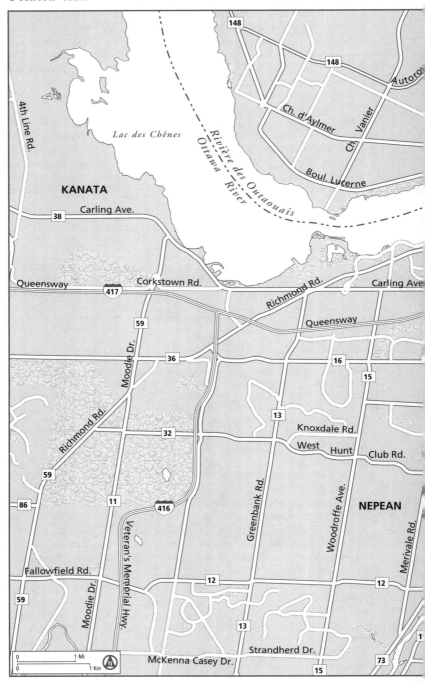

148

148

Autoro

Ch. d'Aylmer

Vanier

Ch.

Boul. Lucerne

Lac des Chênes

Rivière des Outaouais
Ottawa River

4th Line Rd.

KANATA

38 Carling Ave.

Queensway 417 Corkstown Rd.

Richmond Rd.

Carling Ave

59

Queensway

Moodie Dr.

36

16

15

Richmond Rd.

13

32

Knoxdale Rd.

West Hunt Club Rd.

59

86

11

416

Greenbank Rd.

Woodroffe Ave.

NEPEAN

Merivale Rd.

Fallowfield Rd.

Veteran's Memorial Hwy.

59

Moodie Dr.

12

12

13

Strandherd Dr.

73

0   1 Mi
0   1 Km

McKenna Casey Dr.

15

1

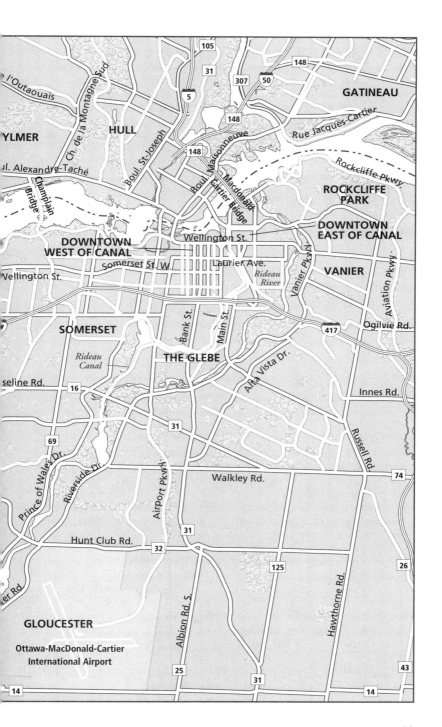

l'Outaouais

GATINEAU

148

31

105

307 50

5

148

148

HULL

YLMER

Ch. de la Montagne Sud

Boul St-Joseph

Boul. Maisonneuve

Macdonald-Cartier Bridge

Rue Jacques-Cartier

Rockcliffe Pkwy.

ul. Alexandre-Taché

Champlain Bridge

ROCKCLIFFE PARK

Wellington St.

DOWNTOWN EAST OF CANAL

DOWNTOWN WEST OF CANAL

Somerset St. W.

Laurier Ave.

VANIER

Vellington St.

Rideau River

Vanier Pkwy.

Aviation Pkwy.

SOMERSET

Bank St.

Main St.

417

Ogilvie Rd.

Rideau Canal

THE GLEBE

Alta Vista Dr.

seline Rd.

16

Innes Rd.

69

Russell Rd.

31

Prince of Wales Dr.

Riverside Dr.

Airport Pkwy.

Walkley Rd.

74

31

Hunt Club Rd.

32

125

26

Albion Rd. S.

Hawthorne Rd.

GLOUCESTER

Ottawa-MacDonald-Cartier
International Airport

25

31

43

r Rd.

14

14

35

prime minister of Canada (24 Sussex Dr.), and Rideau Hall (home of the governor general) are all found on this route. Also on Sussex Drive are the scenic Rideau Falls and the imposing Lester B. Pearson Building, home of the Federal Department of Foreign Affairs. Earnscliffe, the residence of the British high commissioner, was originally the home of Canada's first prime minister, Sir John A. Macdonald. It sits high on a cliff overlooking the Ottawa River.

Downtown, West of the Canal
Ottawa's downtown business district (also refered to as **Centre Town**) is a maze of office towers in an area stretching several blocks to the south of Parliament Hill. There are many excellent hotels, restaurants, and shops in the area. Sparks Street Mall, Canada's first pedestrianized shopping street, is located here.

Somerset Village   This downtown neighborhood, centered on a stretch of Somerset Street between Bank and O'Connor streets, is characterized by a cluster of historic red-brick dwellings. It was revitalized in the mid-1980s after the owners of commercial buildings in the area commissioned a heritage-style streetscape design. Five-globe streetlamps, red-brick sidewalks, trees and shrubs, and benches now line the 19th-century streets. The village encompasses 15 buildings, 13 of which were built around 1900 or earlier, with a lively mix of shops, offices, bars, restaurants, and residential structures. In addition, the Embassy of the Ukraine, the Embassy of Zimbabwe, and the High Commission for Bangladesh are located here.

Somerset Heights   Step into the Far East as you travel further west along Somerset Street to the neighborhood stretching from Bay to Rochester streets. Intriguing markets sell a variety of Asian produce, crafts, traditional Chinese medicinal ingredients, hand-painted silk garments, and many more fascinating treasures. Thai, Vietnamese, and Chinese restaurants appear on every corner, tempting visitors with their distinctive cuisine.

Little Italy   The heart of Ottawa's Italian immigrant population is Preston Street, also fondly known as Corso Italia (both names appear on the official street signs). The area serves as the commercial and cultural center of Little Italy. An abundance of cafes, trattorie, and pizzerias celebrate the essence of Italy—its wonderful cuisine. Irish, French, and Asian Canadians also call the neighborhood home. Every June, the street comes alive with the festivities of Italian Week, culminating in a street party stretching over three evenings.

Westboro Village   Originally a small village on the outskirts of the city, Westboro has retained its friendly small-town atmosphere. This traditional city neighborhood west of downtown has enjoyed a revitalization, which began in the late 1990s. The addition of Richmond Road Mountain Equipment Co-op spurred retail growth in the west end of Westboro's commercial ribbon, and there is hope that the area will eventually link with Wellington Street West to form a shopping district much like the ByWard Market and the Glebe.

The Glebe   Just south of downtown, between the Queensway and Lansdowne Park, lies Ottawa's first suburb. In the 1870s, residential development began to encroach on farmland south of the city. The construction of exhibition grounds at Lansdowne Park and of a streetcar link between the Glebe and the city fueled the growth of this neighborhood. The middle classes settled here in large numbers. Today, the Glebe is an upscale middle-class neighborhood served by a stretch of trendy, high-end stores, services, and eateries on Bank Street. It's well worth spending a morning or afternoon strolling up one side of the street and down the other. If you begin at the north end, take a break near the canal before making your return journey. Brown's Inlet and Park are tucked a block or two west of Bank Street, north of Queen Elizabeth Drive. If you start at the canal end, rest in Central Park, which straddles Bank Street in the vicinity of Powell and Clemow avenues. For winter strolling, take refuge in the atrium at Fifth Avenue Court, about midway down this section of Bank Street.

2 Getting Around
BY PUBLIC TRANSPORTATION

CITY BUSES   **Public Transit** in Ottawa is provided by **Ottawa-Carleton (OC) Transpo.** This is an economical and efficient way to get around since buses can bypass rush-hour traffic through Transitway, a rapid-transit system of roadways exclusively for buses. Routes 95 and 97 are the two main Transitway routes, operating 22 hours a day. All OC Transpo bus routes travel along parts of the Transitway or connect at one of the stations. OC Transpo stations, many of which are located next to major shopping or employment centers, offer convenient transfer points with heated waiting areas, information displays, and phones. Many have bike racks and vendor kiosks.

The regular exact cash fare is C$2.25 (US$1.50) adult single or C$1.25 (US80¢) child. It's cheaper to use tickets, at C80¢ (US50¢) each, since the adult fare is two tickets and the child fare is one ticket. The exception is during weekday rush hours, when some express routes charge a three-ticket fare. Day passes are a good buy at C$5 (US$3) for unlimited rides. You can buy bus passes and tickets at more than 300 vendor locations across the city.

The number of buses that are fully accessible to **people with disabilities** is on the rise, with a target set at 25% of the fleet by the end of 2001. Fully accessible buses, marked by a blue and white wheelchair symbol on the front of the bus, have low floors to provide access for seniors, people with limited mobility, people using wheelchairs, and parents with small children or strollers. The buses lower to the curb so there are no stairs to climb, and drivers can extend a ramp to accommodate wheelchairs.

For persons with permanent or short-term disabilities who are unable to walk to or board regular transit, **Para Transpo** is available. Both visitors and residents can use this service, but you must have the application form signed by an appropriate health professional and register and reserve a day in advance. Call ℂ **613/244-1289** for information and registration, or ℂ **613/244-7272** for reservations.

Public transit throughout **Hull, Gatineau,** and the **Outaouais** region on the Quebec side of the Ottawa River is provided by **Société de transport de l'Outaouais (STO)** (ℂ **819/770-3242**).

LIGHT RAIL TRAIN   The **Light Rail** pilot project is scheduled to begin in 2001. Designed to go where the Transitway doesn't, Light Rail will initially use an 8 kilometer (5 mile) stretch of existing Canadian Pacific rail line running between Greenboro Transitway Station in the south end and Lebreton Flats in the north end of the city, where a new Transitway station will be constructed. Each train, built by the Canadian company Bombardier, will consist of three cars, accommodating 135 seated and 150 standing passengers. The front and rear diesel-powered units will allow the train to travel in either direction on the track without having to turn around. A low-floor design ensures easy access for passengers and a quiet, comfortable ride. Operating hours are expected to be Monday to Friday 6:30am to midnight, Saturday 7am to midnight, and Sunday 7:30am to 11pm. The fare will be the same as the Transitway bus fare.

BY TAXI

You can hail a taxi on the street, but you'll find one more readily at taxi stands in front of most hotels, many important buildings, and some museums. You can also summon a taxi by phone. In the Ottawa area, 24-hour cab companies include **Blue Line** (© 613/238-1111), with a fleet of more than 600 cabs, and **Capital Taxi** (© 613/744-3333). **West-Way Taxi** (©613/727-0101) has drivers who have been trained to transport people with disabilities.

BY TOUR BUS

There are so many interesting buildings, monuments, attractions, and views in Ottawa that hopping on a tour bus is a great idea, especially if it's your first visit to Canada's capital. Tours are fully narrated so you don't miss anything while you're cruising around town. On-and-off privileges are perfect for families—if you or your kids need a break to stretch your legs, or if you see somewhere you'd like to visit, just hop off the bus and join it again later. Tickets are valid for 3 days. The best bet (if your kids are old enough to happily ride on the bus for an hour or more) is to take the full tour on the first day, making a note of the places you'd like to stop and explore. On the second day, execute your grand plan.

Gray Line Sightseeing Tours   Choose an open-top double-decker bus or a vintage trolley bus. Step on or off the bus any time you wish at the following stops: Parliament Hill, Museum of Civilization, Notre Dame Basilica, Rideau Hall, RCMP Museum and Stables, National Aviation Museum, National War Museum, Royal Canadian Mint, National Gallery, ByWard Market, Rideau Canal, Dow's Lake, Experimental Farm, and Canadian Museum of Nature. If you call ahead, the bus will pick you up at your downtown hotel. Tours operate from May to October. Tickets are valid for 3 days and prices are reasonable— a family of four can get a 3-day, on-off privilege ticket for C$54 (US$36). For departure times and other information, call Gray Line at © **800/297-6422** or 613/565-5463.

Capital Double Decker & Trolley Tours   This locally owned and operated tour company also offers open-top double-decker buses and historic trolley buses. Tours are fully narrated. Hotel pick-up and return are free, and you can hop on and off all day. For more information, call © **800/823-6147** or 613/749-3666.

Oakroads   If you want to explore the back roads and scenic routes in the surrounding countryside, take an Oakroads day tour. Travel in a 22-seat luxury coach and stop at small towns and places of natural and historic interest, all within a day's drive of Ottawa. Operating from May to October, a different tour is planned for each day of the week. Rates are C$40 (US$26) per adult, C$25

(US$17) per child, and C$100 (US$66) per family. The tour departs from the corner of Sparks and Elgin streets and from the Capital Infocentre at 90 Wellington St. Call ahead if you want the bus to pick you up from your downtown hotel. For more information, call ✆ **613-748-0144.**

The View from Here

- For views of **Parliament Hill** and the **Ottawa River,** visit Major's Hill Park or Nepean Point.
- To take in the **Ottawa skyline facing south,** as well as **Parliament Hill,** look across from Victoria Island or the Canadian Museum of Civilization.
- For a photo of the stunning architecture of the **Canadian Museum of Civilization,** look across the Ottawa River from Parliament Hill.
- To capture **tulips** on film, visit the numerous public parks and gardens throughout the city during the month of May. Visit the Dutch tulip gardens at the northern tip of Dow's Lake in Commissioner's Park, where 300,000 bulbs create a breathtaking display of color.
- To see beautiful **waterfalls,** visit Rideau Falls and Hog's Back Falls.
- View the **Ottawa skyline facing north** from the Arboretum and the Central Experimental Farm.
- Enjoy a wide vista of the **Ottawa Valley** from Champlain Lookout in Gatineau Park.
- To see the wide sweep of the **Ottawa River** and the **Quebec shoreline,** pay a visit to Rockcliffe Lookout.

BY CAR

So many of Ottawa's attractions are downtown and within walking distance of each other that you can have a wonderful vacation without ever getting behind the wheel of a car. If you traveled to Ottawa by car, leave it in the hotel parking garage unless you're planning to venture out on a day trip. If you reached the city by plane, train, or bus, you could rent a car for a day or two to explore Ottawa's surrounding regions, and spend the rest of the time traveling by city bus, tour bus, and bicycle or on foot.

If you do decided to drive, be prepared for one-way streets, which don't follow any predictable pattern. Keep an eye out, as well, for traffic blocks, designed to prevent vehicles from using residential streets as thoroughfares. Some streets change name several times along their length and others stop abruptly, only to continue a few blocks over. Needless to say, a map is essential if you're driving in city areas. You'll have the added convenience of being able to locate major tourist attractions, parking lots, and other useful destinations.

RENTAL CARS   If you decide to rent a car during the high season, try to make arrangements in advance to ensure the vehicle you want will be available. If you are traveling from outside Canada, you may obtain a reasonable discount by booking before you leave home. The rental fee depends on the type of car, but the starting point is around C$45 (US$30) a day, plus 14% tax. This price does not include insurance, but if you pay with a particular credit card, you might get automatic coverage (check with your credit card issuer before you travel). Be sure to read the fine print of the agreement and to do a complete visual check for damage before accepting the vehicle. Some companies add conditions that will boost your bill if you don't fulfill certain obligations, such as filling the gas tank before returning the car. Major rental companies with offices at Ottawa International Airport and downtown locations include **Thrifty** (*©* **800/847-4389**), **Avis** (*©* **800/879-2847**), **Budget** (*©* **800/268-8900**), **Hertz** (*©* **800/263-0600**), and **National** (*©* **800/227-7368**).

Note: If you're under 25, check with the rental company—some will rent on a cash-only basis, some will rent only if you have a credit card, and others will not rent to you at all.

PARKING   When parking downtown you have a choice of meters or lots. Parking meters are color-coded: Meters with a 1-hour time limit have gray domes, those with a 2-hour limit have green domes, and those for tour-bus parking only have yellow domes. Always read the signs posted near parking meters to find out if there are any parking restrictions. One of the most common restrictions is a ban on parking between 3:30 and 5:30pm on weekdays on certain streets, to improve traffic flow during the evening rush hour. City-owned and private lots charge up to C$10 (US$7) for all-day parking. Your best bet is to use a municipal parking lot, marked with a large green "P" in a circle. On weekends, parking is free at city lots and meters in the area west of the canal, east of Bronson Avenue, and north of the Queensway.

DRIVING RULES   In Ontario, a right turn on a red light is permitted after coming to a complete stop unless posted otherwise, provided you yield to oncoming traffic and pedestrians. Be aware that once you cross the Ottawa River, you enter the province of Quebec, where you *cannot* turn right on a red light. There have been experiments in some communities to introduce right turns on reds, but it strikes fear in the hearts of most Quebec pedestrians, so the jury is still out on whether or not the law will change. Better to err on the side of caution. Wearing your seatbelt is compulsory. Fines for riding without a seatbelt are substantial, and it's the driver's responsibility to ensure that all passengers under 16 are using an approved safety restraint. (Passengers over 16 take on the responsibility themselves of wearing a seat belt.) Speed limits are posted and must be obeyed at all times. Always stop when pedestrians are using the crosswalks, but also be careful of pedestrians crossing against the lights—Ottawans seem to have a mild disregard for pedestrian crossing signals in the downtown core. Beware, as well, of drivers running red lights. Always check that the intersection is clear before advancing when the light turns green, especially if your vehicle is going to be the first one through the intersection.

Tips **Watch for Cyclists!**

With the excellent network of bike pathways in the city, Ottawa has a large population of cyclists. Keep your eyes open for cyclists, especially when opening your car door on the street. Opening your door into a cyclist's path is a traffic violation, and, even worse, could cause serious injury to the cyclist. So always look before opening your vehicle door.

BY BICYCLE

A great way to get around in Ottawa is by bicycle. Ottawa and the surrounding regions offer a comprehensive network of pathways and parkways where people can bike and in-line skate through beautiful natural scenery. A number of city streets also have designated bike lanes. For **maps** of the pathways and more information, drop in to the **Capital Infocentre,** opposite Parliament Hill at 90 Wellington St. (𝄐 **800/465-1867** or 613/239-5000). If you find your planned bike route overly ambitious, hop on the bus: **OC Transpo** has installed bike racks on more than 150 buses, including most buses on routes 2, 95, and 97. Each rack holds two bikes, and loading and unloading is quick and easy. There's no cost to use the rack, other than regular bus fare. The program runs from spring through fall.

If you didn't bring your own equipment, numerous places in Ottawa rent out bicycles and in-line skates. See chapter 7, "For the Active Family," for a list of rental outfits.

Some specific rules apply to cyclists. All cyclists under 18 must wear a **bicycle helmet.** Cyclists cannot ride on the sidewalk and must not exceed speeds of 20 kilometers (12.5 miles) per hour on multiuse pathways. Be considerate of other road or pathway users, and keep to the right. Pass only when it is safe to do so, and if you're on a bicycle use your bell or voice to let others know you're about to pass.

If you're in the vicinity of the Rideau Centre and the ByWard Market, you can **park** your bike at a supervised facility. Located at Rideau and William streets, the facility operates daily 8:30am to 5:30pm, from Victoria Day until Labour Day weekend (third Saturday in May to first Monday in September). The maximum charge is C$2 (US$1.30).

 FAST FACTS: Ottawa

Airport For information on flights, baggage, and air freight and general inquiries, call the appropriate airline company—see "Getting There" in chapter 2. You can also obtain general information from the Infoguide Desk (𝄐 **613/248-2125**) from 9am to 9pm and on the web at **www.ottawa-airport.ca**. The airport is located in the south end of the city at 50 Airport Rd. For information on transportation from the airport to downtown, see "Getting There" in chapter 2.

Air Travel Complaints The Canadian Transportation Agency's Air Travel Complaints Commissioner handles unresolved passenger complaints against air carriers. Information and complaint forms are available at **www.cta.gc.ca** or through Government of Canada Services at 𝄐 **800/O-CANADA** (622-6232).

American Express For cardmember services, including lost or stolen cards, call 𝄐 **800/668-2639**. For traveler's checks, including lost or stolen checks, call 𝄐 **800/221-7282**. There is an American Express Travel Agency, which provides travel and financial services, at 220 Laurier Ave. W. 𝄐 **613/563-0231**.

Area Codes The telephone area code for Ottawa is **613**; for Hull and surrounding areas it's **819**. When calling from Ottawa to Hull, you don't need to use the area code.

ATMs Walk-up cash machines that link to the Cirrus or PLUS networks can be found every few blocks at various bank branches. You can also get cash advances against your MasterCard or Visa at an ATM, but you'll need a separate personal identification number (PIN) to access this service. ATMs generally charge a fee for each withdrawal.

Babysitting   Hotel concierge or front desk staff can usually supply names and phone numbers of reliable sitters.

Business Hours   Most **stores** are open from 9:30 or 10am to 6pm Monday to Saturday, and many have extended hours one or more evenings. Sunday opening hours are generally from noon to 5pm, although some stores are now opening at 11am and others are closed all day. **Banks** generally open at 9:30am and close by 4pm, with extended hours one or more evenings; some are open Saturdays. **Restaurants** open at 11 or 11:30am for lunch and at 5pm for dinner, although many in the ByWard Market district stay open all day. Some **museums** are closed on Mondays from October to April. Many stay open on Thursdays until 8 or 9pm.

Car Rentals   See "Getting Around," earlier in this chapter.

Climate   See "When to Go," in chapter 2.

Currency Exchange   Generally, the best place to exchange your currency is at a bank or by obtaining local currency through an ATM. There are a number of foreign exchange services in Ottawa. **Calforex** in the Rideau Centre, 50 Rideau St. (✆ **800/769-2025** or 613/569-4075), is open daily and provides no-fee American Express traveler's checks and other foreign currency services. **Custom House Currency Exchange** is located at 153 Sparks St. (✆ **613/234-6005**).

Dentists   For emergency dental care, ask the front desk staff or concierge at your hotel for the name of the nearest dentist, or call ✆ **613/523-4185**.

Directory Assistance   For numbers within the same area code, call ✆ **411**. For other numbers, call ✆ **555-1212**, prefixed by the area code of the number you're searching for.

Disability Services   Most of Ottawa's museums and public buildings, as well as many theaters and restaurants, are accessible to travelers with disabilities. For details, refer to the Ottawa visitor's guide, available from the Capital Infocentre, 90 Wellington St. (across from Parliament Hill) (✆ **800/465-1867** or 613/239-5000). Public transit (OC Transpo) is increasingly accessible for passengers with disabilities. For those who are unable to board regular transit, Para Transpo provides alternative transportation. See "Tips for Travelers with Disabilities," in chapter 2.

Doctor   Ask hotel staff or the concierge to help you locate a doctor. Some physicians will visit hotels. Walk-in clinics are available to out-of-province and foreign visitors, but be prepared to pay for services on the spot with cash. For more information, see "Health & Safety," in chapter 2. Telehealth Ontario offers free telephone access to registered nurses, 24 hours, 7 days a week (✆ **866/797-0000**).

Documents   See "Entry Requirements," in chapter 2.

Driving Rules   See "Getting Around," earlier in this chapter.

Drugstores   **Shopper's Drug Mart** has two **24-hour** locations: 1460 Merivale Rd. (at Baseline Rd.) (✆ **613/224-7270**), and Southgate Shopping Centre, 2515 Bank St. (at Hunt Club Rd.) (✆ **613/523-9999**).

Electricity   It's the same as in the United States—110–115 volts, AC.

Embassies/Consulates   All embassies in Canada (more than 100 in total) are located in Ottawa; consulates are primarily located in Toronto, Montreal, and Vancouver. Embassies include the Australian High Commission, 50 O'Connor St., Suite 710, Ottawa, ON K1P 6L2 (✆ **613/236-0841**); the British High Commission, 80 Elgin St., Ottawa, ON K1P 5K7 (✆ **613/237-1530**); the Embassy of Ireland, 130 Albert St., Ottawa, ON K1P 5G4 (✆ **613/233-6281**); the New Zealand High Commission, 727-99 Bank St., Ottawa, ON K1P 6G3 (✆ **613/238-5991**); the South African High Commission, 15 Sussex Dr., Ottawa, ON K1M 1M8 (✆ **613/744-0330**); and the Embassy of the United States of America, 490 Sussex Dr., Ottawa, ON K1N 1G8 (✆ **613/238-5335** or 800/529-4410 for U.S. citizen services).

Emergencies   Call ✆ **911** for fire, police, or ambulance. For Poison Control, call ✆ **613/737-1100**.

Eyeglasses   For same-day service (it may be as quick as 1 hour) on most prescriptions, call **Hakim Optical,** which has five Ottawa locations, including the downtown store at 229 Rideau St. (✆ **613/562-1234**). **Lenscrafters** is conveniently located in major malls, including Bayshore, Place d'Orléans, the Rideau Centre, and St. Laurent Shopping Centre.

Hospitals   The **Children's Hospital of Eastern Ontario (CHEO),** 401 Smyth Rd. (✆ **613/737-7600**), is a pediatric teaching hospital affiliated with the University of Ottawa which services a broad geographical area, including Eastern Ontario and Western Quebec. The hospital has an emergency department. For adult care, the **Ottawa Hospital** is a large academic health sciences center with three campuses, all with emergency departments. The **Civic** campus is located at 1053 Carling Ave. (✆ **613/761-4000**), the **General** campus at 501 Smyth Rd. (✆ **613/737-6111**), and **Riverside** campus at 1967 Riverside Dr. (✆ **613/738-7100**).

Internet Access   You can check your e-mail and send messages at the **Internet Café,** 200 Bank St., at Somerset (✆ **613/230-9000**).

Kids Help Phone   Kids or teens in distress can call ✆ **800/668-6868** for help.

Laundry/Dry Cleaning   Most hotels provide laundry and dry-cleaning services or have coin-operated laundry facilities.

Libraries   The newly amalgamated city of Ottawa now has 33 branches of the Ottawa Public Library. More than half offer programs for children, ranging from a weekly drop-in story time at smaller branches to crafts, puppet shows, bilingual story times, and mother-and-daughter book clubs at larger branches. Drop into any branch to pick up a current brochure or visit the website at www.library.ottawa.on.ca. The main branch is located at 120 Metcalfe Street (✆ **613/236-0301**).

Liquor   You must be 19 years of age or over to consume or purchase alcohol in Ontario. Bars and retail stores are strict about following the law and will ask for proof of age if they consider it necessary. The Liquor Control Board of Ontario (LCBO) sells wine, spirits, and beer. Their flagship retail store, at 275 Rideau St. (✆ **613/789-5226**), has two floors of fine products from around the world, as well as a "Vintages" section with a wide selection of high-quality products. Wine accessories are also available, and seminars and tastings are regularly scheduled. This store is well worth a visit for grown-ups. Ontario wines are available at the Wine Rack and at individual winery outlets. Beer is also available through the Beer Store, with about 20 locations in Ottawa.

Mail Mailing letters and postcards within Canada costs C47¢ (US31¢). Postage for letters and postcards to the United States costs C60¢ (US40¢), and overseas C$1.05 (US70¢).

Maps Maps of Ottawa are readily available in convenience stores and bookstores, as well as at the **Capital Infocentre,** 90 Wellington St. (✆ **800/ 465-1867** or 613/239-5000). For a good selection of maps and travel guides, visit **Place Bell Books,** 175 Metcalfe St. (✆ **613/233-3821**). Specializing in city and country travel books and maps, this bookstore has a hefty selection of vacation guides. Local guide books and scenic photography books of the Ottawa region are also on hand.

Members of Parliament Call the **Government of Canada** information line at ✆ **800/O-CANADA** (622-6232) or 613/941-4823. Your call will be personally answered in the official language of your choice.

Newspapers/Magazines The daily newspapers are the *Ottawa Citizen,* the *Ottawa Sun,* and *Le Droit,* Ottawa's French-language newspaper. Keep an eye out for *Capital Parent* and *Ottawa Families,* two local free publications. *Where Ottawa* is a free monthly guide to shopping, dining, entertainment, and other tourist information. You can find it at most hotels and at some restaurants and retail stores. *Ottawa City Magazine* and *Ottawa Life* are city monthlies. For a great variety of international publications, visit **Mags and Fags,** at 254 Elgin Street (✆ **613/233-9651**), or **Planet News,** at 143 Sparks Street (✆ **613/232-5500**).

Police In a life-threatening emergency or to report a crime in progress or a traffic accident that involves injuries or a vehicle that cannot be driven, call ✆ **911.** For other emergencies (a serious crime or a break and enter) call ✆ **613/230-6211.** For all other inquiries, call ✆ **613/236-1222.**

Post Offices Canada Post, 59 Sparks St., at Elgin Street (✆ **613/844-1545**), offers postal products and services and collector's stamps. Most convenience stores and drugstores offer postal services, and many have a separate counter for shipping packages during regular business hours. Look for the sign in the window advertising such services.

Radio The **Canadian Broadcasting Corporation (CBC)** broadcasts on **91.5FM** and **103.3FM.** For news and talk radio, tune in to **CFRA 580AM.** Ottawa's classic rock station is **CHEZ 106FM.** The local easy-listening music station is **Majic 100FM. The BEAR,** on **106.9FM,** broadcasts a mix of current and classic rock. To keep up with the latest on the sports scene, including broadcasts of the Ottawa Senators and Ottawa 67's, listen to **THE TEAM, SPORTS RADIO 1200.** For country music fans, there's **Young Country Y105FM.**

Safety Ottawa is generally safe, but be alert and use common sense, particularly at night. The ByWard Market area and Elgin Street are busy at night with the bar crowd, so you'll probably want to avoid taking your kids to those areas later in the evening.

Taxes The provincial retail sales tax (PST) is 8% on most goods; certain purchases, such as groceries and children's clothing, are exempt from provincial sales tax. Prepared food, including purchases in restaurants, is taxed at 8%.

Liquor, beer, and wine sold in bars and restaurants are taxed at 10%, and retail purchases are taxed at 12%. For amusement venues, admission charges that are over C$3.95 (US$2.60) are taxed at 10%. The accommodations tax is 5%. In Quebec, there is a 7.5% tax on food, liquor, merchandise, and accommodations. The national goods and services tax (GST) is 7%.

In general, nonresidents may apply for a tax refund. They can recover the accommodations tax, the sales tax, and the GST for nondisposable merchandise that will be exported for use, provided it is removed from Canada within 60 days of purchase. The following do not qualify for rebate: meals and restaurant charges, alcohol, tobacco, gas, car rentals, and such services as dry cleaning and shoe repair.

The quickest and easiest way to secure the refund is to stop at a duty-free shop at the border. You must have original receipts with GST registration numbers. You can also apply through the mail, but it will take several weeks to receive your refund. For an application form and information, write or call the **Visitor Rebate Program,** Revenue Canada, Summerside Tax Centre, 275 Pope Rd., Suite 104, Summerside, PEI C1N 6C6 (© **800/668-4748** within Canada or 902/432-5608 from outside Canada). *Note:* As of November 1, 2001, Quebec no longer provides rebates of provincial sales tax to nonresidents.

Taxis   See "Getting Around," earlier in this chapter.

Telephone   A local call from a telephone booth costs C25¢ (Canadian and U.S. coins are accepted at face value). Watch out for hotel surcharges on local and long-distance phone calls; often a local call will cost at least C$1 (US65¢) from a hotel room. The United States and Canada are on the same long-distance system. To make a long-distance call between the United States and Canada, use the area codes as you would at home. Canada's international prefix is **1.** Phone cards can be purchased at convenience stores and drugstores.

Time   Ottawa is on **Eastern Standard Time. Daylight saving time** is in effect from the first Sunday in April (clocks are moved ahead 1 hour) to the last Sunday in October (clocks are moved back 1 hour).

Tipping   Basically, it's the same as in major U.S. cities—15% in restaurants, 10% to 15% for taxis, C$1 (US70¢) per bag for porters, C$2 (US$1.30) per day for hotel housekeepers.

Transit Information   The public transit system is a bus service provided by Ottawa-Carleton (OC) Transpo (© **613/741-4390**) to the communities of Ottawa, Nepean, Vanier, Rockcliffe, Gloucester, Kanata, and Cumberland. Besides using public roads, OC Transpo has a convenient system of roadways used exclusively by buses—the Transitway. Two main lines operate on the Transitway, with transfers possible at many stations along the routes. Route 95 connects the southwest end of the city with the east via downtown. Route 97 runs between Kanata in the west to the airport in the south via downtown. For more information, see "Getting Around," earlier in this chapter.

Weather   For the weather forecast, check the daily newspaper, catch a radio broadcast, or tune in to the weather channel on TV. Some hotels post this information at the front desk.

4

Family-Friendly Accommodations

Families looking for a place to stay in the National Capital Region are fortunate. With the brisk and reliable business that downtown hotels (and many properties a little farther out) enjoy from government and corporate clients, the choice of accommodations in the city is wide. There is an unusually high proportion of suites, and the downtown core alone offers more than 6,000 rooms.

Although suites don't meet everyone's budget, I firmly believe that a one- or two-bedroom suite with a kitchen is the best bet for families with children. No more perching on the edge of the bed and eating pizza out of a box. No more trying to read by the light of a 40-watt bulb while your little angels are fighting it out in a double bed way past their bedtime. No more crying babies in the small hours, who would go straight back to sleep if only you could zap their bottle in a microwave.

After all, you're on vacation. If you've got a comfortable base with space for everyone to spread out, a place to make meals at your convenience (which will also save you money), two TVs, and maybe a balcony to sneak onto once your kids are asleep, where you can enjoy a glass of wine with your spouse and watch the city lights twinkle … well, it's not a difficult decision, is it?

Still, there are times when you just want a clean place to lay your head for the night, or when you prefer the homey atmosphere of a bed-and-breakfast in a peaceful residential neighborhood, rather than in the midst of the hustle and bustle of the city.

Ottawa offers whatever you're looking for—from Loire Valley Renaissance-style architecture to ultra-modern suites, and from family-run hotels to airport inns, university digs, and homey B&Bs. Many accommodations are within walking distance of the capital's major attractions. Others are only a short drive away. If you're not smack-dab in the middle of things and you don't want to navigate the maze of one-way streets or the dizzying lane changes of the Queensway, Capital Double Decker and Trolley Tours offer free pick-up and drop-off at approximately 50 hotels, inns, and B&Bs during the busy tourist season (see chapter 3, "Getting To Know Ottawa").

PARKING If you have a vehicle with you, remember to factor in the cost of parking when choosing accommodations. Hotel parking rates vary from C$4 (US$2.65) to C$22 (US$14.50) per night in the downtown area. Most lots are underground and some do not allow in-and-out privileges, which restricts your flexibility—and with children in tow, flexibility is a big deal. Overnight street parking is allowed where signs are posted. From November 15 to April 1, a city bylaw prohibits overnight on-street parking from 1 to 7am. When a snowfall of 7 centimeters (3 in.) or more is forecasted (including ranges such as 5 to 10cm, or 2 to 4 in.), the city will issue an overnight winter parking ban, broadcast through the local media. These bans are actively enforced, and those who fail to comply could end up with a C$50 (US$33) ticket.

AN IMPORTANT NOTE ON PRICES The prices quoted in this chapter are **rack rates,** the highest posted rates. Rooms are rarely sold at the full rack rate, but I've quoted rack rates for every property to allow you to compare prices. In each listing, the prices include accommodations for two adults and two children. Discounts can result in a dramatic drop in the rate, typically anywhere from 10% to 50%. Almost every hotelier I spoke with mentioned that weekend specials or family packages are available at various times throughout the year. A 5% accommodations tax and 7% GST (Goods and Services Tax) are added to accommodation charges, but the taxes are refundable to nonresidents upon application (see "Taxes" under "Fast Facts: Ottawa" in chapter 3).

A NOTE TO NONSMOKERS Hotels that reserve floors for nonsmokers are now commonplace, so I don't single them out in this guide. However, people who want a smoke-free room should make that clear when making a reservation. Rooms for smokers are concentrated on particular floors, and the rooms and even the hallways in those areas tend to smell strongly of smoke, even in the cleanest hotels. Never assume that you'll get a smoke-free room if you don't specifically request one.

A NOTE ABOUT POOLS Please be aware that hotel pools are not supervised. If you and your family are among the many who enjoy hotel pools when traveling, remember to use caution.

BED & BREAKFASTS Ottawa has an abundance of gracious, older homes, many of which have been transformed into charming B&Bs. I've selected a few B&Bs that welcome children, but there are numerous others. Some places are more suited to romantic getaways or seniors' sightseeing trips, so mention upfront that you will have your kids with you. For the most part, older, quieter children are more suitable than tots for the B&B environment. Often there are restrictions on the number of guests per room, so it's likely you will have to rent two rooms if your family numbers more than three. Two organizations in the city can help you choose a B&B. The **Ottawa Tourism and Convention Authority (OTCA),** 130 Albert St., Suite 1800, Ottawa, ON K1P 5G4 (© 800/363-4465 or 613/237-5150; www.ottawa.com) has more than two dozen B&Bs as members. **Ottawa Bed & Breakfast** has a select list of accommodations. Contact Robert Rivoire, 18 The Driveway, Ottawa, ON K2P 1C6 (© 800/461-7889 or 613/563-0161). There is also a walk-in accommodation reservation service at the **Capital Infocentre,** 90 Wellington St. (across from Parliament Hill), Ottawa, ON (© 800/465-1867 or 613/239-5000).

CAMPING Across the Ottawa River in Quebec, Gatineau Park's 88,000 acres of woodlands and lakes has two campgrounds. Phillipe Lake Family Campground has around 300 sites. There is also a limited number of canoe-camping sites at La Pêche Lake. For details on these and other camping facilities, contact the **Gatineau Park Visitor Centre,** 318 Meech Lake Rd., Old Chelsea, PQ J0X 1N0 (© 819/827-2020), or call the **National Capital Commission** at © 800/465-1867.

REDUCING YOUR ROOM RATE

Always ask for a deal. Corporate discounts, club memberships (CAA, AAA, and others), and discounts linked to credit cards are just a few of the ways you can get a lower price. In Ottawa, hotels are especially eager to boost their occupancy rates with families on weekends, when their corporate and government clients desert them. Weekend rates and family packages are often available. Even though March break, Winterlude, the Canadian Tulip Festival, and the summer months are all peak tourist times, many hotels offer packages, which may include complimentary museum passes, restaurant vouchers, or other money-saving deals.

1 Downtown (West of the Canal)

This area has the highest concentration of high-rises and the most traffic congestion, complicated by tricky one-way streets and limited meter parking, but it's close to many major attractions. Parliament Hill spreads majestically along the banks of the Ottawa River at the north end of this district. In addition to the Parliament Buildings, where you can catch the Changing of the Guard and the RCMP Musical Ride during the summer, you'll find the National Arts Centre, the Museum of Nature, and many great restaurants and retail stores, especially along Elgin, Bank, and Sparks streets. Many other attractions, including the Rideau Locks, the National Gallery, the Canadian War Museum, the Royal Canadian Mint, ByWard Market, and the Rideau Centre, are just across the canal to the east.

VERY EXPENSIVE

Delta Ottawa Hotel and Suites 🌟🌟   A couple of years ago, the Delta received an award for being the most child-friendly hotel in Ottawa, and the reputation has stuck. Families still flock here on weekends, during March break, and over the summer. In my opinion, the giant two-story indoor waterslide has a lot to do with it. When we visited Ottawa as tourists prior to moving to eastern Ontario, our kids insisted on staying at the Delta because of "that awesome slide." Next to the waterslide (which is separate from the pool), there is a Nintendo area and a well-equipped children's playroom and craft center. A small exercise area overlooks the pool. The hotel offers studios with kitchenettes (fridge, four-ring hot plate, and microwave) and one- and two-bedroom suites with balconies and kitchenettes, so families can prepare their own snacks and meals. Rooms and suites are being refurbished, with completion of all units scheduled for end of 2001.

361 Queen St., Ottawa, ON K1R 7S9. ℂ **800/268-1133** or 613/238-6000. Fax 613/238-2290. www.delta hotels.com. 328 units, 63 with kitchenette. C$315 (US$208) studio; C$169 (US$112) 1-bedroom suite; C$189 (US$125) 2-bedroom suite. Children 18 and under stay free in parents' room. Rollaway/crib free. AE, DC, DISC, MC, V. Parking C$16 (US$11). Small domestic pets accepted. **Amenities:** 2 restaurants; 1 lounge; indoor pool with adjacent waterslide; exercise room; Jacuzzi; sauna; children's center; seasonal children's program; game room; concierge; business center; secretarial services; salon; limited room service; massage; babysitting; washers and dryers; same-day laundry/dry cleaning; executive floor. *In room:* A/C, TV w/ pay movies, dataport, kitchenette in some units, minibar, coffeemaker, hairdryer, iron.

Tips **The Best Seats in the Hotel**

If you're visiting on Canada Day, request a higher-floor room or suite at the **Delta Ottawa,** overlooking the Ottawa River. A few years back, we watched the Snowbirds' airshow over the Parliament Buildings at lunchtime and the fabulous fireworks display in the evening through our upper-floor suite window.

EXPENSIVE

Albert at Bay Suite Hotel ★★ *Value*   This all-suite hotel welcomes families and even goes so far as to provide a free children's program during July and August. The kids' club offers a wide variety of supervised activities for kids ages 3 to 12 daily, from 9am to noon and 1 to 5pm. Although there isn't a pool, a bright and sunny exercise room with a Jacuzzi and an adjacent rooftop patio provides a refuge for parents who want to sneak in and relax while the children are busy at the kids' club. The downtown location is within strolling distance of Parliament Hill (3 blocks), the National Arts Centre (7 blocks), and the Rideau Centre (8 blocks). All units have a kitchen with full-size appliances, including a dishwasher; one or two bedrooms; and two TVs (so there will be no squabbles over channels). Some suites have two bathrooms.

435 Albert St., Ottawa, ON K1R 7X4. ℂ 800/267-6644 or 613/238-8858. Fax 613/238-1433. www.albert atbay.com. 197 units. C$229 (US$151) 1-bedroom suite; C$299 (US$198) 2-bedroom suite. Children 15 and under stay free in parents' room. Rollaway C$10 (US$7), crib free. AE, DC, DISC, MC, V. Parking C$11 (US$7). **Amenities:** Restaurant; Jacuzzi; sauna; seasonal children's program; limited room service; washers and dryers; same-day laundry/dry cleaning; executive suites. *In room:* A/C, TV w/ pay movies, dataport, kitchen, fridge, coffeemaker, iron.

Aristocrat Suite Hotel   With a full kitchen in every unit, the Aristocrat guarantees family-friendly accommodation. Located within walking distance of many downtown attractions and a short stroll from the banks of the Rideau Canal, it's a good base for tourists. The bedrooms and living room are a decent size, but with a table and chairs taking up floor space, the kitchen is a bit short on room. Be prepared to roll up your sleeves to wash the pots—there isn't a dishwasher. Suites have only one TV (in the living room), which may be a nuisance to some families; others may see that as a blessing. There is no pool, but the hotel offers a number of specialty services. If you're arriving by air, the Aristocrat will arrange for a limousine, with a driver to greet your flight inside the airport. As another bonus, you can have groceries delivered to your suite to save you the trouble of shopping. Ask about special family rates.

131 Cooper St., Ottawa, ON K2P 0E7. ℂ 800/563-5634 or 613/236-7500. Fax 613/563-2836. 200 units. C$129 (US$85) studio or 1-bedroom suite; C$179 (US$118) 2-bedroom suite. Children 17 and under stay free in parents' room. Rollaway C$10 (US$7), crib free. AE, DC, MC, V. Parking C$9 (US$6). **Amenities:** 1 restaurant; exercise room; Jacuzzi; sauna; secretarial services; limited room service; massage; baby-sitting; washers and dryers; same-day laundry/dry cleaning. *In room:* A/C, TV, kitchen, coffeemaker, hairdryer, iron.

Best Western Victoria Park Suites ★★   Freshly decorated in 2000, this hotel offers comfortable and spacious studios and one-bedroom suites, all with kitchenettes. Parliament Hill is 10 blocks north, which is a bit far for little legs to walk, but a bus or taxi will whisk you there in no time if you'd rather leave your car in the underground lot. The Museum of Nature, with its huge dinosaurs, creepy insects, beautiful birds, and life-size woolly mammoth family, is just a block away. When the kids' club is running at Victoria Park Suites' sister hotel, the Albert at Bay Suite Hotel, you can take your kids there for free supervised fun and games daily in July and August. Preteens or teens will love the Web TV, connected in all units. If you want to block access to Web TV or even the in-room Nintendo, just ask at the front desk. A complimentary continental breakfast is included in the rates, and CAA members can save a few bucks with free parking.

377 O'Connor St., Ottawa, ON K2P 2M2. ✆ 800/465-7275 or 613/567-7275. Fax 613/567-1161. www. victoriapark.com. 124 units. C$199 (US$131) studio; C$219 (US$145) 1-bedroom suite. Children 16 and under stay free in parents' room. Rollaway/crib free. AE, DC, DISC, MC, V. Parking C$9 (US$6). **Amenities:** Breakfast room; exercise room; sauna; secretarial services; babysitting; washers and dryers; same-day laundry/dry cleaning. *In room:* A/C, TV w/ pay movies, kichenette, fridge, coffeemaker, iron.

Cartier Place and Towers Suite Hotels ⊘⊘⊘ This higher-end suite hotel has wonderful amenities for children. Besides the indoor pool, bathed in natural light streaming through glass doors (which are thrown open in the summer and lead onto a sundeck), there is a well-equipped children's playroom and even a preschool-size play structure in the pool area. An outdoor courtyard features a climbing gym and children's play equipment. On weekends, a ping-pong table is set up in one of the meeting rooms. In the winter months, the novelty of a rooftop skating rink will perk up even the most jaded child traveler. The last major renovation—of floors six, seven, and eight—was completed in 2000, so if you want the latest color scheme and brand-new kitchen appliances, request a suite on these floors. All units are suites with full kitchens and private balconies with garden chairs.

180 Cooper St., Ottawa, ON K2P 2L5. ✆ 800/236-8399 or 613/236-5000. Fax 613/238-3842. www.suite dreams.com. 253 units. C$229–C$269 (US$151–US$178) suite. Children 16 and under stay free in parents' room. Rollaway/crib free. AE, DC, DISC, MC, V. Parking C$12 (US$8). Small pets accepted C$8 (US$5). **Amenities:** Restaurant/lounge; indoor pool; exercise room; Jacuzzi; sauna; children's playroom; outdoor playground; rooftop skating rink; game room; business center; limited room service; babysitting; washers and dryers; same-day laundry/dry cleaning. *In room:* A/C, TV w/ pay movies, dataport, kitchen, coffeemaker, hairdryer, iron.

Crowne Plaza Ottawa ⊘⊘ If you're looking for contemporary luxury in a traditional hotel room, this is a fine place to stay. After more than C$11 million (US$7 million) in extensive renovations, the former Citadel Hotel has been transformed. The public areas reflect a sophisticated Art Deco style, with clean lines, expanses of wood, and a rich, earthy color scheme. The upscale decor continues into the hallways and guest rooms, which have been refurbished with new carpets, draperies, wall coverings, furniture, and redesigned bathrooms. An underground shopping arcade, open primarily during weekday office hours, is accessible from inside the hotel, and there is a large health club with extensive facilities on-site. Kids will love the indoor pool, nicely set in a light-filled space, with patio doors leading onto a courtyard. The well-trained staff are attentive, courteous, and efficient.

101 Lyon St., Ottawa, ON K1R 5T9. ✆ 800/227-6963 or 613/237-3600. Fax 613/237-2351. www.crowne plazaottawa.com. 411 units. C$229 (US$151) double. Children 17 and under stay free in parents' room. Roll-away/crib free. AE, DC, DISC, MC, V. Valet parking C$21 (US$14), self-parking C$14 (US$9). **Amenities:** Restaurant, lounge; indoor pool; health club; Jacuzzi; sauna; concierge; business center; limited room service; babysitting; same-day laundry/dry cleaning; executive floors. *In room:* A/C, TV w/ pay movies, dataport, fridge in some units, coffeemaker, hairdryer, iron.

Lord Elgin Hotel ⊘ This established hotel, with its elegant lobby, is conveniently located near Parliament Hill and the Rideau Centre shopping mall and across from the National Arts Centre. If your kids are yearning for a patch of green to run around on, head across the street to Confederation Park, a small city park, for respite from the dense metropolis of skyscrapers crowding the business district west of the hotel. Walking north along Elgin Street, you'll find plenty of pleasant eateries and shops that will draw your kids like a magnet, including Christmas in the Capital, at no. 231, and Sugar Mountain, at no. 286. Construction of 60 new units, a new exercise area, and an indoor pool is underway, due to be completed in 2002, so expect the occasional hiccup in the hotel's day-to-day operation. The rooms are not overly spacious and the bathrooms are utilitarian. Rooms at the back are quieter, but you lose the view of the park. Staff are formal and efficient.

100 Elgin St., Ottawa, ON K1P 5K8. ℂ **800/267-4298** or 613/235-3333. Fax 613/235-3223. www.lordelgin hotel.ca. 300 units. C$160 double (US$106). Children 17 and under stay free in parents' room. Rollaway/crib free. AE, DC, DISC, MC, V. Valet parking C$14 (US$9). Pets accepted in some rooms but cannot be left alone. **Amenities:** Restaurant, lounge; exercise room; bicycle rental nearby; concierge; salon next door; limited room service; babysitting; same-day laundry/dry cleaning. *In room:* A/C, TV w/ pay movies, dataport, coffeemaker, hairdryer, iron.

Marriott Residence Inn Ottawa ✪✪✪

The units in this all-suites hotel are at least 50% larger than those in standard hotels. For families, this spells comfort and a guaranteed plunge in stress levels, especially if you splurge on a two-bedroom suite, which boasts a well-equipped kitchen, two full bathrooms, and three TVs. If three TVs are just too much to handle, board games and puzzles are available through the front desk. Ask for a kid's pack when you check in, which includes small toys, snacks, and coloring books. The health club's pool has a uniform 1.1 meter (3 ft. 10 in.) depth, so your kids can splash and thrash from end to end. For round-the-clock caffeine cravers and hungry little tummies, there's a 24-hour Tim Hortons right on the doorstep, with access from the main lobby, although in-room coffee, hot chocolate, and popcorn are free. Take advantage of the grocery service—after all, you're on vacation. Just drop off your list before 9am for a late afternoon delivery. Expect cheerful faces and friendly greetings from staff whenever you cross their path. The hotel has been open just over two years, and the furniture and decor still look brand-new, a credit to the meticulous housekeeping. Two one-bedroom suites are equipped for guests with disabilities.

161 Laurier Ave. W., Ottawa, ON K1P 5J2. ℂ **877/478-4838** or 613/231-2020. Central Marriott reservation desk ℂ **800/331-3131**. Fax 613/231-2090. www.residenceinn.com. 171 units. C$179 (US$118) studio; C$299 (US$197) 2-bedroom suite. Rollaway C$12 (US$8), crib free. AE, DC, DISC, MC, V. Parking C$14 (US$9). Pets C$150 (US$99) flat fee; can be left alone if owners can be reached by phone. **Amenities:** 1 room serving complimentary breakfast and snacks; indoor pool; health club; hot tub; sauna; spa next door; concierge; secretarial services; laundry room (some units have washers/dryers); same-day laundry/dry cleaning. *In room:* A/C, TV w/ pay movies, dataport, kitchen (equipment varies with suite size), fridge, coffeemaker, hairdryer, iron.

Minto Place Suite Hotel ✪✪✪ *Value*

Beautifully appointed, spacious suites with kitchenettes or full kitchens make Minto Place one of Ottawa's top choices for family accommodations. Adding to its appeal is direct access to an indoor shopping concourse with a bank, walk-in clinic, post office, food court, car rental outlet, and retail stores. The 19.5 meter (65 ft.) long indoor pool, lit by skylights, is a uniform 1.2 meters (4 ft.) deep and sparkling clean. A sun deck leads off the pool area. In the summer, your kids can sign up for the fun and games at the kids' club. Staff are courteous, pleasant, and experienced in helping families to make the most of their stay in Ottawa.

433 Laurier Ave. W., Ottawa, ON K1R 7Y1. (C) **800/267-3377** or 613/782-2350. Fax 613/232-6962. www.mintohotel.com. 417 units. C$147 (US$97) studio; C$184 (US$121) 1-bedroom suite; C$249 (US$164) 2-bedroom suite. Children 18 and under stay free in parents' room. Crib free. AE, DC, DISC, MC, V. Parking C$12 (US$8) weekdays, C$4 (US$3) weekends. **Amenities:** 2 restaurants; indoor pool; exercise room; hot tub; sauna; seasonal children's program; secretarial services; shopping arcade; limited room service; babysitting; washers and dryers in some suites; same-day laundry/dry cleaning. *In room:* A/C, TV w/ pay movies, dataport, kitchen or kitchenette, coffeemaker, hairdryer, iron.

Sheraton Ottawa Hotel ⭐⭐   The Sheraton is a classy hotel, as you'll note from the moment you enter the elegant lobby and are greeted by the impeccably dressed doorman. A spiral staircase leads to the second floor, but you can opt for the more conventional elevator. Even the restaurant is posh, furnished with rich, dark wood, gleaming brass, and sparkling chandeliers. Rooms are spacious, and the complete refurbishment in 1998 included upgraded vanities and ceramic tiles in the bathrooms. For the kids, there's the all-important indoor pool, with a bank of windows at one end to allow in natural light. If luxurious surroundings are a priority on your vacation, you won't be disappointed here.

150 Albert St., Ottawa, ON K1P 5G2. (C) **800/489-8333** or 613/238-1500. Fax 613/238-2723. www.sheraton. com. 236 units. C$235 (US$155) double. Children 16 and under stay free in parents' room. Rollaway/crib free. AE, DC, DISC, MC, V. Valet parking C$14–$19 (US$9–$13). Small pets accepted. **Amenities:** Restaurant, lounge; indoor pool; exercise room; sauna; concierge; business center; room service; babysitting; same-day laundry/dry cleaning; executive rooms. *In room:* A/C, TV w/ pay movies, dataport, coffeemaker, hairdryer, iron.

⟨ Tips Pool Safety

Hotel pools do not usually provide lifeguards or other supervisory personnel. It is the parents' responsibility to closely supervise their own children in the pool area. Exercise caution when the pool is crowded. It's difficult to keep your eye on your children all the time when there are dozens of swimmers in the water. Enjoy your swim and always follow pool safety rules.

MODERATE

Capital Hill Hotel & Suites   This comfortable but far from ritzy hotel offers families good value and the advantage of a downtown location. Various hotel room and suite accommodations are available, including standard rooms with one queen- or king-size bed, studios with two queen-size beds and a kitchenette, and one-bedroom suites with two queen-size beds, a kitchenette, and a pull-out couch. Around half of the 150 units are equipped with a stove, a small fridge, dishes, and utensils, but none have microwaves or dishwashers. The top two floors (11 and 12) have been refreshed with a bright, neutral decor; floors 9 and 10 are currently being renovated. The room size is average and bathrooms are small. Guests receive complimentary passes to a health club situated in the Rideau Centre shopping mall, a few minutes' walk away.

88 Albert St., Ottawa, ON K1P 5E9. (C) **800/463-7705** or 613/235-1413. Fax 613/235-6047. www.capital hill.com. 150 units. C$129 (US$85) double with kitchenette; C$149 (US$98) 1-bedroom suite. Children 17 and under stay free in parents' room. Rollaway/crib free. AE, DC, DISC, MC, V. Parking C$11 (US$7). Pets accepted. **Amenities:** Restaurant, bar; secretarial services; massage; same-day laundry/dry cleaning; executive rooms. *In room:* A/C, TV w/ pay movies, dataport, kitchenette in some units, coffeemaker, hairdryer, iron.

Ramada Hotel & Suites Ottawa ★ If you're searching for moderately priced accommodation with self-catering, the Ramada fits the bill. The property is situated at the quiet end of Cooper Street just steps from the banks of the Rideau Canal and a few blocks west of the shops and restaurants of Elgin Street. All rooms with two double beds have a kitchenette with a two-ring hot plate and small fridge. A microwave can be supplied on request. One-bedroom suites are equipped with a full kitchen, and a small number have a connecting door to a single room, effectively creating a two-bedroom suite. The bathrooms have heated floors, a luxurious and comforting touch.

111 Cooper St., Ottawa, ON K2P 2E3. © 800/267-8378 or 613/238-1331. Fax 613/230-2179. 233 units. C$147 (US$97) double with kitchenette; C$197 (US$130) 1-bedroom suite. Children 17 and under stay free in parents' room. Rollaway/crib free. AE, DC, DISC, MC, V. Parking C$8 (US$5). Pets accepted. **Amenities:** Restaurant, lounge; exercise room; secretarial services; 24-hour room service; babysitting; washers and dryers; same-day laundry/dry cleaning; executive rooms. *In room:* A/C, TV w/ pay movies, dataport, kitchen or kitchenette, coffeemaker, hairdryer, iron.

INEXPENSIVE

Arosa Suites Hotel If your budget is tight, you may want to consider the Arosa Suites. The living quarters are compact and the decor is dated, but the price is right. A maximum of four occupants plus one baby in a crib is the limit to each one-bedroom suite. Almost half the residents, many of them corporate or government employees, are long-term occupants, but you'll see more families around in the summer. Parking is cheap, but be warned: The parking lot doesn't have room for every vehicle—it's first-come, first-served. Most kitchens have a dishwasher, and all units except three have a private balcony.

163 MacLaren St., Ottawa, ON K2P 2G4. © 613/238-6783. Fax 613/238-5080. www.arosahotel.com. 60 units. C$94 (US$62) 1-bedroom suite. Children 16 and under stay free in parents' room. Crib free. AE, DC, DISC, MC, V. Limited parking C$4 (US$2.50). **Amenities:** Exercise room; washers and dryers; same-day dry cleaning. *In room:* A/C, TV, kitchen, coffeemaker.

Mid-Towne Heritage B&B ★★ (Value) Built in 1891 as a fashionable Victorian family home, this is one of the most charming bed-and-breakfasts in Ottawa. It has been recently restored, with original fireplaces, stained glass, wood, and plaster. The shade trees and gardens are set in one of the last remaining private yards in the city core. The owners reckon their home is the closest B&B to Parliament Hill, which is only a 10-minute stroll away along Wellington Street. This is one of the few B&Bs to offer suites. The second floor offers a choice of two—one with two bedrooms (with twin beds in one to keep the peace between those blanket-hogging kids), a private bathroom, and balcony, and the other with twin beds (plus the option of having two cots in the sitting room) and a private bathroom. The rooms are fresh and pretty, with Victorian decor. The entire building is nonsmoking. As with most B&Bs, the owners accept children at their discretion, and suggest that ages 8 and up are best suited to the tranquil charm of this home. For families who conduct their lives at a gentle pace, this will be a lovely base for an Ottawa vacation.

220 Lyon St., Ottawa, ON K1R 5V7. © 888/669-8888 or 613/236-1169. Fax 613/234-4706. www. bbcanada.com/1863.html. 4 units. C$109–$125 (US$72–$83) suite, including breakfast. Rollaway free. AE, DC, MC, V. Free parking. *In room:* A/C, TV, hairdryer, no phone.

Natural Choice/4 Nature B&B If you're a nuts-and-granola kind of family, you'll feel right at home in this vegetarian, nonsmoking B&B facing the Canadian Museum of Nature. The bedrooms are fresh and bright and decorated with original artwork, in keeping with the relaxed, friendly atmosphere. The hosts

Family-Friendly Ottawa Accommodations

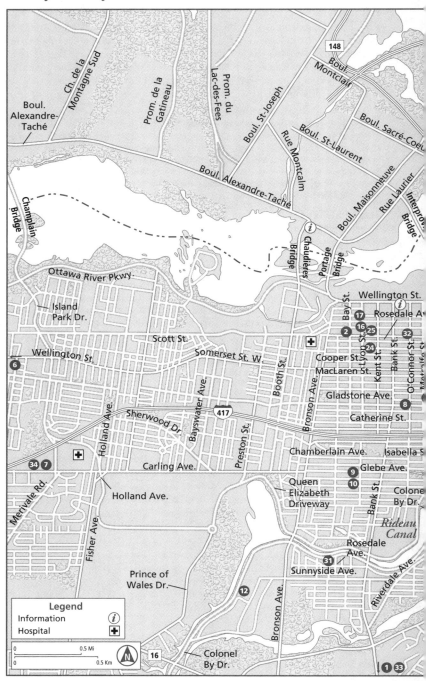

Legend
Information 🛈
Hospital ✚

0   0.5 Mi
0   0.5 Km

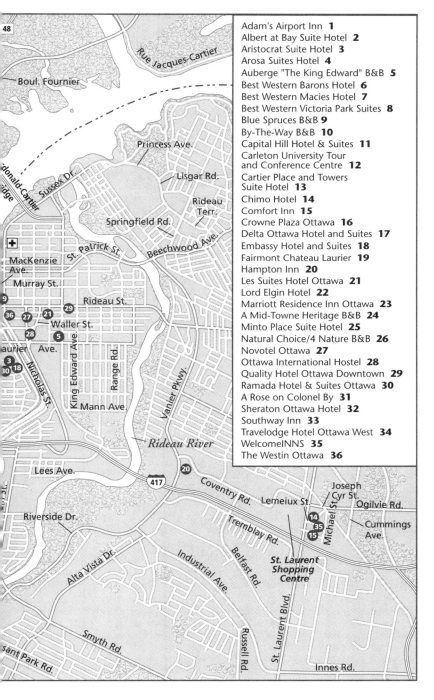

Adam's Airport Inn **1**
Albert at Bay Suite Hotel **2**
Aristocrat Suite Hotel **3**
Arosa Suites Hotel **4**
Auberge "The King Edward" B&B **5**
Best Western Barons Hotel **6**
Best Western Macies Hotel **7**
Best Western Victoria Park Suites **8**
Blue Spruces B&B **9**
By-The-Way B&B **10**
Capital Hill Hotel & Suites **11**
Carleton University Tour
and Conference Centre **12**
Cartier Place and Towers
Suite Hotel **13**
Chimo Hotel **14**
Comfort Inn **15**
Crowne Plaza Ottawa **16**
Delta Ottawa Hotel and Suites **17**
Embassy Hotel and Suites **18**
Fairmont Chateau Laurier **19**
Hampton Inn **20**
Les Suites Hotel Ottawa **21**
Lord Elgin Hotel **22**
Marriott Residence Inn Ottawa **23**
A Mid-Towne Heritage B&B **24**
Minto Place Suite Hotel **25**
Natural Choice/4 Nature B&B **26**
Novotel Ottawa **27**
Ottawa International Hostel **28**
Quality Hotel Ottawa Downtown **29**
Ramada Hotel & Suites Ottawa **30**
A Rose on Colonel By **31**
Sheraton Ottawa Hotel **32**
Southway Inn **33**
Travelodge Hotel Ottawa West **34**
WelcomeINNS **35**
The Westin Ottawa **36**

provide services ranging from massage and craniosacral therapy (gentle manipulation of the skull to relieve pain and tension) to yoga classes and weddings. Their flourishing garden has a picnic table for children and families, as well as a room on the second floor where children can play when meditation and yoga are not in session. Besides the green space outside the Museum of Nature (complete with life-size models of a woolly mammoth family), there's a park within walking distance with a children's playground and wading pool.

263 McLeod St., Ottawa, ON K2P 1A1. © **888/346-9642** or 613/563-4399. www.vegybnb.com. 3 units. C$85–$125 (US$56–$83) per family depending on number of guests, including breakfast. Rollaway free. AE, MC, V. Limited free parking. Pets C$10 (US$7). **Amenities:** Massage and other services available. *In room:* Ceiling fans, no phone.

2 Downtown (East of the Canal)

This area of downtown is bordered by the Ottawa River to the north, the Rideau River to the east, the Queensway to the south, and the canal to the west. You'll find the lively and exciting ByWard Market area in this district, as well as a number of large high-rise hotels, Major Hills Park, Strathcona Park, the University of Ottawa, the National Gallery, the Canadian War Museum, and the Royal Canadian Mint. On the quiet residential streets, embassy residences and B&Bs are interspersed among elegant Victorian and Edwardian homes. Parliament Hill borders the west bank of the canal and the Ottawa River.

VERY EXPENSIVE

Fairmont Château Laurier *★★★* The imposing granite-and-limestone façade of this grand hotel, built in 1912 in the same Loire Valley Renaissance style as Quebec City's Château Frontenac, is one of Ottawa's premier landmarks. If you're looking for tradition, luxury, and attentive service, this is the place to stay—royalty and celebrities have always been attracted to the Château Laurier's grace and beauty. You'll pay for the pleasure, but the surroundings are exceptional. The spacious public areas display the grandeur of another era, as they are gradually being refurnished with the hotel's original furniture, rescued from a storeroom and meticulously restored.

At the check-in desk, little guests can climb a set of steps to the counter and collect their special kids' kit, complete with puzzles, games, and coloring books. The less expensive rooms are rather small but just as elegant as the larger rooms and suites; nine rooms are equipped for guests with disabilities. The upper floors offer impressive views over the Ottawa River to the Gatineau Hills. The extensive health club, built in 1929, has been preserved, and the Art Deco–style 20-metre (65.5 ft.) long pool, with a 1-metre (3 ft. 6 in.) shallow end, is crystal clear. Also in the health club complex is a children's playroom, packed with toys and games for younger children. After working up an appetite in the health club, dress up and head to the hotel restaurant—a new executive chef was appointed in February 2001, causing a flurry of excitement among local foodies.

1 Rideau St., Ottawa, ON K1N 8S7. © **800/441-1414** or 613/241-1414. Fax 613/562-7032. www.fairmont.com. 429 units. C$309 (US$204) and up double; C$429 (US$283) and up suite. Children 17 and under stay free in parents' room. Rollaway/crib free. AE, DC, DISC, MC, V. Valet parking C$20 (US$13), self-parking C$14 (US$9). Pets C$25 (US$17) per day. **Amenities:** Restaurant, outdoor terrace, bar/tearoom; large indoor pool; health club; sauna; bicycle and rollerblade rental; unsupervised children's playroom; small video arcade; concierge; business center; 24-hour room service; massage; same-day laundry/dry cleaning; executive floor. *In room:* A/C, TV w/ pay movies, dataport in some rooms, minibar, fridge available on request, coffeemaker, hairdryer, iron.

The Westin Ottawa ★★ The lobby is grand and the staff are obliging and exceedingly well-mannered at this upscale hotel. The Westin welcomes children and offers all kinds of helpful items and services for guests traveling with kids. Through Westin's kids' club, designed for infants to 12-year-olds, kids get a gift plus a tippy cup or sports bottle at check-in. A free children's movie, child-care services, special laundry pricing, express meal service, and a kids' menu with free drink refills are some of the other advantages of the kids' club. Parents also can request a safety kit, crib, highchair, jogging stroller, or other equipment in advance—rooms are set up in prior to check-in, so there's no need to call the front desk to arrange for those little extras after arrival.

All rooms feature floor-to-ceiling windows to provide the best possible views of the city. Active parents might like a challenging game of squash on one of the three international standard courts, or they might take a dip in the indoor pool, which has an adjacent outdoor sundeck. For those who live to shop, the third floor of the hotel provides direct access to the stores and services of the Rideau Centre.

11 Colonel By Dr., Ottawa, ON K1N 9H4. © **888/625-5144** or 613/560-7000. Fax 613/234-5396. www. westin.com. 487 units. C$325–$355 (US$215–$234) double. Children 18 and under stay free in parents' room. Rollaway/crib free. AE, DC, DISC, MC, V. Valet parking C$22 (US$15); self-parking C$10 (US$7). Pets accepted. **Amenities:** Restaurant, 2 bars; indoor pool; exercise room; hot tub; sauna; concierge; tour/activities desk; shopping arcade; 24-hour room service; massage; babysitting; same-day laundry/dry cleaning; executive floors. *In room:* A/C, TV w/ pay movies, dataport, minibar, coffeemaker, hairdryer, iron.

EXPENSIVE

Les Suites Hotel Ottawa ★★ (Value) An all-suite property, Les Suites was originally built as a condominium complex in 1989. As a result, the one- and two-bedroom suites are spacious and well equipped, with a full kitchen in every unit. Elevators are situated away from the rooms and bedrooms are located at the back of the suites, away from potential hallway noise. For an even quieter environment, ask for a suite overlooking the garden courtyard. The health club and indoor pool are shared with guests of Novotel Ottawa. Complimentary kids' packs are available on check-in, and include coloring books, contest entry forms, and small gifts. The Rideau Centre and the ByWard Market area are on the hotel's doorstep.

130 Besserer St., Ottawa, ON K1N 9M9. © **800/267-1989** or 613/232-2000. Fax 613/232-1242. 243 units. C$210 (US$139) 1-bedroom suite; C$250 (US$165) 2-bedroom suite. Children 18 and under stay free in parents' room. Rollaway/crib free. AE, DC, DISC, MC, V. Valet parking C$13(US$9); self-parking C$13 (US$9). Pets C$25 (US$17) flat fee. **Amenities:** Restaurant; indoor pool; exercise room; hot tub; sauna; concierge; secretarial services; shopping arcade; limited room service; massage; babysitting; washers and dryers; same-day laundry/dry cleaning; executive suites. *In room:* A/C, TV w/ pay movies, dataport, kitchen, coffeemaker, hairdryer, iron.

Novotel Ottawa ★ With refurbishments completed in 1999, the public areas and rooms at this hotel are decorated in Mediterranean hues of blue, orange, and yellow. The result is striking and sunny and a welcome change from the carefully neutral shades common to many hotels. Kids' packs to keep the little ones amused are handed out at check-in, and there's a pool to satisfy your water babies. The hotel doesn't go out of its way to cater to families, but the surroundings are pleasant, the staff are cheerful and attentive, and the Rideau Centre, Parliament Hill, and many of the museums are all nearby.

33 Nicholas St., Ottawa, ON K1N 9M7. © **800/668-6835** or 613/230-3033. Fax 613/760-4765. www. novotel.com. 281 units. C$195 (US$129) and up double. Children 16 and under stay free in parents' room. Rollaway/crib free. AE, DC, DISC, MC. V. Parking C$9–$12 (US$6–$8). Pets accepted. **Amenities:** Restaurant,

bar; indoor pool; exercise room; hot tub; sauna; tour/activities desk; secretarial services; limited room service; massage; same-day laundry/dry cleaning. *In room:* A/C, TV w/ pay movies, dataport, minibar, hairdryer, iron.

MODERATE

Auberge "The King Edward" B&B ★   Conveniently situated close to the Rideau Canal and within easy walking distance of the ByWard Market, the Rideau Centre, and many downtown attractions, the King Edward is a distinguished Victorian home. The front parlour has been turned into a peaceful oasis of tropical plants, accented by a trickling fountain. A second sitting room offers comfortable chairs and sofas, suitable for reading or listening to music. Throughout the home you'll find many period details, including fireplaces, plaster moldings, pillars, and stained-glass windows. The elegant bedrooms, with turn-of-the-century furnishings, are generously proportioned. One room is large enough to accommodate a cot, and the B&B's two other rooms have balconies, giving families a little extra room. Children are welcomed at the discretion of the owner. The entire building is nonsmoking.

525 King Edward Ave., Ottawa, ON K1N 7N3. © **800/841-8786** or 613/565-6700. www.bbcanada. com/kingedward. 3 units. C$75–$80 (US$50–$53) double (max. per room 2 adults or children); C$95 (US$63) large double with cot. Rates include breakfast. MC, V. Free parking. *In room:* A/C, TV, no phone.

Quality Hotel Ottawa Downtown   Almost 40% of the rooms in this hotel are business class and there is no pool, so this property is unlikely be at the top of the list for youngsters. Families do stay here quite comfortably though. The location is prime for downtown and the parking is less expensive than at many other hotels in the area. Located on the southwest corner of King Edward Avenue and Rideau Street, it's easy to find. For the best view of the city and the Gatineau Hills, ask for a corner room or one facing northwest. The adjoining restaurant is a family eatery, serving roadhouse-style Canadian and Continental meals with generous portions.

290 Rideau St., Ottawa, ON K1N 5Y3. © **800/228-5151** or 613/789-7511. Fax 613/789-2434. www.quality hotelottawa.com. 212 units. C$150 (US$99) double. Children 18 and under stay free in parents' room. Rollaway C$12 (US$8), crib free. AE, DC, DISC, MC, V. Parking C$9 (US$6). Pets accepted. **Amenities:** Restaurant/bar; secretarial services; limited room service; babysitting; same-day laundry/dry cleaning; executive rooms. *In room:* A/C, TV w/ pay movies, dataport, coffeemaker.

INEXPENSIVE

Embassy Hotel and Suites   This hotel offers no special concessions for people traveling with children, but all units have a full kitchen (minus dishwasher), so if you're on a budget and want to stay in a downtown suite, keep it in mind. The bathrooms and bedrooms tend to be small, but there is plenty of seating in the living rooms of the one-bedroom suites. Some units have new carpet and linens; others are in need of refurbishing. But the price is on the mark.

25 Cartier St., Ottawa, ON K2P 1J2. © **800/661-5495** or 613/237-2111. Fax 613/563-1353. www.embassy hotelottawa.com. 130 units. C$110–$125 (US$73–$83) studio; C$155 (US$102) 1-bedroom suite; C$205 (US$135) 2-bedroom suite. Children 16 and under stay free in parents' room. Rollaway/crib free. AE, DC, DISC, MC, V. Limited parking C$8 (US$5). **Amenities:** Restaurant, coffeeshop; exercise room; sauna; limited room service; babysitting; coin-op washers and dryers; same-day laundry/dry cleaning. *In room:* A/C, TV, kitchen, coffeemaker, hairdryer, iron.

Ottawa International Hostel   Ever think your kids should be locked up? You can throw them in the clink for the night here—literally. Before becoming a hostel, the building was the Carleton County Gaol (1862 to 1972). Guided tours of the former prison are available. Your family can enjoy a quiet night's

sleep behind bars in the former cells, which have been renovated and enlarged—if the ghost of the last prisoner to be publicly hanged in Canada doesn't disturb you. If you are a Hostelling International member, you'll receive a discounted room rate. There is a daily charge of C50¢ (US30¢) per towel and C$2.50 (US$1.70) for bedlinens. A cosy TV lounge and a communal kitchen with several hot plates and lockers for storing food are available for guests. The dining room is housed in the former prison chapel, and in the summer, guests may use the barbecue in the garden. Washroom facilities, with washbasins, toilets, and showers, are unisex. Families may opt for a private room with bunk beds, which accommodates up to five people, but most likely your kids will want to sleep in the jail cells. Although the space is cramped and the beds are narrow, the experience will be authentic.

75 Nicholas St., Ottawa, ON K1N 7B9. © **613/235-2595.** Fax 613/235-9202. www.hostellingintl.on.ca. 154 units. C$23 (US$15) per adult in dormitory, C$16 (US$11) per child age 10–17 in dormitory; C$54 (US$36) private room (max. 5 people); children 9 and under free. AE, MC, V. Parking C$4 (US$2.65). **Amenities:** Game room; washers and dryers. *In room:* Table-top fans, no phone.

3 The Glebe & South Central

The Glebe is a trendy, upper-middle-class family neighborhood lined with turn-of-the-century red brick homes and a number of larger, elegant houses. Although the area's main street, Bank Street, has wonderful restaurants and shops, hotels and motels are scarce in this district. But some families might be more comfortable staying here than in the high-rises of downtown. Just south of the Glebe lies another quiet neighborhood, where you'll find the Carleton University campus, bordered by Dow's Lake, Bronson Avenue (one of the main arteries to downtown), and the Ottawa River. The two B&Bs in this area are listed as expensive only because a family of two adults and two children would need two bedrooms, effectively doubling the price. However, one or two adults and a child could be accommodated in one room.

EXPENSIVE

Blue Spruces B&B ✶✶   This warmly welcoming home in the heart of the quiet, dignified residential neighborhood known as the Glebe is a delight. The rooms are spotless and fresh looking, yet cosy. The owners have carefully chosen the furnishings to complement this turn-of-the-century property, and they will be happy to detail the origins of their collection of antique prints. The innkeepers' British background guarantees that breakfast is done right—the morning paper is laid on the table, alongside expertly folded floral napkins, fresh scones with homemade preserves, and an appetizer of grilled grapefruit. This home is not suitable for pre-school-age guests, but older children who can conduct themselves with decorum are certainly welcome. Upstairs on the guest bedroom floor, a shared sitting room, opening onto a seasonal sun porch, contains a TV, a fridge, and appliances for making hot beverages. There is also a suite with private sitting room. The entire building is nonsmoking. A walk to the west will bring you to the Dutch Tulip Gardens and Dow's Lake, while a stroll to the east will take you to Bank Street and the plethora of trendy shops and eateries in the Glebe.

187 Glebe Ave., Ottawa, ON K1S 2C6. © **888/828-8801** or 613/236-8521. Fax 613/231-3730. www.bbcanada.com/926.html. 3 units. C$90–$95 (US$59–$63) double; C$125 (US$83) suite. Rates include breakfast. Rollaway free. *In room:* A/C, phone in one unit.

A Rose on Colonel By ★★ *Finds*   This cosy Edwardian-style home, built in 1925, is just steps from the Rideau Canal on a quiet residential street. Before becoming a B&B 2 years ago, the property was leased for many years by the American and French embassies as a diplomatic residence. The atmosphere in this nonsmoking home is warm and friendly, and children are genuinely welcomed. The delightful breakfast room is decorated with a collection of blue glass, strikingly displayed along the windowsills to catch the sunlight. The two bathrooms are shared between three guest rooms. There is only enough space to add a single cot to each bedroom, so you'll need two rooms if your family numbers more than three. A comfy lounge on the second floor is equipped with a fridge, microwave, coffeemaker, and phone. A short walk away is Brewer Park, bordered on its southern edge by the scenic Rideau River. The owner of the B&B will be happy to supply your youngsters with crusts of bread to feed the ducks and swans on Brewer Pond.

9 Rosedale Ave., Ottawa, ON K1S 4T2. © **613/291-7831.** www.rosebandb.com. 3 units. C$88–$126 (US$58–$83) per room. Rate includes breakfast. Rollaway/crib free. AE, V. Free parking. Pets sometimes accepted. **Amenities:** Washer and dryer. *In room:* Ceiling fans, no phone.

INEXPENSIVE

By-The-Way B&B   Situated on a quiet residential street in the Glebe, By-The-Way is a 1960s-era house tucked in the midst of century homes. This is basic accommodation at a reasonable price, and the hosts are pleasant and affable. The owners have thoughtfully created a lower-level suite suitable for families, so you'll get the friendliness of a B&B along with the independence of a separate entrance, kitchenette, phone, and TV. This open-plan suite contains one single and one double bed, and a cot can be arranged to allow a maximum occupancy of four people. The kitchenette is equipped with a fridge, microwave, two-ring hot plate, dishes, and utensils, but no dishwasher. Board games and children's books are available on request. The vanity unit in the spacious bathroom is set apart from the bath and toilet, which can speed things up at bedtime or during the morning rush. A 10-minute walk will take you to the nearest park along leafy, shaded sidewalks.

310 First Ave., Ottawa, ON K1S 2G8. © **613/232-6840.** Fax 613/232-6840. www.magma.ca/~bytheway. 1 unit for families. C$100 (US$66) 4 people. Rate includes breakfast. Rollaway free. AE, DC, MC, V. Free parking. *In room:* A/C, TV, kitchenette, iron.

Carleton University Tour and Conference Centre   During the summer months, Carleton's student residences are open to the public. Combining inexpensive, utilitarian accommodations with the convenience of campus facilities, a stay on campus is appealing to families. A family of four can be accommodated in two twin-bedded dorm rooms with an interconnecting bathroom, and rates include an all-you-can-eat breakfast in the large cafeteria. All buildings are nonsmoking. Athletic and recreational facilities on campus include an indoor pool, squash and tennis courts, a fitness center with a sauna and whirlpool, a game room and video arcade, and plenty of nature trails for walking, biking, or in-line skating. At nearby Dow's Lake you can rent canoes, kayaks, and bicycles. In the summer, the Governor General's Regiment is billeted in two of the residence buildings. Kids will get a kick out of seeing the regiment up close as the soldiers get ready to march up to Parliament Hill each morning. Scheduled to open in the fall of 2001 is a new residence featuring two- and four-bedroom suites with kitchenettes, sitting rooms, and private bathrooms.

1125 Colonel By Dr., Ottawa, ON K1S 5B6. © **613/520-5611**. Fax 613/520-3952. www.carleton.ca/housing/tourandconf. 1,100 units. C$99 (US$65) 4 people in dorm. Rate includes breakfast. MC, V. Parking C$5 (US$3) Mon–Fri, free on weekends. **Amenities:** Cafeteria, fast-food outlet, food court; indoor pool; health club; tennis courts; hot tub; sauna; watersports/bicycle rental at Dow's Lake; game room; video arcade; washers and dryers. *In room:* A/C in some units, no phone.

4 Ottawa East

Just off the Queensway near St. Laurent Boulevard is a little cluster of hotels. It may be too far to walk downtown, but don't let that deter you from staying in this district, because it offers lots of family entertainment. St. Laurent Shopping Centre, with over 230 stores and services, is within walking distance. Several family entertainment venues, including the Silver City movie theater, the Gloucester Wave Pool, and the high-tech adventures of Cyberdome Entertainment, are in easy reach. Take in a game of AAA baseball at Jetform Stadium in season. A couple of minutes' drive north on St. Laurent Boulevard will bring you to the National Aviation Museum, and a couple of minutes in the opposite direction will take you to the Museum of Science and Technology. For families traveling by train, the hotels listed here are all close to the station.

MODERATE

Chimo Hotel   Each unit contains a mini-fridge, allowing you to store cold drinks and snacks for everyone, and you'll also save money by eating out at the fast-food chains and roadhouse-style restaurants that abound in this district. Rooms and bathrooms are average size and in keeping with the price of a night's stay. This hotel is conveniently located near the Lone Star Cafe, if Tex Mex and line dancing are your thing, and it's the closest hotel to the St. Laurent Shopping Centre, for families of shopaholics.

1199 Joseph Cyr St., Ottawa, ON K1J 7T4. © **800/387-9779** or 613/744-1060. Fax 613/744-7076. www.chimohotel.com. 257 units. C$125–$145 (US$83–$96) double. Children 15 and under stay free in parents' room. Rollaway C$15 (US$10), crib free. AE, DC, DISC, MC, V. Free parking. **Amenities:** Restaurant, bar; indoor pool with atrium; exercise room; hot tub; sauna; secretarial services; limited room service; same-day laundry/dry cleaning. *In room:* A/C, TV w/ pay movies, dataport, fridge, coffeemaker, hairdryer, iron, safe.

Comfort Inn East   Most major cities and urban areas across Canada sport at least one of these moderately priced, comfortable hotels. Amenities are sparse, but the rooms are of a consistently good standard, and reliability is important when you're choosing somewhere to spend the night. There is no particular entertainment for children on the premises, but the proximity to the attractions mentioned in the introduction to this section is a plus.

1252 Michael St., Ottawa, ON K1J 7T1. © **800/228-5150** or 613/744-2900. Fax 613/746-0836. www.choicehotels.ca. 69 units. C$120 (US$79) double. Children 17 and under stay free in parents' room. Rollaway C$8 (US$5). AE, DC, DISC, MC, V. Free parking. **Amenities:** Secretarial services; same-day laundry/dry cleaning. *In room:* A/C, TV w/ pay movies, coffeemaker, iron.

Hampton Inn ★★ *Value*   A brand-new hotel that opened in 2000, the Hampton Inn has large guest rooms with high-quality furnishings and oversized bathrooms. Each room is equipped with a kitchenette that includes a microwave, sink, and small fridge (dishes and utensils are not supplied). The indoor pool area is spotless and spacious. A complimentary continental breakfast is served in the lobby lounge, and light fare is available in the evenings. As a result of its new and comfortable accommodations, indoor pool, and competitive pricing, the Hampton Inn has an edge over other options in the area.

100 Coventry Rd., Ottawa, ON K1K 4S3. ℂ **877/701-1281** or 613/741-2300. Fax 613/741-8689. YOWCN01
@hi-hotel.com. 179 units. C$121 (US$80) studio. Rate includes breakfast. Children 17 and under stay free in
parents' room. Rollaway C$15 (US$10), crib free. AE, DC, DISC, MC, V. Free parking. **Amenities:** Breakfast
room/lounge; indoor pool; exercise room; hot tub; secretarial services; massage; babysitting; washers and
dryers; same-day laundry/dry cleaning. *In room:* A/C, TV, dataport, kitchenette, coffeemaker, hairdryer, iron.

WelcomINNS   A clean and comfortable room awaits you here. The small
fridges in each unit will come in handy for storing drinks and snacks. There's no
pool on-site, but the Gloucester Wave Pool is nearby, as are the high-tech pleasures of the Cyberdome, in the St. Laurent Shopping Centre. The prices suit the
amenities you receive at this hotel.

1220 Michael St., Ottawa, ON K1J 7T1. ℂ **800/387-4381** or 613/748-7800. Fax 613/748-0499. www.
welcominns.com. 109 units. Winter C$117 (US$77) double; summer C$127 (US$84) double. Rates include
continental breakfast. Children 17 and under stay free in parents' room. Rollaway C$10 (US$7), crib free.
AE, DC, DISC, MC, V. Free parking. **Amenities:** Exercise room; hot tub; sauna; babysitting; same-day
laundry/dry cleaning. *In room:* A/C, TV w/ pay movies, dataport, fridge, hairdryer, iron.

5 Ottawa West

The hotels listed here are all good bets for families. Retail stores and family-style
restaurants are within walking distance, and although you'll need to drive to
attractions, all of these hotels provide comfortable rooms and pools. If you find
the downtown hotels a little pricey, or if they're full, consider staying in this area.

MODERATE

Best Western Barons Hotel   Although the location is a little far from
the city center, the family-friendly nature of this hotel and its competitive pricing make it a worthwhile place to stay. Its proximity to the Queensway means
that you can drive into the city in 15 minutes. The large regional shopping mall,
Bayshore, is 5 minutes away, and the Corel Centre is only 10 minutes west.
If you need to rent a car, there is a Budget car rental desk in the lobby.

Staff here are cheerful, knowledgeable, and polite. In the summer, ask them
about the "Family Fun Deal," which may include anything from free comic
books to museum and arcade passes or a disposable camera. Families also will
enjoy the clean and bright indoor pool. Exercise equipment is housed behind a
glass wall so parents can work out while keeping a close eye on the goings-on in
the pool. In the summer, a patio and grassy area out back are popular with
guests, who are welcome to use the barbecue. Rooms are larger than average, and
most of the bathrooms have recently been retiled. Families may opt for the convenience of a limited number of one-bedroom suites, which have a sink, small
fridge, and microwave but no dishes or utensils. The two larger suites have a
two-ring hot plate, dishes, and utensils, in addition to the standard kitchenette
fittings.

3700 Richmond Rd., Ottawa, ON K2H 5B8. ℂ **800/528-1234** or 613/828-2741. Fax 613/596-4742.
www.bestwestern.com/ca/baronshotel. 83 units. C$119 (US$79) double; C$124 (US$82) 1-bedroom suite;
Children 17 and under stay free in parents' room. Rollaway C$10 (US$7), crib free. AE, DC, DISC, MC, V. Free
parking. Pets C$10 (US$7). **Amenities:** Restaurant, kids' menu, bar; indoor pool; exercise room; hot tub;
sauna; secretarial services; limited room service; washers and dryers; same-day laundry/dry cleaning; executive rooms. *In room:* A/C, TV w/ pay movies, dataport, kitchenette in some units, coffeemaker, hairdryer, iron.

Best Western Macies Hotel   Macies is one of Ottawa's largest family-
run hotels. Now in their third generation of family management and with more
than 60 years of hospitality experience, the Macies staff are well equipped to deal
with vacationing families. Just pick up the phone and folding cribs, playpens,

baby baths, potties, nightlights, socket covers, and hot water bottles will be at your door. A kid's pack is available at check-in, which includes a disposable camera so kids can capture their own Kodak moments. Westgate Shopping Centre, with around 45 stores and services plus a movie theater, is directly opposite the hotel.

1274 Carling Ave., Ottawa, ON K1Z 7K8. ☎ **800/268-5531** (Canada), 800/528-1234 (U.S.), or 613/728-1951. Fax 613/728-1955. www.macieshotel.com. 123 units. C$104–C$130 (US$69–US$86) double. Children 12 and under stay free in parents' room; C$5 (US$3) ages 13 and up. Rollaway/crib free. AE, DC, DISC, MC, V. Free parking. Domestic, house-trained pets accepted but cannot be left alone. **Amenities:** Restaurant, lounge; large heated outdoor pool; health club; Jacuzzi; sauna; business services; limited room service; babysitting; washers and dryers; same-day laundry/dry cleaning. *In room:* A/C, TV w/ pay movies, fridge, coffeemaker, hairdryer, iron.

Travelodge Hotel Ottawa West   A complete refurbishment of guest rooms began in 1999, and by mid-2001 around one-third of rooms were completed. The business-grade rooms are the most comfortable, furnished with two queen-size beds and new bathrooms. There is one family room known as "Sleepy Bear's Den" with two double beds, a VCR, and a kid-size table and two chairs. The den will be a preschooler pleaser, but be prepared for teddy bear curtains and matching bedspreads. In the summer, two heated outdoor pools give everyone a chance to enjoy the water. WebTV is expected to be launched in 2001.

1376 Carling Ave., Ottawa, ON K1Z 7L5. ☎ **800/578-7878** or 613/722-7600. Fax 613/722-2226. www. travelodge.com. 274 units. C$140 (US$92) Sleepy Bear's Den, C$170 (US$112) business-grade double. Children 11 and under stay free in parents' room; C$10 (US$7) ages 12 and up. Rollaway C$10 (US$7), crib free. AE, DC, DISC, MC, V. Free parking. **Amenities:** Restaurant, lounge; 2 heated outdoor pools; secretarial services; same-day laundry/dry cleaning. *In room:* A/C, TV w/ pay movies, fridge, coffeemaker.

6 The Airport

Ottawa has a shortage of hotel rooms close to the airport, and the two places listed here are much in demand by business travelers. The problem is finally being addressed, with the Southway Inn expecting to almost double its units in late 2001 and plans underway for at least one new hotel to be built near the airport. Nevertheless, if you are traveling to Ottawa by air and would like a room close to the airport on arrival or prior to departure, these hotels are both comfortable. The Southway Inn has more amenities for families than the Airport Inn.

MODERATE

The Southway Inn   If you're seeking accommodations far from the high-rise jungle of downtown, this property in the south end of the city will suit. There are family restaurants and services, including a bank and drugstore, nearby, and if you avoid traveling during rush hour, it's only a short drive from the action of downtown Ottawa. It's a short drive to the airport too. For active kids, the Capital Golf Centre (4km, or 2.5 miles, south) has a championship 18-hole miniature golf course and batting cages. Parents might like to play the public course or try a swing on the 18-hole par-3 course. The indoor pool is bright and pleasant. The Southway Inn is undergoing expansion and expects to open another 74 units in late 2001, 5 of which will have full kitchens.

2431 Bank St. S., Ottawa, ON K1V 8R9. ☎ **800/267-9704** (Canada), 800/262-9704 (U.S.), or 613/737-0811. Fax 613/737-3207. www.southway.com. 96 units. C$155 (US$102) family rate (4 people) double. Rollaway/crib C$15 (US$10). AE, DC, DISC, MC, V. Free parking. Pets C$15 (US$10) first day, C$5 (US$3) each additional day. **Amenities:** Restaurant/bar; indoor pool; exercise room; hot tub; sauna; secretarial services;

limited room service; washers and dryers; same-day laundry/dry cleaning; executive rooms. *In room:* A/C, TV, dataport, kitchen in some units, fridge, coffeemaker, hairdryer, iron.

INEXPENSIVE

Adam's Airport Inn *(★* *(Value*   A 7-minute drive from the airport, this hotel is a good bet for a night's rest at either end of your vacation if you're traveling by air, especially if you have a late arrival or early-morning start. The rates are spot on for what's on offer, which is a clean and comfortable bed, friendly desk staff, and free parking. Just the basics, nicely delivered. Although the building is set back a little way from busy Bank Street, ask for a room at the back over-looking the quiet residential neighborhood. A complimentary continental breakfast and 24-hour coffee are available in the lobby.

2721 Bank St., Ottawa, ON K1T 1M8. *(C* **800/261-5835** or 613/738-3838. Fax 613/736-8211. 62 units. C$85 (US$56) family rate (4 people) in a double. Rollaway C$10 (US$7), crib free. AE, DC, MC, V. Free parking. Pets C$10 (US$7) per day. **Amenities:** Exercise room; washers and dryers. *In room:* A/C, TV, dataport, fridge, hairdryer.

Family-Friendly Dining

Dining out is one of life's great pleasures, and good-quality food and a pleasing atmosphere are its essential ingredients. In this section, I've listed some of the best places to eat in Ottawa, all of which either welcome or tolerate kids, since they will almost certainly be accompanying you if you're reading this book.

I've avoided establishments at extreme ends of the spectrum. At the top end, I've omitted the area's most select fine-dining establishments. Although you may not be refused a table, these are really not places to feed your preschoolers crackers and juice. But if your kids are age 6 and up, and they can hold a knife and fork as well as a conversation, you may want to venture into some of the more sophisticated eateries in town. Ottawa and Hull are home to many excellent restaurants specializing in French cuisine, and local residents will be only too glad to make a recommendation.

Just like everywhere else on the planet, Ottawa has its share of fast-food drive-thrus. You know who they are and what you'll find there. If you must visit them because you need a clean washroom with baby-changing facilities, your little one has to have a drink *right now*, or you have to unload toddlers and preschoolers in the playroom for half an hour because you need some alone time, then by all means go ahead.

As you stroll around the city, be warned that sooner or later you will come face to face with a chip wagon. They hold no appeal for me, but I can't deny their popularity in this part of the country. Besides the usual offering of deep-fried, sliced potatoes, many wagons serve poutine, a Quebecois concoction of fries topped with cheese curds and smothered in gravy. As in most Canadian cities, sausage and hotdog carts edge their way onto downtown sidewalks once the weather begins to warm up in the spring.

One step up from fast-food in paper bags lies a bunch of instantly recognizable chains providing table service. You can drag in fidgety, tired, or noisy offspring and no one will bat an eye—in fact, the staff will probably ply them with crayons and paper placemats. For a list of Ottawa's best chains, see "Chow Down on Chains," below.

If you're lucky enough or savvy enough to be staying in a suite, take advantage of the kitchen and eat at home to keep costs down or when kids are tired and the weather is wet or cold. When you do venture out, try to be seated before the clock strikes 12 for lunch and between 5 and 6pm for dinner if you want to get prompt service (essential with younger children) and to avoid waiting in lines (also crucial when kids are in tow).

Whenever the weather permits, go for the alfresco experience. Nobody will care if food gets dropped on the floor, there's an ever-changing panorama to keep younger ones occupied, the noise generated by your kids is less likely to attract disapproving glances, and secondhand smoke is less of a problem.

The restaurants I've chosen for this chapter are not by any means the only places to enjoy good food in a family-friendly atmosphere. Rather, the idea is to give you a sampling of the broad range of excellent cuisine that awaits you in Ottawa. Bon appetit!

DINING NOTES Dining out in Ottawa does not have to be an expensive venture, but be aware that taxes are high. Meals are subject to 8% provincial sales tax and 7% GST, so when you factor in an average tip, a whopping 30% is added to the bill. Tipping is usually left to the diner's discretion, although some establishments add 15% to the bill for parties of six or more. Wine prices in restaurants are quite high—don't be surprised to find your favourite vintage at double the price you'd pay at the liquor store. Save a little money by ordering an Ontario wine. Niagara vineyards produce some distinguished wines that are increasingly gaining international respect.

1 Restaurants by Cuisine

AFTERNOON TEA

Zoe's at the Fairmont Château Laurier ★★★ (Downtown East of the Canal, $$$, *p. 71*)

AMERICAN

Hard Rock Café ★★ (Downtown East of the Canal, $$, *p. 71*)

ASIAN

Shanghai Restaurant ★ (Chinatown, $$, *p. 80*)

BAGELS

Kettleman's Bagels ★ (the Glebe, $, *p. 78*)

Ottawa Bagelshop & Deli (Wellington Street West, $, *p. 79*)

BAKERY

The French Baker/Le Boulanger Français (Downtown East of the Canal, $, *p. 75*)

Le Moulin de Provence (Downtown East of the Canal, $, *p. 76*)

Wild Oat Bakery and Natural Foods (the Glebe, $, *p. 78*)

BISTRO

The Black Tomato ★★★ (Downtown East of the Canal, $$$, *p. 70*)

CHINESE

Yangtze (Chinatown, $$, *p. 80*)

CREPES

The Creperie (Downtown East of the Canal, $, *p. 75*)

DELI

Dunn's Famous Delicatessen (Downtown West of the Canal, $, *p. 69*)

DESSERTS

Oh So Good Desserts Café (Downtown East of the Canal, $, *p. 76*)

DINER

Elgin St. Diner (Downtown West of the Canal, $, *p. 69*)

ECLECTIC

Marchélino ★★ (Downtown East of the Canal, $, *p. 76*)

FUSION

Savana Café ★★ (Downtown West of the Canal, $$, *p. 68*)

ICE CREAM

Cow's Ottawa ★ (Downtown East of the Canal, $, *p. 75*)

Pasticceria Gelateria Italiana Ltd. (Little Italy, $, *p. 81*)

Piccolo Grande (Downtown East of the Canal, $, *p. 77*)

Pure Gelato (Downtown West of the Canal, $, *p. 69*)

INDIAN
  Haveli (Downtown East of the
    Canal, $$, *p. 74*)
  The Roses Café (Downtown West
    of the Canal, $$, *p. 68*)

ITALIAN
  The Canal Ritz ⭐ (the Glebe, $$,
    p. 77)
  La Roma ⭐⭐⭐ (Little Italy, $$$,
    p. 81)
  Mamma Grazzi's Kitchen ⭐
    (Downtown East of the Canal,
    $$, *p. 74*)
  Oregano's Pasta Market (Down-
    town East of the Canal, $$, *p. 74*)

MEDITERRANEAN
  Bravo Bravo ⭐⭐ (Downtown
    West of the Canal, $$$, *p. 67*)

PIZZA
  Café Colonnade ⭐ (Downtown
    West of the Canal, $$, *p. 68*)

SEAFOOD
  The Fish Market ⭐⭐ (Down-
    town East of the Canal, $$$,
    p. 71)

  Flippers ⭐ (the Glebe, $$$, *p. 77*)

TAKEOUT
  L'Amuse Gueule ⭐⭐ (the Glebe,
    $, *p. 78*)
  BeaverTails (Downtown East of
    the Canal, $, *p. 75*)
  Fettucine's (Downtown West of
    the Canal, $, *p. 69*)
  Luciano's ⭐ (Little Italy, $, *p. 81*)
  Parma Ravioli (Wellington Street
    West, $, *p. 79*)

TEX-MEX
  The Lone Star Cafe (Further Out,
    $$, *p. 81*)

VEGETARIAN
  The Green Door (Further Out, $,
    p. 82)
  Peace Garden Cafe (Downtown
    East of the Canal, $, *p. 76*)

VIETNAMESE
  New Mee Fung ⭐⭐ (China-
    town, $$, *p. 80*)

2 Downtown (West of the Canal)

You'll find loads of delightful restaurants tucked in the side streets and squeezed in between the high-rise buildings of the downtown core. Office workers and suits with cell phones grafted onto one ear fill these eateries at lunchtime on weekdays, but you can beat the crowd if you arrive before noon. Parking may be a challenge, so if you're travelling as a pair of parents, ask the driver to drop off the passengers and then hunt for an empty meter.

EXPENSIVE

Bravo Bravo ⭐⭐ MEDITERRANEAN   The main dining area at the front of this large restaurant is bright and airy with plenty of space between tables. A warm Mediterranean sunset palette, scuffed wooden floors, and a faux stone archway complete the picture. The ceiling is high enough and the music loud enough that families with small children will feel they can stay awhile without disturbing the peace. Check out the display of authentic hand-painted Venetian masks on one of the walls. If you're a risotto fan, have a taste of Bravo Bravo's offerings. The mushroom, pancetta, and onion risotto is creamy smooth and al dente. It will stick to your ribs—and even feed two or three kids from one serv-ing. There isn't a kids' menu, but the kitchen will cheerfully prepare pastas or pizzas with simple toppings for younger folk. Ice-cream freaks please note that Piccolo Grande gelato is on the menu. If you want to savor Bravo Bravo after the kids are asleep, pick up some antipasti and rich, gooey desserts from the takeout section at the entrance.

292 Elgin St. ✆ **613/233-7525.** Reservations recommended weekends only. Main courses C$12–$20 (US$8–$13). AE, DC, MC, V. Mon–Sat 11am–2am, Sun 10:30am–2am.

MODERATE

Café Colonnade ⍟ PIZZA   Pizzas almost fly from the oven onto tables and out the door at this place because Ottawans love Colonnade's pizza. And there's a lot to like—the thick crust with a sprinkling of cheese around the edge, the generous smear of tangy tomato sauce, and the gooey mozzarella that holds the toppings in place. Personal pizzas will fill most grown-up tummies or two kids at lunchtime, or you can order a medium or large and let everyone dig in. Although you really should go there for the pizza, the menu offers pasta, veal, chicken, manicotti, cannelloni, and other dishes. North American fare, including sandwiches and burgers, are also listed. There's no kids' menu, but a half-portion of pasta or an appetizer works just fine. The dining room is spacious and plainly furnished—the focus is clearly on the food. An outdoor terrace stretches along one side of the building, providing a place to hang out on warm summer days and evenings.

280 Metcalfe St. ✆ **613/237-3179.** Pizza C$7–$19 (US$5–$13), main courses C$7–$11 (US$5–$7). AE, DC, MC, V. Sun–Thurs 11am–10pm or 11pm; Fri–Sat 11am–11pm or midnight.

The Roses Café INDIAN   An Indian restaurant is a great choice for a family meal because everyone can spoon as much or as little of each dish onto their plate as they like. Typically, there are a lot of meatless choices and vegetables are presented with delicately spiced sauces, which, from a kid's point of view, act to disguise the taste. The appetizers and accompanying dishes are lots of fun for kids to eat too. Mine love pappadums, thin, crispy chip-like discs that melt in your mouth. With a focus on South Indian cuisine, the Roses menu features the dosa, a rice and lentil flour crepe filled with a variety of Indian-style vegetables. Their butter chicken curry is mildly spiced and has earned a reputation for excellence in the city. Takeout is available. The success of the Gladstone Avenue location prompted the owners to open two more: Roses Café Too, at 3710 Richmond Road, and Roses Café Also, at 349 Dalhousie Street.

523 Gladstone Ave. ✆ **613/233-5574.** Reservations recommended on weekends. Main courses C$6–C$12 (US$4–$8). AE, DC, MC, V. Mon–Fri 11:30am–2pm and 5–10pm, Sat–Sun 11:30am–2:30pm and 5–10pm.

Savana Café ⍟⍟ FUSION   The walls of the Savana Café are warm, vivid, and tropical. Intense Caribbean blue, brilliant green, and exquisite sunset colors put you in the mood for fun, and the food makes you want to sing (reggae, possibly?). With banana or coconut added to many dishes as a sweetener, kids will like the food here. Mine certainly did. West African–style vegetable stir-fry and sweet basil shrimp are two absolutely divine dishes. Or try the two-potato fries, coconut rice, pad thai, satay, or curry chicken—there's something for everyone. Servers are enthusiastic and knowledgeable. Don't be shy to ask for the ingredients of a particular dish or for a recommendation for younger tastebuds. Come hungry because the portions are generous and you won't be able to stop yourself from cleaning your plate.

431 Gilmour St. ✆ **613/233-9159.** Reservations recommended. Main courses C$10–$15 (US$7–$10). AE, DC, MC, V. Mon–Fri 11:30am–3pm and 5–10pm, Sat 5–10pm.

INEXPENSIVE

Dunn's Famous Delicatessen DELI   If you want to sample an authentic Montreal smoked meat sandwich without making the 2-hour trip from Ottawa, dive into Dunn's and sink your teeth into a stack of hand-carved smoked meat, brought in fresh from the Dunn's smokehouse in Montreal. Dunn's opened for business in Montreal in 1927, and the first Ottawa restaurant opened in 1990. The decor is a little scuffed around the edges, but that just adds to its comfortable, mom's kitchen kind of appeal. With customers chattering, dishes clattering, and servers dashing around, no one will notice if your kids' manners are taking a day off. The Elgin Street location never closes, so whether you're hungry for breakfast, lunch, or dinner, Dunn's is ready for you.

220 Elgin St. ✆ **613/230-6444.** Most items under C$10 (US$7). AE, DC, MC, V. Daily 24 hours. Also at 57 Bank St. ✆ **613/230-4005.** Mon–Fri 7am–9pm, Sat–Sun 8am–9pm.

Elgin St. Diner DINER   This is a comfy, neighborhood kind of place where you can saunter in, flop into a chair, and hang out with a coffee while the kids slurp milkshakes and chomp peanut butter and jam sandwiches. Kids' meals, which include a sandwich, burger, or hotdog plus fries and juice, milk, or soda, are only C$3.50 (US$2.30). The breakfast special features two eggs, your choice of bacon, ham, or sausage, home fries, baked beans, toast, and coffee for C$4.50 (US$3), or you can choose from the variety of omelets or pancakes with real maple syrup on the all-day breakfast menu. There are plenty of old-fashioned dinners, including meatloaf, shepherd's pie, and liver and onions. Servers are cheerful, and you can drop in any time—they never close.

374 Elgin St. ✆ **613/237-9700.** Most items under C$10 (US$7). AE, DC, V. Daily 24 hours.

Fettucine's TAKEOUT   If you're staying in a downtown suite with kitchen facilities, pay a visit to Fettucine's and stock your fridge with fresh pasta, sauces, and ready-to-eat salads. The spinach and cheese ravioli is filling and delicious. Other good bets are chicken parmigiana and basil pesto. Lasagna, cannelloni, pasta salad, and Caesar salad are also regular menu items. Everything is made on the premises.

280C Elgin St. ✆ **613/230-4723.** Most items under C$10 (US$7). AE, V. Mon–Sat 10:30am–8pm, Sun 11am–7pm.

Pure Gelato ICE CREAM/CAFÉ   You can never have too much ice cream and it's handy to know a place or two outside the ByWard Market area where you can get the good stuff. Here's one of them. Kids' cones are under C$2 (US$1.30) and the choice is dizzying, with lots of fruit flavors, more than nine chocolate concoctions, and unusual flavors like ginger, Toblerone, and chestnut. Hot, golden malted Belgian waffles are only C$5 (US$3) and you can add gelato for a buck. Plunk the kids down on shiny metallic stools at the long counter and enjoy. For grown-ups, there's a European-style coffee bar.

350 Elgin St. ✆ **613/237-3799.** Most items under C$10 (US$7). V. Sun–Wed 11am–midnight, Thurs–Sat 11am–1am.

3 Downtown (East of the Canal)

By far the greatest concentration of good restaurants and food shops in Ottawa is in the ByWard Market district. East of the Rideau Canal, the area is officially bordered by Sussex Drive, St. Patrick Street, King Edward Avenue, and Rideau Street. The ByWard Market building and seasonal farmer's market run between

CHOW DOWN ON CHAINS

Chains thrive because they deliver a consistent product in a reliable manner. The menu is generally the same at every location, so you can order quickly and be pretty certain of what you'll get. Hosts will bring booster seats, highchairs, paper kids' menus, and crayons. Servers will grin at your kids and top up your coffee. So keep an eye out for these chains when you're out and about. Some have more locations than I've listed here—let your fingers do the walking if your favorite isn't listed below in your neighborhood.

Boston Pizza, 1055 St. Laurent Blvd. (© **613/746-1039**) and 521 West Hunt Club Rd. (© **613/226-3374**), serves pizza, pasta, salads, ribs, and sandwiches for dine-in, takeout, or delivery. **Denny's** is a family-style restaurant at 2208 Bank St. (© **613/731-4828**). You'll find **East Side Mario's** American Italian fare at 1200 St. Laurent Blvd. (© **613/747-0888**). If you crave a good steak, try **The Keg**, 75 York St. (© **613/241-8514**). There's a **Kelsey's** roadhouse-style family restaurant close to the Canada Science and Technology Museum at 1910 St. Laurent Blvd. (© **613/733-2200**). **Mexicali Rosa's** serves up their California-style Mexican food at 895 Bank St. (© **613/236-9499**), 200 Rideau St. (© **613/241-7044**), and Dow's Lake Pavilion at 1001 Queen Elizabeth Dr. (© **613/234-8156**). Seafood is on the menu every day at **Red Lobster**, 1499 St. Laurent Blvd. (© **613/744-7560**). For good old-fashioned food, go to **Rockin' Johnny's Diner**, 1301 Carling Ave. (© **613/761-7405**) and 1129 St. Laurent Blvd. (© **613/744-5666**). A popular BBQ chicken restaurant in Quebec, **St-Hubert** has three locations in the Ottawa area, including one at 1754 St. Laurent Blvd. (© **613/526-1222**). And last but not least, every grandparent's favorite BBQ chicken restaurant is **Swiss Chalet**, 1910 Bank St. (© **613/733-7231**), 96A George St. (© **613/562-3020**), 675 Kirkwood Ave. (© **613/729-1789**), and 540 Montreal Rd. (© **613/746-1777**).

York and George streets. Parking is plentiful, but because of the popularity of the dining and shopping here, spaces are scarce. If you don't luck out on the first or second pass, bite the bullet and park in one of the open-air or underground lots. It may cost a little more, but you're saved the time and stress of driving around in circles, and you can leave your vehicle for hours for a flat fee of C$10 (US$7) or less, whereas most meters in the market allow a maximum of 1 or 2 hours at certain times of the day.

EXPENSIVE

The Black Tomato ★★★ BISTRO   This is one of the best places to eat in the ByWard Market area, with top marks for the food and the surroundings. The kitchen has heaps of culinary talent, so prepare yourself for a hedonistic evening. Parents will appreciate this place more than the kids. It's not a place for toddlers, but bring along kids from about age 5 and up. The kitchen will prepare a small helping of a plain dish for your children if you ask, so do bring them along because you really have to try this place. If the weather is warm, you can retreat to the back patio in the picturesque courtyard. Make the scrumptious Sunday brunch a family event. Three courses (granola or soup; egg special or French toast; dessert or sorbet; and coffee, tea, or juice) are yours for C$14 (US$9). My daughter polished off a wedge of French toast (cut from a round loaf) with strawberries and mango whipped cream, sautéed potatoes, and bacon, while I savored every spoonful of my black bean and corn chowder. Arrive early because the place gets extremely busy, especially in the evening.

11 George St. ✆ 613/789-8123. Reservations accepted only for parties of 8 or more. Main courses C$16–$24 (US$11–$16). AE, MC, V. Mon–Sat 11:30am–10pm or 11pm, Sun 11:00am–10pm or 11pm.

The Fish Market ✶✶ SEAFOOD   Ottawa's original fresh fish restaurant, established in 1979, has an astounding array of fish and seafood from around the world. Young sailors' survivor rations include fish and chips, shrimp and fries, and broiled salmon and rice for C$4 (US$3). Older seafood lovers will find the menu a delight, with fresh oysters, salmon or shrimp pasta, lobster, Alaskan crab legs, scallops, tuna, marlin, and any number of other sea-dwelling creatures to choose from. The menu is refreshed twice a day as supplies ebb and flow in the kitchen. My daughter, who has eaten her fair share of fish and chips in England, declared the battered cod and chips the best she'd tasted this side of the Atlantic. I'm also a fan of fresh fish, having lived by the sea for a number of years, and the steamed mussels with white wine, garlic, and fresh vegetables met with my approval. Watch out for the live trout and lobster tanks at the front door. Upstairs is the more casual Coasters Seafood Grill, with a central fireplace and open kitchen. There are more non-fishy menu choices here than downstairs and prices are a little lower.

54 York St. ✆ 613/2413474. Fish Market main courses C$13 (US$9) and up; Coasters main courses C$9–$13 (US$6–$9). AE, DC, MC, V. Mon–Thurs 11:30am–2pm and 5–10pm, Fri 11:30am–2pm and 5–11pm, Sat 11:30am–2:30pm and 5–11pm, Sun 11:30am–3pm and 5–10pm.

Zoe's ✶✶✶ AFTERNOON TEA   There is nothing more civilized than afternoon tea, and the Château Laurier does it very well, from the white linen to the silver tea service and waiters in waistcoats and bow ties. Tea is served in the late afternoon in the glass-enclosed terrace of Zoe's restaurant (on the right side of the main hotel lobby). Make sure your children bring their best table manners with them, and if they're still apprentices, use this as an opportunity to teach them a little dignity and decorum. Little girls especially will enjoy this experience—you may want to have a girls' day out if you're blessed with daughters as I am. Have a good breakfast on the day you plan to visit and skip lunch because British afternoon tea is a substantial offering. The full tea at the Château Laurier consists of fresh fruit cup, seasonal fruit tartlets, afternoon tea cake, Victorian scones with Devonshire cream and strawberry jam, dainty finger sandwiches (English cucumber and cream cheese, smoked turkey with raspberry mayonnaise, and salmon and dill herb), and tea, coffee, or juice. No less than nine teas are listed and there's not a teabag in sight. Waiters supply you, instead, with a silver-plated strainer to rest on your china cup. You can almost see the ghosts of Edwardian ladies reaching for the teapot.

Fairmont Château Laurier, 1 Rideau St. ✆ 613/241-1414. Reservations recommended. C$20 (US$13) for full afternoon tea. AE, DC, MC, V. Afternoon tea Mon–Fri 3–5:30pm.

MODERATE

Hard Rock Café ✶✶ AMERICAN   If you're a rock music fan, you'll find the collection of memorablilia from rock's most legendary performers jaw-dropping. Make sure you take a walk around the place and don't miss upstairs.

Family-Friendly Ottawa Dining

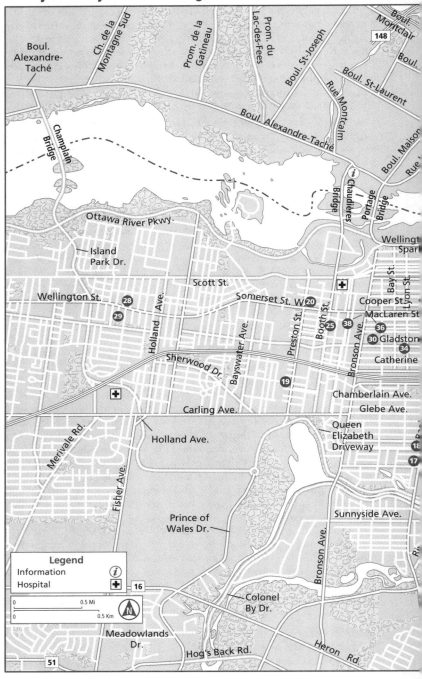

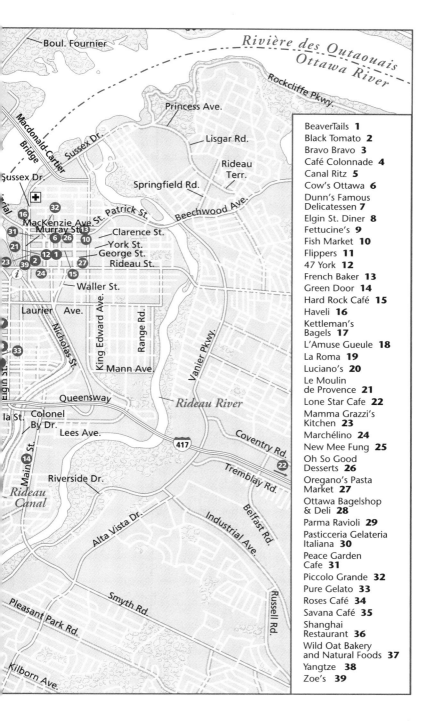

Boul. Fournier

Rivière des Outaouais
Ottawa River

Rockcliffe Pkwy.

Princess Ave.

Lisgar Rd.

Macdonald-Carter Bridge

Sussex Dr.

Sussex Dr.

Rideau Terr.

Springfield Rd.

St. Patrick St.

Beechwood Ave.

16

32

MacKenzie Ave.

31

Murray St. 13

6 26 10

Clarence St.

York St.

21

12 1

George St.

23 39 2 1

27

Rideau St.

i

24

15

Waller St.

Laurier   Ave.

King Edward Ave.

Range Rd.

Vanier Pkwy.

7

Nicholas St.

33

Mann Ave.

Rideau River

Elgin St.

Queensway

Colonel By Dr.

Lees Ave.

417

Coventry Rd.

la St.

22

Tremblay Rd.

Main St.

14

Riverside Dr.

Belfast Rd.

Rideau Canal

Alta Vista Dr.

Industrial Ave.

Russell Rd.

Pleasant Park Rd.

Smyth Rd

Kilborn Ave.

BeaverTails **1**
Black Tomato **2**
Bravo Bravo **3**
Café Colonnade **4**
Canal Ritz **5**
Cow's Ottawa **6**
Dunn's Famous
Delicatessen **7**
Elgin St. Diner **8**
Fettucine's **9**
Fish Market **10**
Flippers **11**
47 York **12**
French Baker **13**
Green Door **14**
Hard Rock Café **15**
Haveli **16**
Kettleman's
Bagels **17**
L'Amuse Gueule **18**
La Roma **19**
Luciano's **20**
Le Moulin
de Provence **21**
Lone Star Cafe **22**
Mamma Grazzi's
Kitchen **23**
Marchélino **24**
New Mee Fung **25**
Oh So Good
Desserts **26**
Oregano's Pasta
Market **27**
Ottawa Bagelshop
& Deli **28**
Parma Ravioli **29**
Pasticceria Gelateria
Italiana **30**
Peace Garden
Cafe **31**
Piccolo Grande **32**
Pure Gelato **33**
Roses Café **34**
Savana Café **35**
Shanghai
Restaurant **36**
Wild Oat Bakery
and Natural Foods **37**
Yangtze **38**
Zoe's **39**

I was impressed by signed guitars from Brian May of Queen and David Bowie, but there are others if your taste in music runs in a different direction. Contemporary bands are featured as well as the old greats, so your kids will recognize at least some of the names. Rock videos blare from TV screens, and when the restaurant is busy, the atmosphere is charged. There are two outdoor patios for summer toe-tapping and table-top drumming. But stop singing along long enough to eat. Burgers, steaks, fajitas, chicken breast, and pot roast are all menu favorites. The kids' menu, printed on the back of a coloring book, offers a main course and beverage for C$7 (US$5). And how good is their hot-fudge sundae, made with Hard Rock Café's unbelievably rich signature ice cream? You'll just have to try it for yourself.

73 York St. ℂ 613/241-2442. Reservations accepted only for parties of 6 or more. Main courses C$8–$25 (US$5–$17). AE, DC, MC, V. Daily 11:30am–late.

Haveli INDIAN   Popular with Ottawans, Haveli specializes in authentic North Indian cuisine, prepared by a team of chefs from various regions of India. The dining room reflects traditional Indian decor, with high-back chairs in intricately carved dark wood and brass plates on the tables. The buffet, served for lunch every day except Saturday (when they are closed for lunch) and on Sunday evenings, allows novice and experienced samplers of Indian cuisine to taste a variety of dishes, from meat curries to tandoori chicken, naan, rice, samosas, vegetables, and salads, plus those little extras that we all love to order: raita, pappadums, pickles, and chutneys. If you're introducing your kids to Indian food for the first time, tandoori chicken, plain pappadums, and rice are good choices. Always taste the food first to check the heat level before offering it to your kids—a bad experience with a chilli pepper can stay with them for a very long time. Takeout is available.

39 Clarence St. ℂ 613/241-1700. Reservations recommended weekends only. Main courses C$10–$16 (US$7–$11). AE, MC, V. Mon–Wed 11:45am–2:15pm and 5:30–9:30pm, Thurs–Fri 11:45am–2:15pm and 5:30–10:30pm, Sat 5:30–10:30pm, Sun noon–2:30pm and 5–9pm. Other location: 194 Robertson Rd. ℂ 613/820-1700.

Mamma Grazzi's Kitchen ⭐ ITALIAN   Mamma Grazzi's is one of those rare places that serves up consistently good food in a knock-out location. Whether you like your pasta dressed with tomato, cream, or olive oil, you'll have several combinations of ingredients to choose from. Housed in a heritage stone building, Mamma Grazzi's is especially delightful in the summer, when you can enjoy the old, cobblestone courtyard out back. The quaint courtyard is flanked by the terraces of a couple of other eateries, creating a European atmosphere. Because they make everything to order, you may have to wait a little, but it's worth it. Try the Italian sodas, infused with orange or lemon. They beat sickly sweet North American soft drinks hands down. The entrance to the restaurant is in a little alleyway off George Street, and you'll have to negotiate stairs wherever you eat—up to the second floor, or down to the ground floor or outdoor terrace.

25 George St. ℂ 613/241-8656. Reservations not accepted. Main courses C$8–$14 (US$5–$9). AE, MC, V. Sun–Wed 11:30am–10pm, Thurs–Sat 11:30am–11pm.

Oregano's Pasta Market ITALIAN   In an historic building in the heart of the market at the corner of William and George streets, Oregano's features a large dining room and two outdoor patios where you can watch the hustle and bustle of the ByWard Market while you eat. As you would expect, there's lots of pasta on the menu, including seashell pasta with shrimp, cannelloni, manicotti, tortellini, and grilled chicken with fettucine. Servings are generous and some pasta dishes can be ordered as half-portions (my half-portion of spaghettini Bolognese was plenty big enough and kept hunger pangs at bay for the entire afternoon). Pizzas with traditional toppings are under C$10 (US$7).You can order pasta with butter, tomato sauce, meat sauce, or just plain for the fussy bunch. The all-you-can-eat buffet, served at lunch and dinner, is an extravagant selection of appetizers, salads, pastas, and pizza. Kids 3 to 6 eat for half price.

74 George St. ✆ **613/241-5100.** Reservations recommended for dinner. Main courses C$10–$14 (US$7–$9); buffet C$9 (US$6) lunch, C$10 (US$7) dinner. AE, DC, MC, V. Mon–Sat 11am–11:30pm, Sun 10:30am–11:30pm.

INEXPENSIVE

BeaverTails TAKEOUT   This fast-food treat, first served in 1978 in the ByWard Market, enjoys a loyal following in Ottawa. Beaver Tails are flat, deep-fried pastries shaped like a beaver tail, with toppings like drizzled chocolate, cinnamon and sugar, garlic, and cheese. They sell well in all seasons, but we like them best outdoors on a cold, crisp, sunny winter day when we've worked up an appetite from skating or skiing (you'll find locations at Blue Mountain ski resort in Ontario and Mont Tremblant in Quebec). If you're more of an indoor kind of family, the St. Laurent Centre in Ottawa also has a stall.

87 George St. ✆ **613/241-1230.** Most items under C$10 (US$7). Summer daily 10am–late. Winter Mon–Wed 10am–6pm, Thurs–Sat 10am–11pm, Sun 10am–8pm.

Cow's Ottawa ICE CREAM   Cow's hails from Prince Edward Island in Canada's Atlantic provinces. Their secret recipe using all natural ingredients, combined with a mixing process that minimizes the amount of air added to the product, results in a smooth, creamy, premium ice cream. They keep inventing new flavors, so you never know what you'll find when you drop in. Our family's favorite is the ice cream studded with miniature filled chocolates. The company has created a unique retail store jam-packed with clothing and all kinds of small, kid-appealing knick knacks that sport the black and white cow. You'll find lots of T-shirts with images of cows in humorous situations. The clothing is good quality and washes well.

43 Clarence St. ✆ **613/244-4224.** Most items under C$10 (US$7). AE, MC. V. Daily Jan–Apr 10am–5pm, May–Sept 10am–10pm, mid-Sept–Dec 10am–6pm.

The Creperie CREPES   I've never met a kid who doesn't like pancakes. French pancakes (crepes) are especially nice because they come with yummy fillings and toppings. As you would expect, the menu is full of savory and sweet crepes. For C$5.50 (US$3.60), kids 10 and under get a ham and cheese or chicken-filled crepe and a drink. Full sized crepes, with chicken, seafood, vegetable, beef, or ham fillings, come in under C$15 (US$10). Dessert crepes (white and dark chocolate, strawberries, bananas, and ice cream in various combinations) are satisfying and sweet. The only drawback to this place is that the ventilation system is poor, which poses a problem when smokers are present.

47 York St. ✆ **613/241-8805.** Reservations recommended summer and weekends. Main courses C$10–$15 (US$7–$10). AE, DC, MC, V. Mon–Tues 11am–10pm, Wed–Fri 11am–11pm, Sat 10am–11pm, Sun 9am–10pm.

The French Baker/Le Boulanger Français BAKERY/CAFÉ   Reputed to have the flakiest, richest, most buttery croissants in the city, the French Baker also has authentic baguettes and other bread and pastry items. If you venture down the long corridor to the back of the small bakery, you'll find a chic gourmet food shop. Selection is limited but delicious. French and Quebecois cheeses are available, and you can sit and sip a coffee or sample the light fare.

119 Murray St. ✆ **613/789-7941**. Most items under C$10 (US$7). AE, MC, V. Mon–Fri 7:30am–6:30pm, Sat–Sun 7:30am–5:30pm.

Marchélino *★★* ECLECTIC   This unique restaurant, situated just inside the east entrance of the Rideau Centre, offers an eclectic mix of gourmet fast food served up at various market-style stalls. Toddlers and preschoolers will love to wander among the beautiful displays of fruits, salads, breads, and pastries and watch the staff at work rolling out dough, baking bread, sliding pizzas in and out of the stone hearth oven, and assembling sushi. Their extensive selection of food to eat in or take out includes chocolate croissants, muffins, cinnamon buns, scrambled eggs with ham and chives, at least seven varieties of soup, customized sandwiches with five kinds of bread and a dozen fillings, grain-fed roasted chicken, pizza with classic or adventurous toppings, Yukon Gold fries, and pasta. Try the rösti, a Swiss dish of shredded potato, pan-fried golden brown and topped with smoked salmon, chicken, or sour cream. Even the coffee is upscale —each cup is ground and brewed individually.

50 Rideau St. (in the Rideau Centre). ✆ **613/569-4934**. Most items under C$10 (US$7). AE, MC, V. Mon–Thurs and Sat 7:30am–9pm, Fri 7:30am–10pm, Sun 7:30am–7pm.

Le Moulin de Provence BAKERY/CAFÉ   At the north end of the ByWard Market building is this wonderful mix of bakery, cafe, and patisserie. Order a bowl of café au lait for yourself and hot chocolate for the kids, and savor a delicate French pastry in the midst of the bustling market. Then grab some cheese or paté, tuck a baguette under your arm, and head home for lunch, in the true European manner.

55 Byward Market. ✆ **613/241-9152**. Most items under C$10 (US$7). V. Daily 7am–7pm.

Oh So Good Desserts Café DESSERTS   You can't miss the delectable desserts here, since the shiny glass showcase is front and center when you enter the door. The rest of the place is dark. Black tables, black chairs, black walls. Large chalk murals featuring a jazz theme give some color to the room. The cakes are displayed on three shelves in the well-lit showcase at kids' height so they can look the peanut butter fudge buster right in the eye. On the day we visited, we counted 34 different cakes. There's only one serving size, which will easily fill two kids. Evenings tend to be busy and very smoky, so a daytime visit is recommended unless it's summer and you can nab a table on the rear patio. Takeout is available.

108 Murray St. ✆ **613/241-8028**. Most items under C$10 (US$7). AE, V. Mon–Thurs 9am–11pm, Fri 9am–midnight, Sat 9am–midnight, Sun 11am–11pm.

Peace Garden Cafe VEGETARIAN   A tiny oasis in the leafy inner court of the Times Square Building, Peace Garden is a great place to retreat when you feel the need to escape from noisy city streets. There are a few small tables in the courtyard next to a tinkling fountain and a counter with stools to climb onto, if your kids like that kind of thing (mine do). If you're hungry, soup, salads, sandwiches, and a variety of Indian, Malaysian, Italian, and Greek specialties will fit the bill. It's also a great place just to sip a spicy Indian chai tea or a cool, fresh mango lassi (yogurt drink). To boost your energy after a day of sightseeing, ask the server to recommend one of their power juices.

47 Clarence St. ✆ **613/562-2434**. Most items under C$10 (US$7). MC. Mon–Wed 7:30am–8pm, Thurs–Fri 7:30am–9pm, Sat 9am–10pm, Sun 10am–8pm.

Piccolo Grande ICE CREAM   "Gelato is your fantasy," says Piccolo Grande. Dream up any flavor of gelato and Piccolo Grande will do their best to make it for you, although you may have to give them a few days to work on it. If it's one of their regular flavors (they have almost 80, so they can't keep them all in the store at once) and you'd like a liter or more, they will try to get it for you within 48 hours. Of course, they may already make your ultimate ice cream. Close your eyes and think of amaretto, mochaccino, pear, or zabaglione. If your kids would wrinkle their noses at those, what about caramel chocolate chip, banana peanut butter, pumpkin, cinnamon, or strawberries and cream? Apple, grape, or tangerine sorbet? Cranberry, mango, or honeydew melon sherbet? Your kids will go crazy trying to decide. You can eat a tasty and inexpensive lunch there, too. Homemade soups, salads, Italian sandwiches, pasta, and lasagna are all available to eat in or take out. There are only 40 seats inside and lunchtime can get very busy. After 7pm they serve only gelato. If you're not in the market area, you can still get Piccolo Grande's wonderful product at two restaurants—Vittoria Trattoria, at 825 Bank St. in the Glebe, and Bravo Bravo, at 292 Elgin St. in the downtown area west of the canal—and at Nicastro's groceteria, at 1558 Merivale Rd. Now start dreaming.

55 Murray St. ✆ **613/241-2909**. Most items under C$10 (US$7). V. Summer Mon–Sat 9am–midnight, Sun 9am–11pm. Winter Mon 9:30am–5pm, Tues–Thurs 9:30am–7pm, Fri–Sat 9:30am–11pm, Sun 11am–6pm.

4 The Glebe

Strung along Bank Street between the Queensway and the Canal lies the trendy shopping and dining district known as the Glebe. Have your plastic ready because there will be lots of treasures to tempt you. When you need a break from all that frenzied shopping, take refuge in a cafe, restaurant, or gourmet food shop until your energy levels begin to rise once more. With a population base that includes young professional families, the Glebe caters to children, albeit upscale ones.

EXPENSIVE

Flippers ⓚ SEAFOOD   Flippers has been serving fresh fish to Ottawans since 1980. Seafood restaurant staples (bay scallops, salmon, shrimp, and mussels) are treated with respect and prepared with style. Specials include Alaskan king crab legs, Arctic char, and bouillabaisse. Children 6 and up will be comfortable here. Some dishes can be ordered in reduced portions and there are kid-appealing menu choices—English-style fish and chips, grilled Atlantic salmon, and pasta. A papier-mâché mermaid perches in one corner of the room, and glass fish mobiles hang from the ceiling.

819 Bank St. (Fifth Avenue Court). ✆ **613/232-2703**. Reservations accepted only for parties of 6 or more. Main courses C$11–$18 (US$7–$12) and up. AE, DC, MC, V. Daily 11:30am–2pm and 5pm–10pm.

MODERATE

The Canal Ritz ⓚ ITALIAN   With its converted boathouse setting, the Canal Ritz offers a constantly changing view of the Rideau Canal. In summer, boats sail past the tables on the spacious terrace, and in winter, skaters glide past on the world's longest skating rink. The children's menu offers a choice of pizza, pasta, or chicken, a refreshing change from the usual burger fare. If you're looking for grown-up food, the thin-crust designer pizza is topped with pears, dried figs, and smoked gouda. For lunch, try the Canal Ritz salad with fresh salad greens, herb-marinated shrimp, feta, cucumber, and tomatoes. The bread here is wonderful—loaves are satisfyingly dense, with a hint of sweetness and a crisp but not crumbly crust. The parking lot is on the south side of Fifth Avenue, directly opposite the restaurant.

375 Queen Elizabeth Dr. ℂ **613/238-8998.** Reservations recommended. Main courses C$10–$15 (US$7–$10). AE, DC, MC, V. Daily 11:30am–11pm.

INEXPENSIVE

L'Amuse Gueule TAKEOUT Having spent many vacations in France, I can attest that the wonderful dishes coming from the French chef/owner's kitchen at this gourmet food shop are as good as any you'll get on the Continent. If boeuf bourguignon or carrot salad appear in the display case, snap them up. Takeout dinner entrees change weekly and feature a different dish every day, from herb-roasted grain fed chicken to lobster-filled crepes. There are a few tables and chairs inside, but this is mainly a takeout and catering shop. Order a gourmet picnic basket filled with tasty dishes or pick up some local and imported cheeses and a baguette or two, then head to the banks of the canal for a leisurely family picnic.

915 Bank St. ℂ **613/234-9400.** Main courses C$10–$12 (US$7–$8). MC, V. Tues–Fri 10:30am–7pm, Sat 9:30pm–7pm.

Kettleman's Bagels 🌟 BAGELS Kids love coming here as much for the entertainment of watching the bakers at work as for the bagels. From the mounds of dough, bakers cut off strips, shape them into circles, and slide them into the open wood-burning oven on long planks. The freshly baked bagels are delicious on their own, but try one of the spreads or fillings. Little kids (and big kids!) love peanut butter and jam on a plain toasted bagel, the pizza bagel (half a bagel served open-faced with pizza toppings), and Kettleman's famous pretzel, a soft, salted, hand-rolled pretzel. There are two additional locations: Carling Avenue in the west end and Place d'Orléans Drive in the east end.

912 Bank St. ℂ **613/567-7100.** Most items under C$10 (US$7). Daily 24 hours. Other locations: 2177 Carling Ave. ℂ **613/722-4357**; 1222 Place d'Orléans Dr. ℂ **613/841-4409.**

Wild Oat Bakery and Natural Foods BAKERY If you need a break while trolling the cool shops along Bank Street in the Glebe, this is a good spot to dash in and grab a bite. Seating is limited, so you may have to take your food outside

---

☕ Coffee Break

Old-fashioned coffee and donut shops still abound in small-town Ontario, but in the big cities, chains with a more sophisticated (and expensive!) twist dominate the downtown street corners. In Ottawa, **Second Cup, Starbuck's,** and **Grabbajabba** are the names you're most likely to see downtown. The coffee-based drinks in these trendy cafes tend to be tasty, but by the time you've plied your kids with a drink and snack each, the bill for your much-needed jolt of caffeine may be a little hard to swallow. Keep your eyes open for **Tim Hortons,** a more down-to-earth chain in terms of coffee selection and prices. There are a couple of downtown locations, but most branches are out in the suburbs, where they attract drive-thru business. Tim's serves great donuts and coffee, as well as inexpensive sandwiches, soup, and chili.

and walk as you eat. Ready-to-eat small pizzas and samosas make a good light lunch, and you can follow them with brownies, squares, or one of the large cookies lined up in wicker baskets on the counter. We've sampled chocolate chip, peanut butter, ginger, maple and hemp seed, and oatmeal raisin and haven't found a dud among them. Wheat-free, yeast-free, and naturally sweetened baked goods are available. Browse the shelves for organic pasta, vegetables, and other healthy food items.

817 Bank St. ✆ 613/232-6232. Most items under C$19 (US$7). Mon–Fri 8:30am–8pm, Sat 9am–6pm, Sun 10:30am–5:30pm.

5 Wellington Street West

This residential neighborhood west of downtown is quieter than the Glebe, but there are also some interesting shops to be found here (see chapter 9, "Shopping with Your Kids"). Spend some time strolling the street and refuel at the eateries below. Watch for the seasonal farmer's market on Parkdale Avenue to browse the local fresh produce.

INEXPENSIVE

Ottawa Bagelshop & Deli BAGELS   Here you'll find bagels and much much more. This hotchpotch of bakery, deli, cafe, and gourmet food shop is a warren of shelves jam-packed with a bewildering variety of ethnic goodies. Venture toward the back and you'll find the bagel counter, where you can buy bags of bagels to take home. Turn to your right and go up the steps to enter the eat-in section. A European coffee counter, a buffet table with hot and cold food, and a sandwich counter round off the eatery. The prices for sandwiches and filled bagels are posted on a board. If you choose the buffet, which includes BBQ chicken, Italian sausages, rice, and lots of salads, the cashier will weigh your plate and charge you an amount based on C$7.25 (US$5) per pound. Try the cheese blintzes—they're light and creamy with just a touch of sweetness. The place is a real neighborhood haunt for locals, packed with everyone from school children to mothers and babies and seniors.

1321 Wellington St. W. ✆ 613/722-8753. Most items under C$10 (US$7). AE, MC, V. Mon–Thurs and Sat 6:30am–7pm, Fri 6:30am–8pm, Sun 6:30am–6pm.

Parma Ravioli TAKEOUT   With its spacious open kitchen behind the retail counter, Parma Ravioli is a wonderful place for kids to learn how pasta is made. You're likely to see something different each time you visit. Cooks in white jackets and tall hats knead dough, mix pasta fillings, and assemble ravioli right before your eyes. After you've finished watched the show, take home oodles of Italian goodies—bread, rolls, focaccia, fresh pasta, ravioli, lasagna, manicotti, pasta sauces, and Italian desserts.

1314 Wellington St. ✆ 613/722-6003. Most items under C$10 (US$7). Mon–Wed 9:30am–6pm, Thurs–Fri 9:30am–6:30pm, Sat 9am–6pm, Sun 10am–5pm.

6 Chinatown

Ottawa's Asian community has settled primarily around Somerset Street West. The main street is lined with Asian grocery stores and restaurants. Highlighting just a few eateries is a difficult task because there are so many good places to eat Asian food in the city, and not all are in Chinatown.

MODERATE

New Mee Fung *★★* VIETNAMESE   Meticulous attention to detail in the composition and presentation of the dishes results in a memorable dining experience. This small restaurant is clean, simply furnished, and casual, making it ideal for families. With lots of finger foods, dishes that require assembly (you can roll up your chicken in rice paper), and chopsticks to master, the kids will be kept busy. Each dish on the extensive menu is coded. Just jot down the numbers on the scrap of paper the smiling server gives you and wait for a splendid feast to arrive. Many dishes feature grilled chicken, beef, and pork, and there's a good selection of soups, spring rolls, salads, and noodles. Our grilled marinated chicken was accompanied by fresh mint, basil, and lettuce; soft, paper-thin discs made from rice flour for wrapping morsels of food; glass noodles sprinkled with chopped peanuts, carrots, bean sprouts, and cucumber salad; and delicately flavored dipping sauce. Takeout is available.

350 Booth St. ℂ **613/567-8228.** Main courses C$5–C$12 (US$3–$8). MC, V. Wed–Mon 10am–10pm.

Shanghai Restaurant *★* ASIAN   Serving a mixture of Cantonese, Szechuan, and Asian dishes, Shanghai is one of the top restaurants in Ottawa's Chinatown. Spicy dishes are marked with an asterisk to guide diners. You'll find some familiar Canadian Chinese dishes on the menu, but allow yourself to be tempted by spicy Thai chicken with sweet basil, ginger-teriyaki vegetable fried rice, Shanghai crispy beef, or shrimp with bok choy and roasted garlic. The coconut-curry vegetables in a spicy peanut sauce go well with a bowl of steamed rice. After 8pm the menu switches to finger foods and light snacks as the younger crowd moves in, so come early if you're planning a family dinner. Takeout is available.

651 Somerset St. W. ℂ **613/233-4001.** Reservations recommended weekends only. Main courses C$7–$15 (US$5–$10). AE, MC, V. Tues–Wed 11am–2pm and 4:30pm–11pm, Thurs–Fri 11am–2pm and 4:30pm–1am, Sat 4:30pm–1am, Sun 4:30pm–11pm.

Yangtze CHINESE   Both Cantonese and Szechuan cuisine are served in this spacious dining room. Large, round tables will seat 8 to 10 comfortably, and a Lazy Susan in the center of the table allows everyone to help themselves from the communal dishes. Families and groups are welcome here for all-day dining. Many dishes familiar to North American diners are on the menu—kung po shrimp, sweet-and-sour chicken, broccoli with scallops, beef with snow peas, chow mein, and fried rice. House specialties include chicken in black-bean sauce, pepper steak, and imperial spareribs. Takeout is available.

700 Somerset St. W. ℂ **613/236-0555.** Reservations recommended. C$7–$15 (US$5–$10). AE, MC, V. Mon–Thurs 11am–12:30am, Fri 11am–1am, Sat 10am–1am, Sun 10am–12:30am.

7 Little Italy

Preston Street, also known as Corso Italia, is the heart of Ottawa's Little Italy. Food is the soul of Italy, and when you stroll up one side of Preston Street and down the other, you'll find ristorantes, trattorie, and caffès galore. Many of them have outdoor patios, and all offer a warm Mediterranean welcome. I've selected a fine-dining restaurant, a casual cafe, and a pasta shop to give you a taste of Corso Italia. Go and explore and you'll discover many more treasures.

EXPENSIVE

La Roma (★)(★)(★) ITALIAN   A well-established Preston Street ristorante, La Roma has a solid reputation for good-quality traditional Italian cuisine. The elegant ivory and burgundy dining room is sophisticated and charming. Service is impeccable. Children ages 6 and up who are experienced diners will be quite welcome here. Choose from a wide variety of chicken, veal, pasta, and other Italian specialties, accompanied by Italian bread. Grown-ups take note: The all-Italian wine list is impressive, so sneak a peak even if you're not ordering a bottle. I recommend the breast of chicken with lemon sauce, with a light, creamy, and dreamy tiramisu and espresso as the grand finale.

430 Preston St. © 613/234-8244. Reservations recommended. Main courses C$12–$20 (US$8–$13). AE, DC, MC, V. Mon–Fri 11:30am–2pm and 5–11pm, Sat–Sun 5–11pm.

INEXPENSIVE

Luciano's (★) TAKEOUT   Drive 5 minutes from downtown almost to the top of Preston Street, park behind the building, and stock up on ravioli, agnolotti, and tortellini stuffed with yummy fillings like sundried tomato, spinach and ricotta, and butternut squash. Choose fresh spaghetti, fettucine, linguine, or rigatoni and some homemade sauces—Bolognese, clam, tomato, putanesca, mushroom, pesto, or pepper. Buy some oven-ready portions of lasagna and cannelloni, a baguette and olive oil, and a tub of gelato, and you have dinner—home-cooked meals should always be so easy.

106 Preston St. © 613/236-7545. Most items under C$10 (US$7). MC, V. Mon 1–6pm, Tues–Thurs 9am–6pm, Fri 9am–8pm, Sat 9am–5:30pm.

Pasticceria Gelateria Italiana Ltd. (★) ICE CREAM/CAFE   A decidedly European atmosphere prevails in this mix of pastry shop, ice-cream store, and neighborhood cafe. The beautifully sculpted Italian pastries are a feast for the eyes. For a filling and inexpensive lunch, help yourself at the hot pasta bar for C$5 (US$3). Kids who clear their plates can be rewarded with a cone or dish of gelato. When the weather's nice, take the crew outside on the terrace.

200 Preston St. © 613/233-6199. Most items under C$10 (US$7). V. Mon–Sat 7:30am–11pm, Sun 8am–11pm.

8 Further Out

Here are a couple more places to try. They're all no more than a 10-minute drive from downtown.

MODERATE

The Lone Star Cafe TEX-MEX   If you're staying at one of the hotels near the St. Laurent Centre or live in the east end of Ottawa, soak up a little southern hospitality and down-home cooking at the newest location of the Lone Star Cafe. The owner, a native of Houston, Texas, played for the Ottawa Roughriders football team a number of years ago before opening a restaurant to remind him of home. Now part of a chain of 11 restaurants across Canada, the original restaurant remains at 780 Baseline Road in Ottawa. Corn tortilla chips are cooked up fresh in the kitchen every morning and afternoon, and their taste far exceeds the store-bought variety. Service is brisk and cheerful, with servers sporting cutesy names like Moonshine and Chili Pepper. Try mesquite-grilled chicken, which has a lovely smoky BBQ flavor. Young 'uns 10 and under can choose from tacos, fajitas, chicken wings, or the usual burgers, hot dogs, and fries for C$5 (US$3.30). If you're into country music or line dancing, get a sitter and come on out later in the evening for a stomping good time.

1211 Lemieux St. ✆ **613/742-9378.** Reservations accepted for parties of 8 or more, except Fri and Sat evenings and Sun. Main courses C$8–$19 (US$5–$13). AE, DC, MC, V. Mon–Wed 11:30am–10pm, Thurs 11:30am–11pm, Fri 11:30am–midnight, Sat noon–midnight, Sun noon–10pm. Other location: 780 Baseline Rd. (Ottawa West) ✆ **613/224-4044.**

INEXPENSIVE

The Green Door VEGETARIAN   An ideal family destination, this casual eatery has tables set up cafeteria style and a U-shaped buffet with a dessert station in the middle. Grab a tray, wander past hot vegetable stir-fries, tofu dishes, pasta, salads, breads, fresh fruit, cakes, and pies. If you're not a dedicated vegetarian but you've always wanted to try tofu or soy milk, here's your chance. A lot of the offerings are certified organic. You won't see meat anywhere, and if dairy products are contained in dishes, there's a sign to let you know. This is truly a place where parents can say "pick anything you like" and know it will be nutritious and healthy. Pricing is easy—just hand your plate to the cashier and you'll be charged by weight. With prices set at C$17 (US$11) a kilogram (2.2 lb.), your stomach will be full before your wallet is empty. If you're heading out to a park, put together a picnic lunch. Servers will supply takeout containers and paper bags.

198 Main St. ✆ **613/234-9597.** C$17 (US$11) per kg (2.2 lb.). AE, MC, V. Tues–Sat 11am–9pm, Sun 11am–3pm.

6

What Kids Like to See & Do

The nation's capital and the surrounding region has so many attractions, museums, parks, pathways, and festivals that you could jam pack every day of your vacation in Ottawa and still not see and do everything. But be realistic and scale down your expectations. It's better to spend quality time on a few attractions than to dash madly around trying to experience it all. You can always come back for a second visit. When you do, schedule your trip for a different season of the year, so you can enjoy all the region has to offer.

Put your children's needs first when planning your itinerary and everyone will have a more enjoyable vacation. You're on a family vacation, so plan activities that all ages will enjoy. Be sure to schedule in plenty of time for relaxation and naps if your children are very young. Visit a few carefully chosen destinations and then let off steam in one of the area's many beautiful parks and greenspaces. You can run, walk, bike, or in-line skate along the network of pathways throughout the region (see chapter 7, "For the Active Family"). In winter, lace up your skates and glide along the canal. Take a swim in the hotel pool or splash in a wave pool in the east or west end of the city. If shopping is one of your family's pastimes, stroll through one of the large indoor malls, the pedestrianized Sparks Street downtown, or one of the neighborhood shopping areas (see chapter 9) "Shopping with Your

Kids"). Remind yourself that you're on vacation, not competing in an endurance contest.

The night before a museum visit, some parents read their kids a relevant story. Others buy postcards on entering a museum or gallery and accompany their youngsters on a scavenger hunt to find the pictured object or work of art. You probably have your own preferred ways of getting your youngsters psyched for sightseeing. If you're new at this, the best advice you can follow is not to overschedule. Don't expect them to act like adults. Young children have short attention spans. When they start to fidget, let them have 20 minutes in a playground, sit on a park bench and eat an ice cream cone, or take them to a movie.

If you're only in Ottawa for a short break, concentrate your sightseeing in and around the downtown area. You'll find that many of the major attractions are within walking distance of each other along Wellington Street and Sussex Drive or on streets leading off these two roads.

When planning which attractions to visit, keep in mind that many museums put on special programs and workshops for children and families on weekends and during school holidays (one week in mid-March, the months of July and August, and two weeks surrounding Christmas and New Year). Call the **Capital Infocentre ✆ 800/465-1867** or 613/239-5000 for exact dates as they vary slightly from year to year.

SUGGESTED ITINERARIES BY AGE GROUP

For Preschoolers

If you have 1 day In the summer, start the day with a parade. Head for the corner of Elgin Street and Laurier Avenue. Every day at 9:30am (weather permitting), 125 soldiers in busbies and scarlet tunics assemble at Cartier Drill Hall and march up Elgin Street to Parliament Hill for the **Changing of the Guard Ceremony.** Watch the procession pass by and then join in behind, marching to the beat of the military band. Watch the ceremony on the "Hill" and then follow the relieved unit back down Wellington Street When you reach the **Plaza Bridge** over the Rideau Canal (between Parliament Hill and the Chateau Laurier), walk down the steps to the **Ottawa Locks.** Hold your children's hands at all times because there are no safety barriers at the locks. If you have a stroller, use the ramp which is accessible from Confederation Square on the south side of the bridge. Stroll through **Major's Hill Park** and use the pedestrian walkway to cross the **Alexandra Bridge** to the **Canadian Museum of Civilization.** Enjoy the spectacular view of the Parliament Buildings, the Ottawa skyline, and the Ottawa River. Have a bite to eat and a rest in the restaurant or cafeteria in the museum, then head straight for the **Children's Museum,** located within the same building and included with the ticket price. Spend an hour or so inside, then explore **Adventure World,** an outdoor exhibition park at the museum. By this time, you'll be ready to drop, so splurge on a taxi back to your hotel. If you're visiting in **winter,** take a taxi from your hotel to the **Canadian Museum of Civilization** (note the

museum is closed on Mondays in winter) and plan to spend the morning there. Visit the **Children's Museum** first, then explore the main exhibition halls. If the weather allows a brisk walk, head over the **Alexandra Bridge** and walk south along **Sussex Drive** and eat in one of the many restaurants in the **ByWard Market** or experience lunch at the **Marchelino** in the **Rideau Centre.** If your family likes to skate, take a spin on the **Rideau Skateway.** There are plenty of access points along the canal. Skate rentals, warm-up stations, hot chocolate, and snacks are available. If you're looking for an indoor activity, spend the afternoon in the **Canadian Museum of Nature.**

If you have 2 days In the summer, start your day at the **ByWard Market.** Pick up picnic supplies and then buy a day pass for one of the city tour buses—either a double decker bus or an old-fashioned trolley bus. The buses run every 45 minutes and a day pass allows you hop-on-and-off privileges along the way. Hop off at the **Canada Agriculture Museum** and head for the animal barns. Pick up an events list at the main entrance to the museum and check the day's activity schedule. You may be lucky enough to make ice cream, milk a cow, or shear a sheep. Enjoy your picnic lunch in the **Ornamental Gardens** or the **Arboretum.** Hop back on the bus and head for the **Canadian Museum of Nature.** In **winter,** start the day with a trip to the **Canada Museum of Science and Technology,** the **Canada Aviation Museum,** or the **Canadian Museum of Nature** if you opted for canal skating on Day 1. All three museums have snack bars; the

Museum of Science and Technology's is the most substantial. In the afternoon, splash around at **Gloucester Wave Pool** or burn energy at **Cosmic Adventures** indoor playground.

If you have 3 days   Visit either the **Canada Museum of Science and Technology** or the **Canada Aviation Museum** in the morning. In **summer,** go to **Dow's Lake** next, have lunch at one of the restaurants, and either play on the grass or rent a small boat and get out on the water. If you prefer to put your feet up and let someone else do the navigating, take a boat tour on the **Ottawa River.** In cold weather, stay indoors and either visit another of the museums suggested above, or go back to your hotel, enjoy the pool, and maybe rent a family movie.

If you have 4 days   Relax and explore the pathways along Ottawa's waterways, either on foot or by bike. You can rent cycling equipment for transporting toddlers and preschoolers. If you want a park, **Strathcona Park** is one of the best. There's a wading pool, playground, and castle ruins to explore, complete with a slide and animal statuettes. In winter, play in the snow in one of the parks or hit one of the malls if the weather is cold or snowy. If you want to get out of the city, take a drive up to **Gatineau Park.** The park is active in all seasons. Hike, stroll, cycle, snowshoe, or cross-country ski along the trails. There are short circular trails for little legs such as the **Hickory Trail,** which is stroller and wheelchair accessible in summer. There are sandy beaches on the lakes. Another option is a visit to **Turtle Island Aboriginal Village** to enjoy traditional and contempo-

rary Native entertainment, food, and cultural displays. In summer, take a trip on the **Hull-Chelsea-Wakefield Steam Train.** (Allow a full day for this excursion.)

For Ages 6 to 8

If you have 1 day   Same as Day 1 for Preschoolers.

If you have 2 days   Same as Day 2 for Preschoolers, but substitute the **RCMP Stables** for one of the museums if appropriate. Call the **RCMP Musical Ride Stables** at least a day ahead to find out the best time to visit the stables. You may be lucky enough to watch the Mounties and horses practicing their choreography.

If you have 3 days   For half the day, visit the **RCMP Stables, Canada Museum of Science and Technology,** or the **Canada Aviation Museum.** Have lunch at **Dow's Lake Pavilion** and rent a small boat or take a drive along the canal back downtown and relax on a boat tour on the **Ottawa River.** Hang out at one of the lock stations for a while and watch the boats moving through the locks. In winter, take in another museum— consult the section on "Kids with Special Interests," later in this chapter for ideas.

If you have 4 days   Same as Day 4 for Preschoolers, but rent bikes for everyone and travel along the city's **bikepaths.** Take a map so you can plan a route, including places to stop and play or rest for a while. If you go to **Gatineau Park** in the summer, bring a fishing pole (and your fishing license!) and try your luck.

For Ages 8 to 10

If you have 1 day   Same as Day 1 for Preschoolers, but instead of climbing around Adventure World, tour the main exhibits at the **Canadian Museum of Civilization** after you've spent some time in the **Children's Museum.** When you arrive at the Museum of Civilization, purchase tickets for an **IMAX** show later in the day. Go out for dinner to one of the more adventurous restaurants.

If you have 2 days   Same as Day 2 for 6- to 8-year-olds, but visit the **Canada Museum of Science and Technology** instead of the Canada Agricultural Museum. Check the schedule for demonstration times and buy tickets for the simulator ride when you arrive. If there's a sports event or live theatre that appeals to you, treat the whole family to an evening out.

If you have 3 days   Same as Day 3 for 6- to 8-year-olds, except in winter try out **Carlington Snowpark** where you can go tubing or snowboarding and get towed back up the hill after descending a choice of 10 snow slides.

If you have 4 days   Same as Day 4 for 6- to 8-year-olds, but plan a longer excursion. The kids may prefer in-line skates to bikes in summer. For thrill seekers, plan a white water rafting expedition. In winter, rent cross-country skis or snowshoes in **Gatineau Park.** If you're downhill enthusiasts, take your pick from more than half a dozen ski resorts.

For Preteens

If you have 1 day   In summer, arrive at **Parliament Hill** between 9am and 10am to reserve spaces for the family on one of the tours of the Parliament Buildings later in the day, then wait to watch the **Changing of the Guard Ceremony.** Stroll across **Alexandra Bridge** to the **Canadian Museum of Civilization.** If there are younger siblings in the family, take a peek at the **Children's Museum** first. Otherwise, buy tickets for an **IMAX** presentation later in the day, and visit the main exhibits at the Museum of Civilization. Head back across the bridge by foot or taxi and poke around the **ByWard Market,** keeping an eye out for somewhere to have dinner later. If you want more shopping, wander around the **Rideau Centre.** In winter, you can tour the Parliament Buildings as a "walk-in." Line-ups are rare. If Parliament is sitting, you may be able to view the proceedings from the public gallery. After ascending the Peace Tower to view the city, take a taxi to the **Canadian Museum of Civilization** and spend the rest of the day there, or leave mid-afternoon and go skating on the canal.

If you have 2 days   In the summer, start the day with a bus tour, hopping off at the **Canadian Museum of Nature.** There's a small park outside the museum where you can enjoy a picnic lunch. In winter, walk to the Museum of Nature if your hotel is nearby, or take a taxi. Pick a second museum for the afternoon, based on your kids' interests. Schedule some shopping time and eat out.

If you have 3 days   Same as Day 3 for 8- to 10-year-olds. In the evening, go for a swim in the hotel pool, order a pizza, and watch a movie.

If you have 4 days   Same as Day 4 for 8- to 10-year-olds. Other choices for a day out include **Great Canadian Bungee Jump, LaFleche Caves,** or **Diefenbunker Cold War Museum.**

1 Top 10 Attractions for Kids

PARLIAMENT HILL ★★★   **All ages.**

The Parliament Buildings, with their steeply pitched copper roofs, dormers, and towers, are impressive, especially on first sighting from river or road. In 1860, Prince Edward (later King Edward VII) laid the cornerstone for the buildings, which were finished in time to host the inaugural session of the first Parliament of the new Dominion of Canada in 1867. Entering through the south gate off Wellington Street, you'll pass the Centennial Flame, lit by then Prime Minister Lester B. Pearson on New Year's Eve 1966 to mark the passing of 100 years since Confederation. In June, July, and August you can meet the Mounties on Parliament Hill. They're friendly—and love to have their photo taken. If you're visiting the capital between mid May and early September, your first stop on Parliament Hill should be the Info Tent, where you can pick up free information on the Hill and free same-day tickets for all tours. The best time to get tickets is between 9am and 10am, but you can usually select a tour time of your choice. Between September and May, get same-day tickets from the Visitor Welcome Centre, directly under the Peace Tower. All visitors to the buildings are required to go through a security screening system similar to those used in airports.

Where to Eat   Parliament Hill is in the center of Ottawa off Wellington Street, so stroll along Sparks or Elgin streets or visit the ByWard Market area for a variety of restaurants. In cold weather, head for the Rideau Centre and eat in the food court or in the Marchélino.

Tips **Summer Information**

During the busy summer months, drop by the information tent on the lawn in front of the Parliament Buildings between 9 and 10am. You can reserve a spot on the free tour of the Centre Block for later in the day and avoid the long line-ups.

CANADA'S GOVERNMENT: THE BASICS

Canada functions as a democracy, which means its government consists of elected representatives chosen by its citizens. Based upon the British structure of federal government which was established when Canada became self-governing, the **Parliament of Canada** consists of the head of state (**Queen Elizabeth II,** who is represented by the **Governor General**), the **Senate** (equivalent of the British House of Lords) and the **House of Commons.**

The parliamentary duties of the **Governor General** include summoning **Parliament** following each general election, announcing the present Government's objectives at the beginning of each session of **Parliament** through the Speech from the Throne, and approving all bills passed by the **Senate** and the **House of Commons.**

The **Senate** is made up of 104 **Senators,** who represent regions and provinces. They are appointed by the **Governor General** on the advice of the **Prime Minister.**

The **House of Commons** has 301 seats. **Members of Parliament (MPs)** are elected to represent their constituents in each of these 301 ridings, or political districts, for up to five years.

A Parliament is made up of one or more sessions during its lifetime. Parliament sits about 27 weeks of the year, beginning in September and usually lasting until June. Breaks are scheduled to allow **Senators** and **MPs** to spend time working in their regions and ridings.

The **Senate** and the **House of Commons** each meet on a regular basis to deal with issues of national concern and to debate bills (legislative proposals) which are introduced by **Cabinet Ministers, Senators,** or **private Members. Question Period** is often the most lively part of each sitting day. During **Question Period, Cabinet Ministers** are held accountable for their department's activities and also for the policies of the **Government.**

To oversee the proceedings of the **Senate** and the **House of Commons,** maintain order, and to enforce parliamentary rules and traditions, each House has a **Speaker,** who sits on a ceremonial chair at one end of the Chamber, with the **Government** on the right and the **Opposition** on the left. The **Speaker of the Senate** is appointed on the advice of the **Prime Minister.** The **Speaker of the House of Commons** is a current **MP,** elected by his or her peers.

The Buildings *★/★* **Ages 8 and up.** Parliament is composed of three sprawling building blocks—the **Centre Block,** straight ahead, and the flanking **West Block** and **East Block.** This is the heart of Canadian political life, containing the **House of Commons** and the **Senate.** You can attend sessions of the House of Commons to observe the 301 elected members debating in their handsome green chamber with its tall stained-glass windows. Parliament is usually in recess from late June until early September and occasionally between September and June, including the Easter and Christmas holidays. Otherwise, the House usually sits on weekdays. The 104 appointed members of the Senate sit in an opulent red chamber with a mural depicting Canadians fighting in World War I. A fire destroyed the original Centre Block in 1916; only the **Library of Parliament** at the rear was saved. The West Block, containing parliamentary offices, is closed to the public, but you can visit the East Block, housing offices of prime ministers, governors-general, and the Privy Council. Four historic rooms are on view: the original governor-general's office, restored to the period of Lord Dufferin (1872 to 1878); the offices of Sir John A. Macdonald and Sir Georges-Etienne Cartier (the principal fathers of Confederation); and the Privy Council Chamber with anteroom.

Fun Fact **Faces in the Sky**

There are hundreds of gargoyles, grotesques, bosses and other unusual animal shapes carved into the sandstone of the outer walls of the Parliament Buildings. Keep your eyes open for these entertaining sculptures!

Library of Parliament *★/★/★* **Ages 8 and up.** A glorious 16-sided dome, hewn from Nepean sandstone, supported outside by flying buttresses, and paneled inside with Canadian white pine, the library is designed in the Gothic Revival style and was opened in 1876. Inside, a variety of textures, colors, and hand-crafted detail is evident. The floor is an intricate parquet design of cherry, walnut, and oak. The pine paneling features thousands of flowers, masks, and mythical beasts. The center of the room is dominated by a white marble statue of the young Queen Victoria, created in 1871. The Library will be closed for several years beginning in 2001 while major repair work is undertaken. Call to find out when the Library is scheduled to re-open to the public.

Moments **The Bells are Ringing**

Concerts of the 53-bell Carillon of the Peace Tower are presented weekdays in July and August at 2pm (one-hour concert). From September to June, there is a 15-minute noon concert most weekdays.

The Peace Tower ★★   **All ages.** The imposing 92-meter (302 ft.) campanile dominating the Centre Block's façade is the **Peace Tower.** It houses a 53-bell carillon, a huge clock, an observation deck, and the Memorial Chamber, commemorating Canada's war dead, most notably the 66,650 who lost their lives in World War I. Stones from the deadliest battlefields are lodged in the chamber's walls and floors. Atop the tower is a 10.5-meter (35 ft.) bronze mast flying a Canadian flag. When Parliament is in session, the tower is lit. The elevator in the tower is unusual. See if you can sense the 10-degree angle off vertical that the elevator travels for the first 29-meters (98 ft.) of the journey. It's well worth the trip—the views from the observation deck are marvelous in every direction.

Tips **Peace Tower View**

Visit the Peace Tower and enjoy the view from the Observation Deck, but be aware that it closes half an hour before the last Centre Block tour of the day.

Guided Tour of Centre and East Blocks ★★★   **Ages 8 and up.** Free guided tours of the Centre Block, which may include the House of Commons, the Senate, the Hall of Honour, and the Library of Parliament, are available in English and French all year. Guides tell animated stories and interesting anecdotes about the buildings and the people who have worked there. When Parliament is sitting, the tours do not visit the House of Commons or the Senate, but visitors are invited to sit in the public galleries and watch the proceedings. Please note the Library will be closed several years for repairs beginning in 2001. Tour times vary; call the Capital Infocentre at © **800/465-1867** or 613/239-5000 for information.

Fact **The Whispering Wall**

On the grounds to the east of the Centre Block, find the statues of Robert Baldwin and Sir Louis-Hippolyte Lafontaine. The pedestal below has been nicknamed the whispering wall. Try it out by standing at the end of the curved bench which has a carved mace and asking another person to stand at the other end where a sword has been carved. Now, using only whispers, talk to each other. It really does work.

Self-Guided Tour of the Grounds   All ages. With the help of an outdoor self-guiding booklet called **Discover the Hill,** available from the Capital Infocentre across the street from the Parliament Buildings, you can wander around

What Kids Like to See & Do

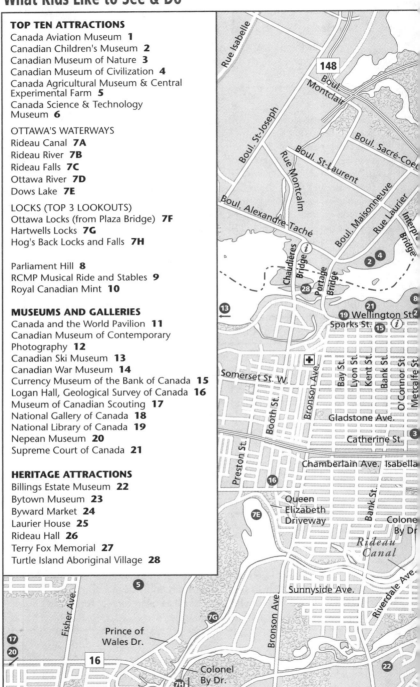

TOP TEN ATTRACTIONS
Canada Aviation Museum **1**
Canadian Children's Museum **2**
Canadian Museum of Nature **3**
Canadian Museum of Civilization **4**
Canada Agricultural Museum & Central
Experimental Farm **5**
Canada Science & Technology
Museum **6**

OTTAWA'S WATERWAYS
Rideau Canal **7A**
Rideau River **7B**
Rideau Falls **7C**
Ottawa River **7D**
Dows Lake **7E**

LOCKS (TOP 3 LOOKOUTS)
Ottawa Locks (from Plaza Bridge) **7F**
Hartwells Locks **7G**
Hog's Back Locks and Falls **7H**

Parliament Hill **8**
RCMP Musical Ride and Stables **9**
Royal Canadian Mint **10**

MUSEUMS AND GALLERIES
Canada and the World Pavilion **11**
Canadian Museum of Contemporary
Photography **12**
Canadian Ski Museum **13**
Canadian War Museum **14**
Currency Museum of the Bank of Canada **15**
Logan Hall, Geological Survey of Canada **16**
Museum of Canadian Scouting **17**
National Gallery of Canada **18**
National Library of Canada **19**
Nepean Museum **20**
Supreme Court of Canada **21**

HERITAGE ATTRACTIONS
Billings Estate Museum **22**
Bytown Museum **23**
Byward Market **24**
Laurier House **25**
Rideau Hall **26**
Terry Fox Memorial **27**
Turtle Island Aboriginal Village **28**

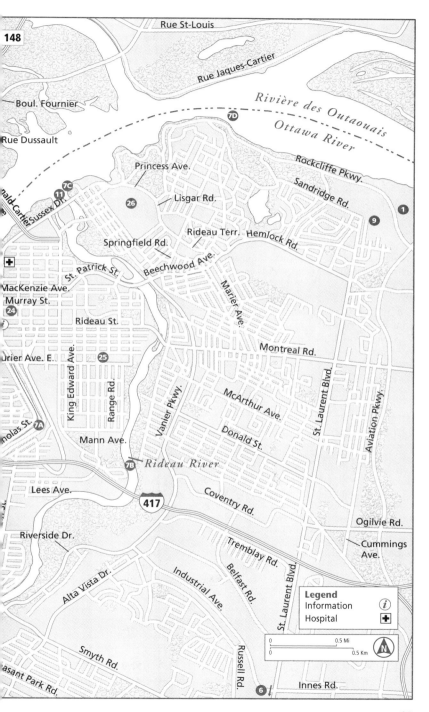

Rue St-Louis

Rue Jaques-Cartier

Rivière des Outaouais

Ottawa River

Boul. Fournier

Rue Dussault

Rockcliffe Pkwy.

Sandridge Rd.

Princess Ave.

Lisgar Rd.

Rideau Terr. Hemlock Rd.

Springfield Rd.

Beechwood Ave.

St. Patrick St.

MacKenzie Ave.

Murray St.

Rideau St.

urier Ave. E.

King Edward Ave.

Range Rd.

Marier Ave.

Montreal Rd.

St. Laurent Blvd.

Aviation Pkwy.

McArthur Ave.

Vanier Pkwy.

Donald St.

Mann Ave.

icholas St.

Rideau River

Lees Ave.

417

Coventry Rd.

Ogilvie Rd.

Riverside Dr.

Tremblay Rd.

Cummings Ave.

Alta Vista Dr.

Industrial Ave.

Belfast Rd.

St. Laurent Blvd.

Smyth Rd.

Russell Rd.

asant Park Rd.

Innes Rd.

Legend
Information *i*
Hospital ✚

| 0 | | 0.5 Mi |
| 0 | | 0.5 Km |

Parliament Hill and explore the monuments, grounds, and buildings. Stroll the grounds clockwise around the Centre Block—they're dotted with statues honoring such prominent historical figures as Queen Victoria, Sir Georges-Etienne Cartier, William Lyon Mackenzie King, and Sir Wilfrid Laurier. Behind the building is a promenade with sweeping views of the river. Here too is the old Centre Block's bell, which crashed to the ground shortly after tolling midnight on the eve of the 1916 fire. At the bottom of the cliff behind Parliament (accessible from the Ottawa Locks on the Rideau Canal), a pleasant pathway leads along the Ottawa River. In July and August, you may be lucky enough to meet one or two of the historical characters from early Confederation times and exchange a word or two with them.

Changing of the Guard ⭐⭐⭐   **All ages.** Late June to late August, a colorful half-hour ceremony is held daily on the Parliament Hill lawn (weather permitting). Two historic regiments—the Governor-General's Foot Guards and the Canadian Grenadier Guards—compose the Ceremonial Guard. The parade of 125 soldiers in busbies and scarlet tunics (guard, color party, and band are all the different sections of the parade) assembles at Cartier Square Drill Hall (by the canal at Laurier Avenue) at 9:30am and marches up Elgin Street to reach the Hill at 10am. On arrival at the Hill, the Ceremonial Guard splits, one division of the old guard positioned on the west side of the Parliament Hill lawn and two divisions of the new guard, or "duties," on the east side. The ceremony includes the inspection of dress and weapons of both groups. The colors are then marched before the troops and saluted, and the guards compliment each other by presenting arms. Throughout, sergeant-majors bellow unintelligible commands that prompt the synchronized stomp and clatter of boots and weapons. Finally, the outgoing guard commander gives the key to the guard room to the incoming guard commander, signifying that the process has been completed. The relieved unit marches back down Wellington Street to the beat of their drums and the skirl of bagpipes.

Tips **Join the Parade**

It's much more fun to march behind the Guards as they parade to Parliament Hill for the Changing of the Guard ceremony than to stand on the sidewalk and watch them pass by. Make your way to Cartier Square Drill Hall on Laurier Avenue beside the Queen Elizabeth Driveway (© **800/465-1897**) before 9:30am on parade days and walk the route with them, or join in behind as they pass by.

Sound and Light on the Hill   **All ages.** Every evening between June and early September, Canada's history unfolds and the country's spirit is revealed through music, lights, and giant images projected on the Parliament Buildings. This dazzling half-hour display of sound and light is free of charge and limited bleacher seating is available.

Moments **Oh Canada!**

If you're a Canadian citizen, take a moment or two to look up at the Canadian Flag on top of the Peace Tower and reflect on how proud and thankful you feel to be part of the great country that is Canada.

Test Your Knowledge of Parliament Hill

1. How many female speakers of the House of Commons have there been?
2. How tall is the Peace Tower?
3. How was the library saved during the terrible fire of 1916 that destroyed the rest of the Parliament Buildings?
4. What color is the carpet in the Senate Chamber?
5. What or who stands in the center of the Parliamentary Library?
6. How many bells are there in the Carillon of the Peace Tower?
7. When was Canada's now-familiar red and white flag raised for the first time on the Peace Tower?
8. Who carved the frieze in the House of Commons foyer which depicts the History of Canada, and how long did it take to complete?
9. What stone is primarily used on the exterior and interior of the Parliament Buildings?
10. What images can be seen in the stained glass windows of the House of Commons?
11. Who lit the Centennial Flame in 1967?
12. How long does it take for the copper roof panels to turn green?

ANSWERS: 1. Two. 2. 92.2 meters (302.5 feet). 3. A quick-thinking employee closed the iron doors to prevent the fire from spreading there. 4. Red. 5. A white marble statue of Queen Victoria. 6. 53. 7. February 15, 1965. 8. Sculptor Eleanor Milne took 11 years to create the beautiful stone frieze. 9. Nepean sandstone from Ontario is used on the exterior and Tyndall limestone from Manitoba is used inside. 10. The floral emblems of Canada's provinces and territories. 11. Prime Minister Lester B. Pearson. 12. About 30 years.

CANADIAN CHILDREN'S MUSEUM ⭐⭐   **Ages 4 to 11.**
Children absolutely love to play in this museum. Every exhibit is child-sized and the layout of the museum strongly encourages exploration. The Children's Museum has a strong commitment to learning by discovery and opportunities for children to exercise their imaginations abound. Hands-on activities and programs use real materials from the Museum's collection. Visitors touch, climb, build, manipulate, move, and create. Through this highly interactive hands-on learning, children learn about the world and its many cultures. The overarching theme is the Great Adventure which takes children on a trip around the world. When children enter the museum they receive a passport they can use to help them plan which exhibits or "countries" to visit. Stationed throughout the museum are special kiosks where kids can stamp their passports to record their visits to different "countries." For example, they can step inside a child-sized Japanese family home. In the tatami (straw-matting) room kids are invited to try the art of origami (Japanese paper folding) or write their own haiku poetry in the garden. Other exciting adventures include exploring an Egyptian pyramid, crawling into a Bedouin tent, putting on an Indonesian shadow puppet show, sitting astride a camel, driving a Pakistani tour bus, or building a brick wall.

Because of the scale of the interactive buildings and stations, kids immediately feel comfortable here and they do tend to zip around from place to place like an out-of-control pinball if you don't exercise a little parental guidance. Anyway, this museum is fun for parents too, so get down on your hands and knees and get involved. Kids from 0 to 14 are the target group, but the kids who will get the most out of the museum (and may want to stay all day) are probably 4- to 11-year-olds. Programs, workshops, and theatre performances are scheduled year round. Educational activities, day camps, sleepovers, and birthday parties are part of the fun too. Call ahead to find out about upcoming special events. During the summer months, you get double the fun because the outdoor exhibition park Adventure World is open. Play chess on a giant chessboard, hop along with hopscotch, or shoot some marbles. The Art-rageous Adventure exhibit area hosts visual arts activities for children. The Waterways exhibit has a boatmaking yard where you can design, build, and launch your own model watercraft. Kids can climb on a log-pulling tugboat or take an imaginary tour in the waterplane. The Canadian Children's Museum also has a temporary exhibition gallery—Kaleidoscope—that features 4 to 6 new exhibitions each year. After exiting the museum, take a look in the Children's Boutique, which is jammed with all kinds of games, toys, books, and other items designed to appeal to kids.

Where to Eat   See Canadian Museum of Civilization, p. 98.

100 Laurier St., Hull, QC. Within the Canadian Museum of Civilization (CMC). ✆ **819/776-7001.** Admission included with CMC ticket. For directions see Canadian Museum of Civilization (CMC), p. 98.

Fact **Museum Central**

Did you know that Ottawa has the highest concentration of museums in Canada?

CANADIAN MUSEUM OF NATURE ⭐⭐⭐   **All ages.**
This is a superb place to explore the wonders of the natural world and merits either a full day (with a good break halfway through) or a couple of visits to see all the exhibits—and everything is worth seeing, all four floors of it. The architecture of the historic building is remarkable. Built of local sandstone, the design includes towers, arched windows, magnificent stained glass windows and a grand central staircase. In addition to the permanent exhibits, special exhibitions are held, and day camps, sleepovers, and birthday parties are popular with all ages. A cafeteria with a brown-bag lunch area is situated on the lower level. If the weather is fine, plan a picnic lunch and eat outdoors in the shadow of the life-size woolly mammoth family on the lawn.

Galleries   The first place that every visitor wants to see is the **Dinosaur Exhibit.** All of the museum's skeletons date from 90 to 65 million years ago and were discovered in the Badlands of southern Alberta and Saskatchewan. Real fossilized bones are on display, augmented by plaster and fiberglass pieces where necessary. Second on most kids lists? The **Creepy Critters Gallery,** which is alive with insects, rodents, and reptiles. It's not for the squeamish—only a pane of glass separates you from the hundreds of crawling, scurrying, and slippery creatures. See cockroaches, slugs, rats, snakes, leeches, spiders, and toads in habitats that replicate their natural living conditions. If you prefer cuddly, furry creatures, pay a visit to the galleries on the second floor east which display preserved specimens of **Canadian birds and mammals** in highly detailed dioramas. Have a seat at the listening post and have fun trying to identify different birdcalls. Next, drop into the **Viola MacMillan Mineral Gallery** and feast your eyes on glittering gemstones and precious metals. Move along to the Activity Centre where you can take the helm of a deep-sea research submarine, visit a gold mine, and travel in an experimental time machine to learn about the **evolution of the Earth.** The **Plant Gallery** has hundreds of living plants, everything from ferns and mosses to coniferous plants and flowers. Between June and September, a colony of bees collect pollen to make honey. An exhibit on obtaining medicines from plant sources rounds out the "green" gallery.

Fun Fact **Day for Night**

Do you know how the head gardener at the Museum of Nature keeps the plants looking so green and lush? Look up at the ceiling. When the museum is closed, these lights are switched on to simulate bright daylight at a greater intensity than would be possible naturally in the relatively dark conditions of the Museum during the day.

High-Definition Cinema   Highly entertaining and educational nature films are on show in the recently installed high-definition cinema, the highest quality digital video technology available. Movies change frequently and are all approximately 45 minutes long. Generally there are two screenings daily in each official language and admission is included with your entrance fee to the museum.

Exploration Station   On the third floor west, the Exploration Station encourages young people to interact with natural history specimens. Kids age 2 to 6 can climb aboard the Nature Train on weekends between 10am and noon and dress up in costumes, play with puppets, listen to songs and stories, and investigate real samples of shells, minerals, and fossils. Older children, ages 6 to 14, are encouraged to bring in items collected from nature and get help in identification or trade their offerings with someone else. Nature interpreters are on hand to guide youngsters in building natural history collections of their own. This facility, called the Trading Post, is open on Thursdays from 6pm to 7:30pm and weekends between 1pm and 4pm.

Where to Eat   There's a cafeteria on site with a brown-bag area. There's a grassy area with picnic tables in front of the museum, as long as you don't mind sharing the space with a life-size replica of a woolly mammoth family.

Victoria Memorial Museum Building, 240 McLeod St. ℂ **800/263-4433** or 613/566-4700. Admission C$6 (US$4) adults, C$5 (US$3) seniors and students, C$2.50 (US$1.65) children 3–12, children 2 and under free. Thurs half-price until 5pm; free 5pm–8pm. Mid Oct–Apr Tues–Sun 10am–5pm, Thurs until 8pm. May–Labour Day (first Mon in Sept) daily 9:30am–5pm, Thurs until 8pm. Labour Day–mid Oct daily 10am–5pm, Thurs until 8pm. Located between O'Connor and Elgin sts., one block south of Gladstone Ave. Note that McLeod St. is a one-way street running west, so enter off Elgin.

(Fact From Fire to Fossils

Following the fire that destroyed the Parliament Buildings in 1916, emergency quarters were set up for the government in the building which is now the home of the Canadian Museum of Nature. The House of Commons sat in the Auditorium for four years, and the Senate occupied the Hall of Invertebrate Fossils (no joke intended). In 1919, the body of Sir Wilfrid Laurier lay in state in the Auditorium.

OTTAWA'S WATERWAYS ★★ All ages.

Ottawa's origins are inextricably linked to its waterways, since it was the settlement that grew up around the canal construction site that eventually became Ottawa. Modern day Ottawa enjoys the canal and river primarily for leisure and pleasure. The city's beauty is enhanced by the extensive network of parkways, pathways, and parks that follow the shores of the Rideau Canal, Rideau River, and Ottawa River.

Rideau Canal ★ The **Rideau Canal** is actually a continuous chain of beautiful lakes, rivers and canal cuts, stretching 202 kilometers (125 miles) between Ottawa and Kingston, and often described as the most scenic waterway in North America. The **Rideau Canal** waterway has been designated a National Historic Site and is one of nine historic canals in Canada. Parks Canada has the responsibility of preserving and maintaining the canal's natural and historic features and providing a safe waterway for boats to navigate. The canal and locks that link the lakes and rivers of the Rideau Valley were constructed between 1826 and 1832 to provide a safe route for the military between Montreal and Kingston in the wake of the War of 1812. Colonel By, the British engineer in charge of the project, had the foresight to build the locks and canal large enough to permit commercial traffic to access the system rather than build the canal solely for military use. As things turned out, the inhabitants of North America decided to live peaceably. The canal became a main transportation and trade route and communities along the canal grew and thrived. With the introduction of railroads in the mid-19th century, the commercial traffic subsided and the canal gradually became a tourist destination due to its beauty and tranquility. The locks have operated continuously since they first opened.

Rideau River The Ottawa section of the Rideau River bisects the city, with the Rideau Canal running roughly parallel for the final 8 kilometers (5 miles) leading to the Rideau Falls. The Rideau River is part of the Rideau Waterway, a collective name for the entire system of lakes, rivers, and canal cuts that make up the route between Ottawa and Kingston. In 2000, the river gained the designation of a Canadian Heritage River. Many city parks are located along its banks, including Rideau Falls Park, New Edinburgh Park, Strathcona Park, Rideau River Park, Brewer Park, Vincent Massey Park, Hog's Back Park, and Mooney's Bay Park.

Rideau Falls ★ Located just off Sussex Drive where the Rideau River empties over a cliff into the Ottawa River, Rideau Falls is surrounded by a beautifully landscaped park. A footbridge spans the Rideau River and the 30-meter (98 ft.) falls are illuminated in the evening. Canada and the World Pavilion, which re-opened in 2001 as a permanent attraction, is located here in the park.

Ottawa River   Historically, the Ottawa River was a major transportation corridor for moving people and goods. When the Europeans settled in the area, the water was harnessed to generate power for the lumber industry. This majestic river is now enjoyed by canoeists, white water enthusiasts, and other outdoor adventurers.

Dow's Lake ✦   The pretty lake that adjoins the Rideau Canal in central Ottawa was once a mosquito-infested swamp and outbreaks of malaria were common amongst canal construction workers in the early 1800s. No one wanted to cut a canal through the swampland. Colonel By, the British engineer in charge of the canal construction, solved the problem by damming a branch of the Rideau River that used to run where Preston Street is now and flooded the swamp. If you visit Dow's Lake when the water levels are low, you may see tree stumps here and there. These stumps are all that remain of the old white pines that grew in the area before the basin was flooded. Dow's Lake is a popular site in the summer. Pedal boats and canoes are available for rental and the Pavilion has restaurants with terraces overlooking the lake. In winter you can rent skates and go for a twirl or spin on the ice.

Locks ✦   Rivers often have rocky sections with shallow, fast-flowing water. Naturally this presents a challenge to navigation and locks were devised to enable boats to safely move uphill and downhill through the water in a controlled manner. There are **45 locks** manned by **24 lock stations** along the main channel of the 202 kilometers (125 miles) **Rideau Canal.** The waterway rises a total of 50 meters (164 ft.) from Kingston on Lake Ontario to Upper Rideau Lake, then drops 83 meters (273 ft.) to the Ottawa River in Ottawa, ending in the 30 meter (98 ft.) Rideau Falls. In Ottawa there are three places where you can watch the locks in action. The most popular spot is downtown Ottawa at the point where the first locks were built. If you stand on the north side of the **Plaza Bridge** (between Parliament Hill and Chateau Laurier) and look down, you'll have a wonderful view of the eight **Ottawa Locks,** which connect the Canal to the Ottawa River, a drop of 24 meters (80 ft.). Travel time through the locks is about 1½ hours. You can go down a stairway beside the bridge (or go down a ramp from the south side of the bridge) right to the level of the locks and watch them in operation. Be extremely careful to keep your children right beside you because there are no safety barriers next to the water. The **Bytown Museum** is alongside the locks. Upstream along the Canal, the next two locks are **Hartwells Locks,** which take about half an hour to navigate. The entrance to the locks is off Prince of Wales Drive south of **Dow's Lake.** The **Central Experimental Farm** borders this section of the Canal and there's an extensive network of paved and gravel bike paths. A little further upstream are the **Hog's Back Locks,** reached by road at 795 Hog's Back Road. An interpretative trail links the locks with Hog's Back dam. There's a bonus at Hog's Back—a swing bridge is part of the lock system, designed to accommodate vessels requiring a clearance greater than 2.8 meters (9.4 ft.). The bridge swings on demand except during peak traffic periods on weekdays. The parkland in this area surrounds the spectacular **Hog's Back Falls,** situated at the point where the Rideau meets the Rideau River. They're named after rocks that are said to bristles on a hog's back. A refreshment pavilion, parking. ties are available.

How Does a Lock Work?

In simple terms that you can explain to your kids, here's how a boat "climbs" up the river. Just reverse the steps for going down.
- The boat approaches the bottom gates of the lock, which has a water level the same as the river on the downstream side.
- The lockmaster turns the crank to swing the lock gates open on the downstream side and the boat enters.
- The lock gates are closed behind the boat.
- Valves on the upstream side of the lock are opened to let water into the lock until the water level in the lock is the same as the water on the upstream side.
- The gates on the upstream side of the lock are opened and the boat leaves the lock.

Boat Tours   There are several companies operating river and canal tours. Reservations are recommended for all tours. **Ottawa Riverboat Company** (© 613/562-4888) offers a 90-minute tour on the 280 passenger *Sea Prince II*, the largest tour boat in Ottawa. Bilingual guides provide commentary as you tour past famous buildings and landmarks as seen from the Ottawa River. **Paul's Boat Lines** (© 613/225-6781) cruises the Ottawa River and the Rideau Canal. On the Ottawa River, the 150-passenger *Paula D* takes visitors on a 90-minute cruise, with spectacular views of the Parliament Buildings, Rideau Falls, and other sites. On the canal, you can glide along in one of three low profile tour boats for a 75-minute cruise. For a unique tour of the city, hop on the **"Amphibus"** (© 613/223-6211), a hybrid vehicle which cruises on the water and tours on land. The bright red 42-seat vehicle, named Lady Dive, is a relative newcomer to the Ottawa tourist scene but it has stirred up a lot of interest. The 90-minute tour begins at the corner of Sparks and Elgin streets, driving along city streets past historic sites and city landmarks, then plunges into the Ottawa River for a relaxing cruise. For more detailed information on boat tours, see "On The Water," later in this chapter.

The Rideau Canal joins the Ottawa River with a series of eight locks just east of the Parliament Buildings. The canal winds south for approximately 8 kilometers (5 miles), opening out into Dow's Lake roughly two-thirds of the way along, and eventually joins the Rideau River at Mooney's Bay on the west side of Riverside Dr. at Hog's Back Rd. The canal is bordered by Prince of Wales Dr. and Queen Elizabeth Parkway on the west side and Colonel By Dr. on the east side. The Rideau River follows a similar course to the east of the canal.

...UM OF CIVILIZATION (★★★   **All ages.**

...stitutions, the Canadian Museum of Civilization ...f million visitors each year. The museum is a ...rary exhibits that explore human history ...nce to Canada. The museum is located ...l, its stunning award-winning archi- ...The building's flowing curves ...ure. Inside the museum, the ...make their way around the ...re the Canadian Chil- ...X theatre.

You'll enter the building at street level, which is also the level that the **Canadian Children's Museum** is on. I'd recommend visiting the **Children's Museum** first, especially if you have kids under 10. Let them run around and play there first, take a break for a drink and a snack or lunch (you can choose from formal dining or a cafeteria; both offer spectacular views over the Ottawa River towards the Parliament Buildings), and then walk through the **main exhibit halls** of the museum. If you want to see an **IMAX** presentation the same day, buy your tickets when you pay the museum entrance fee. You'll save a few dollars and you will also ensure a seat in the theatre. **IMAX** shows often sell out in advance of show time, particularly in the peak tourist season. You can register for a 45-minute guided tour of the Grand Hall or the Canada Hall for an extra C$2.50 (US$1.70) per person or just wander on your own. Before you begin your exploration of the museum, be sure to drop off coats, umbrellas, and other outdoor gear at the complimentary cloakroom and collect a stroller or wheelchair if needed. There is paid underground parking with an inside entrance to the museum. If your kids are up to the challenge, you could spend the whole day here, especially if you take in an IMAX show and visit the **outdoor adventure playground** (summer only). Don't forget to visit the museum boutique and the children's boutique. For **visitors with disabilities,** there are designated bays on level one of the parking arcade, elevator access to all floors, and access ramps installed where necessary. Spaces are reserved in the IMAX theater and the performance/lecture theater for wheelchairs.

Grand Hall ⟨★/★⟩   From the street level lobby, descend the escalator to the showpiece of the museum—the magnificent Grand Hall. This enormous exhibition hall features a display of more than 40 totem poles, representing the culture of the Native peoples of Canada's Pacific Northwest Coast. Six Native house facades have been constructed in the hall, based on architectural styles of different coastal nations over the past 150 years. The Grand Hall also has a performance stage where storytelling sessions, demonstrations, and performances are held regularly. At the far end of the Hall, a forest setting has been created in a room displaying prehistoric artifacts and articles from the Tsimshian people of British Columbia. Just inside the entrance on the right, a ghostly animated face may unintentionally frighten very young children. Further along the exhibit, you may want to steer preschoolers away from a menacing model of a warrior, which, when combined with the room's low lighting, also presents a scary image. But don't let that stop you from taking a walk through. The "forest" was the place my kids remembered the best after their first visit several years ago.

Canada Hall ⟨★/★/★⟩   This impressive exhibit takes visitors on a journey through a thousand years of Canada's social, cultural, and material history. The Canada Hall is a presentation of full-scale tableaux and buildings which have been constructed in the architectural style of specific periods in history using materials (solid wood beams and planking, plaster, stucco, stone, etc.) and methods in use at the time. The sights and sounds of the country's past unfold before you, beginning with the landing of the Norsemen on Newfoundland's coast in A.D. 1000. As you move through the hall, you move west through the country and forward in time. Look below deck in a full-scale stern section of a 16th century Basque whaling ship, see the crude process of rendering whale blubber into oil in a Labrador whaling station, and peer into a farmhouse in the St. Lawrence Valley in 18th century New France. You'll walk into the public square of a town in New France and have the liberty of opening doors and peeking through windows into the lives of the inhabitants. You may be lucky enough to meet one of the colorful historical characters who roam the exhibits from time to time, interacting with the public and adding a new dimension to the museum experience. A lumber camp shanty, a Conestoga wagon, and the main street of a small Ontario town in the Victorian era are a few more sights you'll see during your exploration of Canada's heritage.

First Peoples Hall   The purpose of the First Peoples Hall is to provide a venue to showcase the cultural, historical, and artistic accomplishments of Aboriginal peoples in Canada. Exhibits include an Art Gallery dedicated to contemporary Aboriginal art.

Special Exhibitions   A large hall with three distinct exhibition spaces is dedicated to short-term displays encompassing all museum disciplines—archeology, ethnology, folk culture, and history. Call the museum to see what's on in the **Special Exhibitions Hall, Arts and Traditions Hall,** and the **Gallery** or just drop in and be surprised.

Canadian History Galleries   Special exhibitions in this space change on a regular basis. Recent exhibitions include The Story of Glass and Glass-Making in Canada. Until March 30, 2003, The Story of Dolls in Canada is on display. Over 400 dolls, including Inuit and First Nations dolls, rare antiques, and a collection of contemporary dolls made by Canadian artists are included in the exhibition.

Canadian Postal Museum   This museum is housed within the Canadian Museum of Civilization and admission is included with the main museum ticket. Discover the story of postal communications from coast to coast and around the world. Interactive displays and a high-tech station attract kids and grown-ups to learn more about the world of stamps. All kinds of memorabilia are on display, from toys and quilts to mailboxes and mailbags. A new permanent exhibition was opened in 2000 which shows the role the post has played in Canada's history and features a complete post office from Quebec. Temporary exhibitions range from an introduction to stamp-collecting and an opportunity to design your own stamp to displays of postage stamps from around the world with specimens from the Canadian Museum's International Philatelic Collection.

Canadian Children's Museum ★★   This hands-on just-for-kids museum, housed within the Canadian Museum of Civilization, is a hit with the 2 to 12 crowd. Admission is included with the main museum ticket, although the hours may vary slightly from the main museum hours. You can just visit the Children's Museum if you wish, but the price will be the same. See the separate entry earlier in this chapter for details of the Children's Museum.

IMAX Theater ★★   This amazing theater is the only one of its kind in the world. Combining the technology of IMAX and IMAX DOME, the feeling is one of being wrapped in sight and sound. The IMAX screen is amazing enough—it's seven stories high and ten times the size of a conventional movie screen. To experience the full effect, a 23-meter (76 ft.) diameter hemispheric IMAX DOME moves into place overhead once the audience is seated. All 295 theater seats tilt back to give the audience a comfortable and clear view of the dome. Not all films use the entire screening system. Advance ticket purchase is recommended as shows often sell out in advance. Tickets can be purchased in person at the museum box office (discount if purchased with a museum entrance ticket) or through Ticketmaster. All ages admitted. Plan to arrive 20 minutes before show time, as latecomers will not be admitted.

Where to Eat   You have a choice of a restaurant or cafeteria on site. If the weather's nice, you can take a picnic to Jacques-Cartier Park which is on the banks of the Ottawa River right beside the Canadian Museum of Civilization

100 Laurier St., Hull, QC. © **800/555-5621** or 819/776-7000. IMAX Theater information © **819/776-7010.** IMAX tickets at museum box office or call Ticketmaster © **613/755-1111.** Museum admission (prices subject to change) C$8 (US$5.30) adults, C$7 (US$4.65) seniors, C$6 (US$3.90) students, C$4 (US$2.65) children, C$20 (US$13.20) family (maximum 5 members). Sun half price. Free every Thurs 4pm to 9pm, the Sun before Heritage Day, Museums Day, Canada Day (July 1), Remembrance Day (Nov 11). Admission free for members. IMAX ticket sold separately. May 1 to June 30 daily 9am to 6pm, Thurs until 9pm (Children's Museum closes at 6pm). July 1 to first Tues in Sept, Sat to Wed 9am to 6pm, Thurs and Fri 9am to 9pm. First Wed in Sept to second Tues in Oct daily 9am to 6pm, Thurs until 9pm (Canadian Children's Museum closes at 6pm). Second Wed in Oct to April 30, Tues to Sun 9am to 5pm, Thurs until 9pm (Canadian Children's Museum until 7pm), closed on Mon Dec 24, 9am to 3pm. Closed Dec 25. Easter Mon 9am to 5pm. IMAX Theater hours may differ from museum hours. From the Ottawa River Pkwy. or Wellington St. downtown, take the Portage Bridge to Hull and turn right onto Rue Laurier. The museum is on your right, just a couple of minutes drive. From the east side of the canal, take Sussex Dr. and cross the Alexandra Bridge into Hull. The museum is on your immediate left as you exit the bridge.

CANADA AGRICULTURE MUSEUM & CENTRAL EXPERIMENTAL FARM ★★   All ages.

In the heart of south central Ottawa lies one of the many green spaces that contribute to Ottawa's reputation as the "green capital." More than a thousand acres of farmland make up the **Central Experimental Farm** (CEF). The major tenant of the CEF, occupying more than three quarters of the property, is a crop research center, part of the federal government department of Agriculture and Agri-Food Canada. There are three sites within the CEF open to the public, and they're all great destinations for families. Plants are the focus of the **Arboretum** and the **Ornamental Gardens,** both with free admission. The **Agriculture Museum,** which charges a modest entrance fee, features animal barns, special exhibits, and a chance to experience a traditional farm in action. The **Arboretum** covers around 65 acres of rolling land between the Rideau Canal and Prince of Wales Drive and showcases a wide variety of trees and shrubs, some dating back to 1889 when the Arboretum was established. The Arboretum is open daily from sunrise to sunset and is a very popular place for families to picnic and play in the summer. In the winter, the hills are used for tobogganing. The **Ornamental Gardens** are displayed in an eight acre section of the CEF. Gardening parents will love to stroll around the perennial collection, rose garden, annual garden featuring some of the best new annual flower varieties in North America each year, hedge collection with 65 different species, rock garden, and Macoun Memorial Garden with its sunken pool and stone embankments. While you're admiring the flowers, the kids can frolic in the sun. A delightful way to spend an afternoon. The **Agriculture Museum** offers city slickers (and country bumpkins for that matter) a chance to get up close and personal with all things agricultural. The five acre site is a unique blend of modern working farm and museum. Several heritage buildings are on the site, including a dairy barn, mixed animal barn, and a cereal barn. Several barns have recently been added. A beef and horse barn, designed specifically to accommodate the needs of both animals and visitors, opened early in 2000. Two more places to visit on the farm, open seasonally, are a rare breed barn and a poultry house. There's always something going on at the Agriculture Museum, whether it's a festival, special exhibit, day camp, or demonstration. If you're planning a visit, call ahead so you can catch one of the special days on the farm. Activities are planned with kids in mind and everyone from babies to grandparents will enjoy meeting the animals and learning about the farm. Programs and special events focus on how science and technology meshes with modern agriculture and shows visitors the processes by which Canadians get their food, fibres, and other agricultural products.

Where to Eat   Bring a picnic in summer and enjoy your lunch in the extensive grounds of the Experimental Farm. Dow's Lake Pavilion and Preston Street (Little Italy) are close by if you have a car.

Corner of Experimental Farm Dr. and Prince of Wales Dr. ℂ **613/991-3044.** Admission to exhibits and animal barns of Agriculture Museum C$5 (US$3) adult, C$4 (US$2.50) students and seniors, C$3 (US$2) children 3–15, children under 3 free, C$12 (US$8) family (max 2 adults and 3 children). Animal barns daily 9am–5pm except Dec 25, exhibits and barn boutique daily 9am–5pm Mar 1–Oct 30. Take Prince of Wales Dr. and follow the signs. The museum is just west of Prince of Wales Dr. between Carling Ave. and Baseline Rd.

WHAT'S ON AT THE AGRICULTURE MUSEUM
This calendar of events will give you a good idea of the oodles of activities going on. Events are subject to change; please call ahead to avoid disappointment.

Spring
• Special exhibits re-open for the season. In 2001, the exhibits were "Bread: The Inside Story," which demonstrated how wheat is sown, grown, harvested, and made into bread. The "Barn of the 1920s" exhibit links with the bread theme by displaying the machinery of a wheat farm from that era.

• During the school break periods in Ontario and Quebec in March, special programs are scheduled which include feeding the animals, grooming calves, churning butter, and baking bread.

• Easter weekend features lots of family fun with rabbits to pet, newborn lambs and goats to visit, and hatching chicks. Join the Easter egg hunt on the grounds of the museum.

• Mother's Day and Museums Day are celebrated together with special family oriented activities to acknowledge the important role of mothers on the farm.

• The annual sheep shearing festival features demonstrations of sheep shearing, hoof trimming, Border Collies herding sheep, wool crafts, and children's activities.

• Visit on Spring Planting Day and help to plant oats, beans, barley, and wheat on the farm.

Summer
• Meet the cows and goats on Dairy Day. Make cheese, separate cream, churn butter, see how cows were milked in the past and how they're milked today.

• Father's Day is marked with a day of activities to enjoy with Dad.

• Canada Day at the farm. Celebrate Canada's birthday with a day of family events, crafts, games, hay rides, and ice cream making.

• One-week summer day camps are held in July and August for kids aged 4 to 14. They'll learn all about farming and food production through barn visits, daily chores, crafts, and games. For information call ℂ **613/991-3053.**

• August is Grains Month. Special demonstrations include pasta making, bread making, and grain grinding.

Fall

- Labour Day weekend has special events scheduled. Maybe you'll see farm machinery, learn about organic farming, see rare breeds of farm animals, or meet horses, ponies, and donkeys.
- Fall Harvest Celebration takes place on Thanksgiving Weekend. Make apple cider, sample apple varieties, wander through a maze, take a hay ride, or enjoy the entertainment.
- Barnyard Hallowe'en. Decorate pumpkins and discover how they grow and take part in a trick-or-treat scavenger hunt in the barns. You're invited to come in costume for this one.

Winter

- The barns are open daily 9am to 5pm except Christmas Day throughout the winter, but the exhibits and shop are closed.
- Between Christmas and New Year, special holiday activities are scheduled.

Ongoing

- Barnyard Buddies is a series of one-hour workshops for three- to five-year-olds and their caregivers. Each week the fun includes a craft, story, songs, and a snack. Registration required. Call ✆ **613/991-3053.**

CANADA SCIENCE & TECHNOLOGY MUSEUM ⍟⍟   **All ages.** This kid-friendly hands-on museum has eye-catching exhibits at every turn. My eight-year-old was still going strong after a three hour visit. One of the most intriguing long-term exhibits is **Canada In Space.** Discover the story of Canada's role in space. Various tools such as Radarsat, MSAT, the Canadarm, and the International Space Station Alpha can be explored. A space flight simulator will take you on a virtual voyage in a six-seat cinema pod that moves to the action on the huge screen. There are motionless seats at the rear of the cinema for those who prefer a more sedate experience. You need to purchase tickets for this ride and it's easiest to do that when you first enter the museum. Take note of the ride time so you don't miss your trip to outer space. The **Locomotive Hall** will have your kids wide-eyed as they stand next to four huge steam locomotives, meticulously restored and maintained. You can climb in the cabs of some of them and you can also see a caboose, business car, old number boards, and hear sound effects which give the feeling of a live locomotive. Designed especially for kids, the **Energy Discovery Hall** helps young visitors to learn about energy as they explore dozens of interactive displays set in familiar environments such as a city park, nature trail, house, and an amusement park. There's a special toddler and pre-school section with a talking tree trunk, animals which make sounds, giant pinwheel flowers demonstrating wind energy, a tickling waterfall, and other imaginative displays. A major exhibition on **communications** is one of the largest of its kind in Canada and illustrates the history of electric and electronic communications in Canada. Lively, short **demonstrations** on different topics are held frequently during the day, so ask at the desk when you arrive and take in a show or two during your visit. Lots of programs and workshops are scheduled so call ahead if you want to take part. Plan at least a half-day visit here. In the summer, have a picnic in the **Technology Park** out front. Visit the Cape North Lighthouse, radar antenna, pump jack, Convair Atlas rocket, telescope, windmill, and steam locomotive. Give your kids a while to burn off some energy in the playground, which features an oversized sand box with kiddy construction tools and water games. A cafeteria indoors serves light meals and snacks. The Museum's giftshop, located close to the main entrance, is a wonderful place to shop, with a science/technology/educational theme running throughout. The Museum is fully wheelchair accessible and parking is free.

Where to Eat   There's a cafe on site. In front of the museum there is a small park with picnic tables. On St. Laurent Boulevard there are a number of family restaurant chains.

1867 St. Laurent Blvd. ℂ **613/991-3044** (general information), ℂ **613/991-3053** (reservations and program information). www.science-tech.nmstc.ca. Admission C$6 (US$4) adults, C$5 (US$3) seniors and students, C$2 (US$1.30) children 6 to 14, children 5 and under free, C$12 (US$8) family (maximum 2 adults and 2 children). Simulator ride C$5 (US$2.50) per person. Tues–Sun 9am–5pm and all statutory holidays except Dec 25.

ROYAL CANADIAN MINT ⍟   Ages 5 and up.

Established in 1908 to produce Canada's **circulation coins,** the **Royal Canadian Mint** enjoys an excellent reputation around the world for producing high quality coins. Since 1976, when a plant was built in Winnipeg, Manitoba, for the high-speed, high-volume production of circulation coins, the **Royal Canadian Mint** has concentrated on producing **numismatic (commemorative) coins.** The **Royal Canadian Mint** is also the oldest and one of the largest gold refineries in the Western Hemisphere and is known and respected around the globe as a premier **gold refinery.** Just gaining entry to the building is an experience at the **Royal Canadian Mint.** First you peer into the ticket booth beside a huge pair of iron gates to buy your tour tickets (you can also visit the boutique without taking the tour). As a security guard watches the entrance (also equipped with a surveillance camera), one of the gates swings open momentarily to allow you to step inside the compound and then clanks shut behind you. When you enter the stone "castle," you find yourself in a foyer with a set of stairs leading upwards on your left and an elevator straight ahead. Both will take you to the **boutique,** which displays the many coins and souvenirs available for purchase in well-lit glass show cases around the room. This is the time to nudge the grandparents to get their wallets out and buy a coin set for their grandchildren. There are washrooms here and a place to hang your coats in winter. When it's time for the tour, you're ushered into a small theater to watch a short film on a selected aspect of the mint's activities. Young children may fidget a bit, but before long you're ushered to the viewing gallery which winds its way through the factory. There is a lot to see here, and the tour guide outlines the process of manufacturing coins as you move along the corridor above the factory floor. The first view of a manufacturing facility can be overwhelming for kids, so bring them right up to the windows and take the time to point out specific activities, from the rollers that transform the cast bars into flattened strips, to tubs of blanks that have been punched from the strips, workers hand-drying the blanks after washing, right to the final inspection and hand-packaging of the finished coins.

Where to Eat   The ByWard Market area is your best bet for somewhere to grab a snack or meal. It's only a short walk southeast of the Mint.

320 Sussex Dr. ℂ **800/276-7714 (Canada)** or 613/993-8990. Admission C$2 (US$1.30) adults and children 7 and over, free for children 6 and under, C$8 (US$5) family. Weekends half-price. Victoria Day (third Mon in May)–Labour Day (first Mon in Sept) Mon–Fri 9am–8:30pm, Sat–Sun 9am–5:30pm. Rest of the year daily 9am–5pm. Call for advance reservations for guided tours. From the Queensway, take the Nicholas St. exit (118). Turn left on Rideau St. and right onto Sussex Dr. The Mint is on your left.

CANADA AVIATION MUSEUM   All ages.

One of the best collections of vintage aircraft in the world is on display here and the museum is definitely family oriented. People of all ages will find something to catch their interest here, as you stroll through the huge **exhibition hall** and trace the history of aviation from its beginning to the jet age. You can come close (but not enough to touch; aircraft are fragile machines) to more than 50 aircraft inside the building and around half a dozen more outside in the summer months. There are video terminals dotted around the hall if you're in an educational mood. Several interactive displays, designed to teach the principles of flight, are simple enough for children to operate and understand. On weekends, Thursday evenings, and daily in the summer, visit the **Helicopter Studio,** a fun activity center for children and their families. Look for the yellow helicopter. Inside the center, you'll find a puppet theater, books, craft materials, paper airplanes, building blocks, and lots more stuff to keep kids happy. Take a virtual flight through the Grand Canyon on the **Hang Glider Simulator,** only C$3 (US$2) a ride. Entertaining demonstrations are scheduled throughout the day—everything from wind tunnels to flying a Cessna 150. If you're looking for something a little different, try an **evening program** with scheduled events and dinner or an **overnight stay** where you can explore the Museum by flashlight and sleep under the wings of an airplane. Weekly **day camps** run in the summer with scheduled events including a visit to Ottawa International Airport and a flight in a Cessna 172 aircraft; advance registration is recommended. If you are an aviation buff, or just love to fly, take advantage of a rare opportunity and splurge on a **vintage aircraft flight,** available from May to autumn. A 15-minute ride in an **open cockpit bi-plane** costs C$75 (US$50) per adult or C$110 (US$73) for an adult and child. You can also choose to fly in a two-seater de Havilland Canada **Chipmunk** with a canopy that enables clear views as you soar in the sky; price is C$75 (US$50) for a standard 15-minute ride. If you fancy a float plane, the de Havilland **Beaver** takes off from the Ottawa River and can take up to seven passengers at a time; advance reservations are required for the float plane. Cost is C$50 (US$33) per adult with a minimum of two passengers per trip. When you're back on terra firma, don't forget to take a turn through the **Aeronautica Boutique,** which stocks scale models of aircraft, books, posters, prints, toys, clothing, and kites. When your kids feel the need for refreshment and exercise, visit the indoor snack bar and outdoor playground. Free strollers and wheelchairs are available at the front entrance, plus a thoughtful addition: electric vehicles for physically challenged visitors and the elderly. There's also a library specializing in the history of aviation with an emphasis on the Canadian experience. The library is primarily open by appointment for visitors with a special interest in aviation.

Where to Eat   There is a small snack bar on site and an outdoor picnic area. Nearby St. Laurent Boulevard has a number of family restaurant chains.

11 Aviation Pkwy. (Rockcliffe Airport). © **800/463-2038** or 613/993-2010. Admission C$6 (US$4) adults, C$4 (US$2.50) seniors and students, C$2 (US$1.30) children 6–15, children under 6 free; C$12 (US$8) family (1 or 2 adults with children). Admission free to all Thurs 5pm–9pm. May 1–Labour Day (first Mon in Sept) Mon–Sun 9am–5pm, After Labour Day to April 30 Tues–Sun 10am–5pm. Thurs until 9pm all year. Closed Mon except holidays and school breaks. From downtown, travel northeast on Sussex Dr. (changes name to Rockcliffe Pkwy.) to Aviation Pkwy. Follow signs; museum is on the left.

All About the Mounties

The Royal Canadian Mounted Police (RCMP) is Canada's national police force. Their mission is to preserve the peace, uphold the law, and provide quality service in partnership with the communities they serve.

The idea of a mounted police force was conceived by Sir John A. Macdonald, Canada's first Prime Minister and Minister of Justice. In order to open the Western and Northern frontiers of the young country for settlement and development in an orderly manner, law enforcement officers were needed. In 1873, the North-West Mounted Police was created, inspired by the Royal Irish Constabulary and the mounted rifle units of the United States Army. A year later, approximately 275 officers and men were dispatched to Northwestern Canada.

Over the years, the force expanded and developed into the present day organization, which numbers around 20,000 employees in total. The RCMP is unique in the world because it provides policing services at the national, federal, provincial, and municipal levels. A federal policing service is provided to all Canadians, plus three territories and eight provinces (Ontario and Quebec are the exceptions) are policed at the provincial level. Under separate agreements, the RCMP serves almost 200 municipalities and more than 190 First Nations communities.

The present day RCMP's role is multi-faceted. Here's a list of the programs and services.

- Prevent and investigate crime.
- Maintain order.
- Enforce laws.
- Contribute to national security.
- Ensure the safety of state officials, visiting dignitaries, and foreign missions.
- Provide vital operational support services to other police and law enforcement agencies.

RCMP MUSICAL RIDE AND STABLES ⭐⭐ **Ages 5 and up.**
The **Mounties** are beloved by Canadians and renowned the world over for their courage, integrity, and poise. They are also well known for their personable manner with the public, and this courtesy extends to their open invitation to the public to visit the **Training School and Stables** of the **RCMP Musical Ride.** The Musical Ride is a visual display by specially trained officers and horses who perform intricate riding drills and figures set to musical accompaniment. Free tours are available all year around. In the summer months, you'll find larger groups and more frequent tour schedules. In the winter, it's advisable to call ahead and set up a time with the coordinator, although it's not essential. When we called to ask about tours, we found out that there was a full dress rehearsal scheduled for the indoor arena in two days time. We had the rare treat of watching the complete **Musical Ride** from a comfortable glassed-in gallery—in the company of the Irish Ambassador and his family, no less, which was an unexpected pleasure. We also had a tour of the stables and met several horses, including one who pulls the

RCMP Musical Ride: Facts & Figures

- The choreography of the Musical Ride is based upon traditional cavalry drill movements.
- The horse, scarlet tunic, and lance of the Ride are symbols of the Force's early history.
- The first Musical Ride was performed at Regina Barracks in Saskatchewan in 1887.
- The Ride is performed by 32 regular member volunteers (male and female) who have at least two years police experience and who have taken a training course to qualify for the Ride.
- When on tour, the Ride team consists of 36 horses, 36 constables, 1 farrier, and 4 officers.
- The requirements for the horses' eligibility are very specific. They must be black, 16 to 17 hands high, and weigh between 523 kilograms (1150 lbs.) and 635 kilograms (1400 lbs.). Stallions must be registered Thoroughbred and broodmares are part Thoroughbred.
- Young horses, called remounts, begin training at 3 years of age. At 6 years old, they begin training specifically for the Musical Ride and take their first trip with the Ride.
- The saddle blankets feature the Force's regimental colours (blue and yellow) and bear the fused letters MP.
- The maple leaf pattern you can see on the horses' rumps is made with a metal stencil. Using a damp brush, the horses' hair is brushed across its natural lie to make it stand up.

Queen's carriage when she's in town. My daughter was thrilled to feed them some raw carrots which she had saved in her pocket from a lunch time salad. The beauty and grace of the horses will move you and entertain your kids. The tour guides are friendly and willing to answer questions you or your kids might have about the Musical Ride or the Mounties in general. If you don't happen to visit on a day when a practice is in session, or if the Ride is away on tour (which happens often during the summer), try and get tickets to one of their shows. They're always in Ottawa for the annual Sunset Ceremony in late June, including a performance on July 1st (Canada Day), and they perform in the area at other times between May and October. There's a boutique open in the main tourist season which stocks a variety of Mountie clothing, souvenirs, and toys.

Where to Eat   St. Laurent Boulevard has a number of family restaurant chains.

Corner of Sandridge Rd. and St. Laurent Blvd. ℂ **613/993-3751** or 613/998-8199. Free admission. Donations accepted. May 1–Oct 31 Mon–Fri 8:30am–3:30pm. June–Oct also open weekends 10am–4pm. Nov 1–Apr 30 Mon–Fri 9am–12:30pm. From downtown, follow Sussex Dr. (changes name to Rockcliffe Pkwy.) to Aviation Pkwy. Follow signs; the Musical Ride Centre is at the northeast corner of Sandridge Rd. and St. Laurent Blvd.

2 Museums & Galleries

Canada and the World Pavilion   **All ages.** Located at Rideau Falls Park on Sussex Drive, only a short walk from downtown, this 12000-square foot pavilion opened in the spring of 2001. This permanent exhibition of Canada's achievements and role on the international scene was built following the success of a temporary interpretation center launched in 1995. Admission is free and you can help your kids discover the unique stories of Canadians who have made an impact on the world in the fields of, sports, the arts, international relations, science and technology. Learn about animators, comedians, the game of hockey, Olympic athletes, and the International Space Station. Operate a myoelectric arm, maneuver a wheelchair just like Rick Hansen's, rummage through the ever-changing contents of the Discovery Cart, or have fun with an adventure kit designed specially for kids 10 and under. Find out what Canadians are doing throughout the world to promote social justice, sustainable development, and basic human rights.

Rideau Falls Park, Sussex Dr. Free admission. For further information call the Capital Infocentre at ℂ **800/465-1867** or 613/239-5000. From downtown, travel northeast along Sussex Dr. The Pavilion is adjacent to Rideau Falls on your left.

Canadian Museum of Contemporary Photography   Ages 5 and up.
Wedged between the Fairmont Chateau Laurier Hotel and the Ottawa Locks of the Rideau Canal in a reconstructed railway tunnel, lies the Museum of Contemporary Photography. The exhibition galleries feature the work of Canada's most dynamic photographers and change quarterly. If you have younger children, come on a Family Sunday, when there are activities geared to the whole family. Hands-on workshops, drop-in activities, tours, and music make the Museum fun for all ages. Other family events scheduled throughout the year. For family event information, call ℂ **613/990-2659.** Strollers and a wheelchair available for use.

1 Rideau Canal. ℂ **613/990-8257.** Admission free. May–early Sept daily 10am–6pm, Thurs until 8pm. Sept–Apr Wed–Sun 10am–5pm, Thurs until 8pm. The museum is sandwiched between the Ottawa Locks and the Fairmont Chateau Laurier, just east of the Parliament Buildings.

Canadian Postal Museum   Ages 5 and up. Tracing the history of mail delivery across the vast landscape of Canada, the Postal Museum is housed within the Canadian Museum of Civilization. For details, see the Canadian Museum of Civilization entry earlier in this chapter.

Canadian Ski Museum   Ages 8 and up. If your family likes to participate in winter sports, drop into the Canadian Ski Museum to learn about the history of skiing and how it evolved into the high tech, high speed sport of today. Lots of old equipment and memorabilia are on display. Handmade wooden skis with strips of sealskin on the base to prevent backslipping are a long way from the parabolic skis of today. The evolution of downhill skiing is explained, with credit for the world's first ski tow going to an enterprising Quebecer in the 1930s. After visiting the Museum, you can browse the outdoor adventure equipment and supplies in **Trailhead,** the retail store on the main floor of the building. There are a number of other outdoor stores in the neighborhood of Westboro to explore as well—**Bushtukah** at 206 Richmond Road, **Mountain Equipment Co-op** at 366 Richmond Road, and **The Expedition Shoppe** at 369 Richmond Road. The Canadian Ski Museum entrance is at the side of the building housing Trailhead. Look for a blue door which opens to a stairway leading to the second floor.

1960 Scott St. ℂ **613/722-3584.** Free admission. Mon–Sat 9am–5pm, Sun 11am–5pm. Guided tours are available.

Canadian War Museum   **Ages 6 and up.** The Canadian War Museum is the country's military history museum and serves as a living memorial to men and women who have served in Canada's armed forces. Three floors of permanent exhibitions tell the story of Canada in conflict, from the days of New France, through the two terrible wars of the 20th century, to Canada's role as peace-keepers today. The personal stories of people whose lives have been affected by war are told and many exhibits feature authentic artifacts and memorabilia. On the third floor, the Discovery Room has interactive areas for children and parents. Costumes include a Viking warrior and a modern air force pilot. Try out a trench periscope. Listen to the beat of a military drum and learn the signals that drummers sent to the soldiers in their regiments. Special events, concerts, war films, and historical re-enactments are frequently scheduled. The museum boutique has a small children's section with toy tanks and other military themed amusements. For teens and adults, there is a good selection of books, posters, videos, CD-ROMs, and miniatures. You can order custom reproductions of war art, photos, and images of artifacts through the boutique. Your ticket includes entry to **Vimy House** at 221 Champagne Avenue North, about a 15-minute drive from the War Museum. Vimy House is the museum's research and collections facility where military vehicles, tanks, artillery, weapons, war art, uniforms, and much more can be seen. Opening hours vary so enquire at the War Museum before you set off to visit.

330 Sussex Dr. ℂ **800/555-5621** or 819/776-8600. Admission C$4 (US$2.50) adult, C$3 (US$2) seniors and youths, C$2 (US$1.30) children 2–12, C$9 (US$6) family (max 3 adults, 2 children or youth). Free admission Thurs 4pm–8pm. Half-price Sun. Free admission for Canadian veterans, retired military personnel, and accompanying families. Free admission for members of the Canadian Forces with identification and cadets in uniform. Summer daily 9:30am–5pm, Thurs until 8pm. Winter Tues–Sun 9:30am–5pm, Thurs until 8pm. From the Queensway, take Nicholas St. exit (exit 118). Turn left on Rideau St., right onto Sussex Dr. The Museum is on your left.

Tips Memorial on the Web

The Canadian Virtual War Memorial is being built as an electronic tribute to the Canadians and Newfoundlanders who have lost their lives in major conflicts since 1884. The website also serves as a searchable database so people can look for men and women in their own families who have given their lives for their country. Canadians are invited to submit digitized images of photos, letters, postcards, medals, and other war memorabilia. Visit **www.virtualmemorial.gc.ca** for instructions on how to add your family's war memorabilia to the Virtual War Memorial.

Currency Museum of the Bank of Canada   **Ages 5 and up.** This museum, housed in the center block of the Bank of Canada, traces the development of money from around 500 B.C. to the present day. Kids will get a kick out of some of the unusual articles used as currency, including teeth, grain, cattle, glass beads, shells, fish-hooks and cocoa beans, as well as the more familiar paper and metal. With eight galleries to wander through and a spacious, light-filled atrium in the entrance hall, you can spend a pleasant hour or two here whether you're escaping from the summer heat or the bite of the winter wind. You can visit on your own or pre-register for a guided tour.

245 Sparks St. ℰ **613/782-8914.** For tour reservations call ℰ **613/782-8852.** Free admission. Tues–Sat 10:30am–5pm, Sun 1pm–5pm, all year. Mon 10:30am–5pm May 1–Labour Day (first Mon in Sept).

Logan Hall, Geological Survey of Canada   Ages 6 and up. For those with an interest in rocks, minerals, fossils, meteorites, and ores, the small museum at Logan Hall is a good choice to spend an hour or two. Interactive displays, geological maps, and videos will test your knowledge of geology, teach you how to pan for gold, and help you learn about the Geological Survey of Canada's research projects. Logan Hall is named after Sir William Logan, who founded the Geological Survey of Canada in 1842.

601 Booth St. ℰ **613/995-4261.** Free admission. Mon–Fri 8am–4pm.

Museum of Canadian Scouting   Ages 5 and up. If there's an eager Beaver, Cub, or Scout in your family, take a little detour out to The Boy Scouts of Canada National Headquarters on Baseline Road between Clyde Avenue and Merivale Road. This small museum in the lobby of the Scouts Canada building has exhibits featuring the history of Canadian scouting. You can view archival books related to scouting, a collection of uniforms and badges, and photos and letters which belonged to the founder of Scouting, Lord Baden-Powell. While you're there, visit the **Scout Shop Camping Centre.** The Scout Shop has lots of practical, neat, useful, and sometimes unusual camping equipment, plus books, Beaver, Cub, and Scout uniforms and accessories, and small toys. Call for opening hours.

1345 Baseline Rd. ℰ **613/224-5131** (Museum enquiries) or **613/224-0139** (Scout Shop). Free admission. From the Queensway take Maitland Ave. south (exit 126) to Baseline Rd. Turn left on Baseline. The museum is on your left.

National Gallery of Canada ☆☆   **Ages 7 and up.** Architect Mosha Safdie, famed for his Habitat apartment block and Musée des Beaux-Arts in Montreal, designed this rose-granite crystal palace that gleams from a promontory overlooking the Ottawa River. A dramatic long glass concourse leads to the Grand Hall, offering glorious views of Parliament Hill. Natural light also fills the galleries, thanks to ingeniously designed shafts with reflective panels. Pause on the balcony of the central atrium and look down on a garden of triangular flowers and a grove of trees that repeat the lines of the pyramidal glass roof. The museum displays about 800 examples of Canadian art, part of the 10,000 works in the permanent collection. Among the highlights are Tom Thomson and the Group of Seven, early Quebecois artists, and Montreal Automatistes. European masters are also represented, form Corot and Turner to Chagall and Picasso, and contemporary galleries feature pop art and minimalism, plus abstract works from Canadians and Americans. For families, visit the Artissimo kiosk 11am to 4pm on weekends and during school vacations. Kids ages 3 and up accompanied by an adult can create their own masterpieces. Family workshops are designed for parents and kids to learn more about art, its interpretation and its origins. Art programs for children which run for several sessions are also available. For information or registration for these programs, call ℰ **613/990-4888.** Special programs are available for guests with multiple disabilities or intellectual disabilities. Tactile workshops and tours for visually impaired and blind visitors are occasionally held. Music concerts are scheduled frequently. Facilities include two restaurants and a gift and book store. Wheelchairs and strollers available.

380 Sussex Dr. ✆ **800/319-2787** or 613/990-1985. Admission free to permanent collection. Admission C$5–12 (US$3–8) for special exhibitions. May–mid-Oct daily 10am–6pm, Thurs until 8pm. Mid-Oct–Apr Wed–Sun 10am–5pm, Thurs until 8pm. From the Queensway, take Nicholas St. exit (exit 118). Turn left on Rideau St., right onto Sussex Dr. The Museum is on your left.

National Library of Canada   Ages 10 and up. The National Library is responsible for collecting and preserving Canada's published heritage. Anyone who registers at the Library can use the resources to find information on Canadian literature, music, history, genealogy, literary manuscripts, artists' books, and rare books. There are also tapes, records, and CDs in the Music Collection and personal papers and memorabilia in the Literary Manuscript Collection. Exhibitions and displays are staged regularly. Literary and musical events are held throughout the year. Children's authors, storytelling workshops, musical concerts featuring pianists, medieval ensembles, folksingers, and cellists, and other events will entertain the whole family.

395 Wellington St. ✆ **613/992-9988** (public programs); ✆ **613/995-9481** (reference services). Admission free; some events require tickets and fee. General hours weekdays 8:30am–5pm. Public programs weekdays 9am–4pm; reference services weekdays 10am–5pm; reading room daily 7am–11pm; exhibitions daily 9am–10:30pm.

Nepean Museum   Ages 4 and up. This small museum focuses on local history of the city of Nepean, now part of the new city of Ottawa. Exhibits encourage kids to interact. The Discovery Room, decorated as a Victorian general store, has dress-up clothes, weigh scales, and a cash register. Art supplies and a computer are also on hand.

16 Rowley Ave. ✆ **613/723-7936.** Free admission. Tues–Fri 10am–4pm, weekends 1pm–4pm.

Supreme Court of Canada   Ages 12 and up. While you would not bring young children into the public gallery while the court is in session, you may want to offer teenagers the experience of witnessing an appeal, depending on the circumstances of the case being heard. The Supreme Court is a general court of appeal for both criminal and civil cases and is the highest court of appeal in the country. Three sessions are held through the year between October and June and an average of 120 cases are heard annually. Weekdays 9:45am to 12:30pm and 2pm to 4pm are the usual times to hear appeals. Law students take members of the public on guided tours, which take about half an hour and are recommended for all ages. From May to August tours are held daily on a continuing basis, and the rest of the year tours are available by prior arrangement on weekdays. The architecture of the building is impressive to behold and the grand entrance hall is magnificent. Try and drop in, even if your little ones prevent you from witnessing a session from the public gallery.

301 Wellington St. ✆ **613/995-4330.** For tour reservations, call ✆ **613/995-5361.**

3 Heritage Attractions

Billings Estate Museum   All ages. This well-preserved family home dating from 1827 is one of Ottawa's oldest properties. Built for Braddish and Lamira Billings, two of Ottawa's founding settlers, the Billings Estate includes several outbuildings on the 3.4-hectare (8.4 acre) site. You can browse the collections of family heirlooms, furnishings, tools, paintings, and documents on your own or take a guided tour. Hands-on activities, special events, and workshops are scheduled on a regular basis. Stroll the lush lawns, colorful flower beds, wooded slopes, and old pathways. Enjoy tea on the lawn in the summer months, served several afternoons each week.

2100 Cabot St. © **613/247-4830.** Admission C$2.50 (US$1.70) adults, C$2 (US$1.30) seniors, C$1.50 (US$1) children 5–17, under 5 free. May–Oct, Sun–Thurs noon–5pm. Closed Thanksgiving weekend. Hours subject to change; call ahead.

Bytown Museum   **Ages 5 and up.** Housed in Ottawa's oldest stone building (1827), which served as the Commissariat during the construction of the Rideau Canal, this museum displays articles belonging to Lieutenant-Colonel By, the canal's builder and one of young Ottawa's most influential citizens. In addition, artifacts reflect the social history of the pioneer families in four period rooms and a number of changing exhibits. The rooms depict a 1850 Bytown kitchen, a French Canadian lumber camp shanty, a Victorian parlour, and the exhibit which will be of the most interest to kids—an early toy store. Until the mid 19th century, toys were either made at home or by a specialist toy-maker. Factory made toys were a product of the second half of the 1800s. The museum is situated beside the Ottawa Locks, between Parliament Hill and the Fairmont Chateau Laurier Hotel.

Beside Ottawa Locks. © **613/234-4570.** Admission C$2.50 (US$1.70) adults, C$1.25 (US$.80) students, C$6 (US$4) family. Dec–Mar by appointment. Apr–mid-May daily 10am–2pm. Mid-May–mid-Oct daily 10am–4pm. Mid-Oct–Nov 10am–2pm.

ByWard Market 👁️👁️ **All ages.** In a compact area bordered by St. Patrick Street on the north, King Edward Avenue on the east, Rideau Street on the south, and Sussex Drive on the west, there is a lively district known as the ByWard Market. In the heart of the area, one block east of Sussex Drive between York and George streets, lies the ByWard Market building and the outdoor stalls of the farmer's market, where you can buy outstanding fresh local produce, flowers, and other products such as maple syrup. Outdoor markets are a wonderful place to stroll with your children. The activity and bustle of the market and the fun of choosing a selection of fresh fruit and vegetables to take home and enjoy is a world away from trudging up and down supermarket aisles. To complement the fresh produce, you'll find gourmet food vendors inside the Market building. There are dozens of excellent food retailers in the district, and I urge you to venture inside and taste what's on offer. Here's a few places to keep a look-out for, just to get you started: Le Boulanger Français/The French Baker, 119 Murray St.; Chilly Chilies, 55 ByWard Market; House of Cheese, 34 ByWard Market; International Cheese & Deli, 40 ByWard Market; L'Ami des Gourmets, 55 Murray St.; Lapointe Fish, 46 ByWard Market; Le Moulin de Provence, 55 ByWard Market; The Tea Party, 119 York St. Throughout the year, the ByWard Market hosts family-oriented events on weekends as a thank you to their customers and to make the community surrounding the market a little brighter. Events include a Mother's Day celebration with special restaurant menus, an outdoor fashion show, a jazz band, free hay rides, and farm animals on display. On the first Sunday in June, a display of 150 vintage, classic, and high performance cars is held. Annual events later in the year include Bytown Days when 19th century Ottawa is revisited, a search for the world's biggest pumpkin, and an old-fashioned Christmas comes to the Market with carolers riding around the Market district in a horse-drawn carriage adorned with sleigh bells.

History of the ByWard Market

The ByWard Market area is the oldest part of Ottawa. Following the War of 1812, the British were looking for an alternative water passage between Montreal and Kingston. The Rideau River was chosen, despite the fact that a canal would have to built to bypass the Rideau Falls, the only point of contact between the Ottawa and Rideau Rivers. Wrightsville was a thriving lumber town on the north shore of the Ottawa River, but a settlement was needed for canal workers on the south shore adjacent to the construction site. Accordingly, a shantytown grew up in the area between the Rideau River and the canal which came to be known as Lower Town (now known more commonly as downtown, east of Canal). Market Square was the heart of Lower Town, and the ByWard Market building was originally much larger than it is today. The opening of the Rideau Centre shopping mall adjacent to the Market led residents and visitors to rediscover the district and the ByWard Market is now one of the trendiest places in Ottawa for shopping, dining, and entertainment.

From the Queensway, exit at Nicholas St. (exit 118). At Rideau St., turn right and then left on King Edward Ave. From King Edward Ave., turn left onto George, York, Clarence, or Patrick. Or you can turn left onto Rideau St., right on Sussex Dr., and then turn right onto George, York, Clarence, or Murray.

Laurier House   Ages 8 and up. This fine Victorian residence, built in 1878, was home to two prime ministers, spanning over 50 years of occupancy by two of Canada's most important and influential political figures. A tour of this home helps to put a human face on Canada's politics and history. Prior to 1896, there was no official residence provided for the Prime Minister. Sir Wilfrid Laurier, Canada's first French-Canadian prime minister, was the first resident of Laurier House, purchased by the Liberal Party to house their leader. Several rooms contain furnishings and mementos of Laurier's but the majority of the house is restored to the era of William Lyon Mackenzie King, Canada's longest serving Prime Minister and the second occupant of the house. Apparently King held séances in the library, and his crystal ball is on display. A reconstruction of Prime Minister Lester B. Pearson's study contains the Nobel Peace prize medal he won for his role in the 1956 Arab-Israeli dispute. Strathcona Park is just across the street from Laurier House, so after you've done a quick tour (if your kids are the young and restless type), wander over to the park, check out the wonderful children's playground there and watch the swans glide along the Rideau River.

335 Laurier Ave. E. © **613/992-8142.** Admission C$2.50 (US$1.70) adults, C$2 (US$1.30) seniors, C$1.25 (US$.80) youth, free for children 5 and under. Apr–Sept Tues–Sat 9am–5pm, Sun 2pm–5pm; Oct–Mar Tues–Sat 10am–5pm, Sun 2–5pm. From the Queensway, take the Nicholas St. exit (exit 118). Turn right on Laurier Ave. E. The museum is on your left.

Rideau Hall ★★   **All ages.** Rideau Hall has been the official residence and workplace of Canada's Governor General since 1867 and is considered to be the symbolic home of all Canadians. The public is welcome to wander the 32 hectares (79 acres) of beautiful gardens and forests. Outdoor concerts and cricket matches are held in the summer and there's ice-skating on the pond in winter. Free guided tours are offered of the residence. The Governor General's

Awards are presented here annually, honoring Canadians for extraordinary accomplishments, courage, and contributions to science, the arts, and humanity. Two receptions are held annually for the public—the Garden Party in June and the New Year's Day Levee. The Ceremonial Guard is on duty at Rideau Hall during July and August. The first Changing of the Guard Ceremony, held in late June, features a colorful parade led by a marching band. Relief of the Sentries is a ceremony performed hourly 9am to 5pm during the summer. The Visitor Centre, operating daily between May and September, has family activities, a play structure, and hands-on activities for children.

1 Sussex Dr. ✆ **800/465-6890** or 613/991-4422. www.gg.ca. Admission to all tours and activities is free. Grounds are generally open daily 9am–sunset; subject to change without notice. From the Queensway, take the Nicholas St. exit (exit 118), turn left on Rideau St., right on Sussex Dr. The entrance to Rideau Hall is on your right just after you cross the Rideau River.

Turtle Island Aboriginal Village   All ages. During the summer months, Turtle Island Tourism Company sets up an Aboriginal summer village on historic Victoria Island on the Ottawa River. Live demonstrations of traditional and contemporary Native singing, drumming, and dancing are staged. Listen to an ancient legend or story in an authentic tipi, enjoy traditional Aboriginal foods and visit the cultural displays. On show are tipis, birch bark canoes, totem poles, and Cree Hunt Camps. Fun for all ages. The Trading Post craft shop stocks arts and crafts made by the local Aboriginal community. A special three-hour program takes you to the Gatineau Hills where you sit by the fire with Native guides, walk through the woods, and learn about the First Peoples' relationship with nature. Wilderness survival retreats and outdoor adventure programs are held; one to five days in length. You can reach Victoria Island from the Chaudieres Bridge by car or via the Portage Bridge if you're walking or cycling.

12 Stirling Ave. ✆ **877/811-3233** or 613/564-9494. www.aboriginalexperiences.com. In the summer, the village operates in an outdoor location on Victoria Island in the Ottawa River. Victoria Island is just west of the Parliament Buildings, and lies below the Chaudières and Portage bridges.

4 Kid-Friendly Tours
ON LAND

Amphibus   All ages. For a unique tour of the city, hop on the "Amphibus," a hybrid vehicle which cruises on the water and tours on land. The bright red 42-seat vehicle, named Lady Dive, is a relative newcomer to the Ottawa tourist scene but it has stirred up a lot of interest. The 90-minute tour begins at the corner of Sparks and Elgin streets, touring past historic sites and city landmarks, then plunges into the Ottawa River for a relaxing cruise. Reservations recommended.

Sparks St. and Elgin St. ✆ **613/223-6211.** Tickets C$24 (US$16) adult, C$22 (US$15) student, C$20 (US$13) child, C$65 (US$43) family (2 adults, 2 children; additional children C$10 (US$7)). May, June, Sept, Oct daily 9am–5pm, tours every 2 hours. July, Aug daily 9am–9pm, tours hourly.

Capital Double Decker and Trolley Tours   All ages. This locally owned and operated tour company offers authentic open-top double decker buses and historic replica trolley buses. Fully narrated tours. Free hotel pickup and return. The most popular ticket is a three-day pass which allows you to hop on and off at any of the 20 designated stops at your leisure. Cost for a family three-day pass is C$56 (US$37). Other tours available. Discounts on other attractions when you buy your tickets. Tickets available from the main kiosk at the corner of Sparks and Metcalfe streets downtown and the Capital Infocentre. Call for more information.

Kiosk at corner of Sparks St. and Metcalfe St. ✆ **800/823-6147** or 613/749-3666. Seasonal.

Grayline Sightseeing Tours   All ages. Choose an open-top double decker bus or vintage trolley bus. Step on or off the bus any time you wish at these stops: Parliament Hill, Museum of Civilization, Notre Dame Basilica, Rideau Hall, RCMP Museum and Stables, National Aviation Museum, National War Museum, Royal Canadian Mint, National Gallery, ByWard Market, Rideau Canal, Dow's Lake, Experimental Farm, Museum of Nature. If you call ahead, they'll pick you up at your downtown hotel. Tours operate from May to October. Tickets are valid for three days and prices are reasonable—a family of four can get a three day, on-off privilege ticket for C$54 (US$36).

For departure locations and times and other information call Gray Line ℂ **800/297-6422** or 613/565-5463. Seasonal.

Oakroads   All ages. If you want to explore the back roads and scenic routes in the countryside surrounding Ottawa, take an Oakroads day tour. Travel in a 22-seat luxury coach and stop at small towns and places of natural and historic interest, all within a day's drive of Ottawa. Operating May to October. A different tour is planned for each day of the week. Call ahead if you want them to pick you up from your downtown location.

Departs from corner of Sparks and Elgin sts. and Capital Infocentre ℂ **613/748-0144.** Tickets C$40 (US$26) adult, C$25 (US$17) child, C$100 (US$66) family. Seasonal.

Orient Express Rickshaws   All ages. Although we're not in the Orient, traveling by rickshaw in the summer is a convenient way to get around downtown and it's lots of fun. The rickshaws carry two or three people, pulled by strong and friendly young men. You can take a half-hour tour of the cobblestone ByWard Market courtyards complete with entertaining stories of days gone by for C$25 (US$17) or use the rickshaws as a taxi service. They're on a cellular dispatch system and you can book ahead by phone. You can also usually find them on George Street in the ByWard Market area.

George St., ByWard Market. ℂ **613/860-SHAW(7429).** www.rickshaws.net. Mid May to Labour Day (first Mon in Sept).

GUIDED WALKING TOURS

For an entertaining evening, join in the **Haunted Walk of Ottawa** (Ages 8 and up) and hear the city's ghost stories and the dark side of Ottawa's history. Follow a black-cloaked storyteller, lantern in hand, and stroll through the quiet streets. They welcome families on the tour and claim that many of their fans are in fact children. The historical stories will probably be over the heads of very young children, but unless your child is very easily frightened, they'll most likely enjoy themselves. There aren't any nasty surprises or theatrical incidents on the tour, as the guides prefer to tell the stories and take you to the sites of hauntings and ghost sightings—they leave the rest up to your imagination. The walks take place entirely out of doors, so dress for the weather. The tour takes about one and a half hours and the total distance covered is about 1.6 kilometers (1 mile). Call for information on French language tours and Hallowe'en tours. Tickets may be purchased in advance by phone with a major credit card or within the hour before the tour begins from the tour guide.

Tour departs from D'Arcy McGee's Irish Pub, 44 Sparks St. at Elgin St. ℂ **613/730-0575.** Tickets C$12 (US$8) adults, C$8 (US$5) seniors and students, children 10 and under with an accompanying adult are free. May–Oct Mon–Wed 8pm, Thurs–Sat 8pm and 9pm. Sun 8pm on holiday weekends only.

Ottawa Walks   **Ages 8 and up.** Guided walking tours of the ByWard Market, Rideau Canal, historical Ottawa, and more.

1536A Beaverpond. © **613/744-4307.** Tickets C$5.75 (US$3.80) adults, C$4 (US$2.50) seniors and students, children free, C$11.50 (US$8) family. Operates year round with tours scheduled daily 9am–9pm. Call for more information.

SELF-GUIDED WALKING TOURS

Art Walk   **All ages.** The National Capital Commission has produced a guide describing seven public art walking tours in Ottawa and Hull. You will see statues of prominent historical figures, contemporary sculptures made of wood, stone, papier mache, metal, and fiberglass, war memorials, statues of Canadian heroes, totem poles, murals, and monuments. Tours vary from 35 minutes to one hour in length. Available free from the Capital Infocentre, 90 Wellington St.

Parliament Hill   **All ages.** A free booklet available from the Capital Infocentre gives a detailed description of a self-guided walking tour of Parliament Hill. See entry under "Parliament Hill," earlier in this chapter.

Moments   **A Great Canadian Hero**

Across from the Centre Block of Parliament Hill, in front of the Capital Infocentre on Wellington Street, stands a proud memorial to Canadian Terry Fox (see _"Terry Fox: A Symbol of Hope and Courage,"_ below). Many Canadian schoolchildren raise money for cancer research every September by taking part in a sponsored run/walk in memory of Terry Fox. Take a few minutes to show your kids the statue and talk with them about the courage and determination of this great Canadian hero.

Path of Heroes   **All ages.** The Government of Canada has produced a guide with seven walking tours around the heart of the National Capital Region. The walks vary in length from 15 minutes to one hour. Each tour has a different theme: The Heroic Heart; Remembrance, Culture, and Honour; Pictures and Visions; Canada and the World; Bridges and Meeting Places; Across Space and Time; and finally Lore, Law, and Money. The guide suggests places to stop along the way at designated buildings, vistas, and statues that tell the stories of Canadian heroes. Available free from the Capital Infocentre, 90 Wellington St.

ON THE WATER

Amphibus   This hybrid vehicle takes passengers on a 90-minute tour beginning on land and then plunging into the Ottawa River for a relaxing cruise. See entry under "On Land," above.

Ottawa Riverboat Company   **All ages.** Take a 90-minute tour on the 280-passenger _Sea Prince II,_ the largest tour boat in Ottawa. Bilingual guides provide commentary as you tour past famous buildings and landmarks as seen from the Ottawa River. Refreshments are available on board. Reservations recommended. Cruise tickets available at the ticket booth in Confederation Square, Ottawa Riverboat Dock (at the foot of the Ottawa Locks just west of the Fairmont

Terry Fox: A Symbol of Hope & Courage

In 1977, a young 18-year-old Canadian, **Terry Fox,** was given the devastating news that he had bone cancer and his right leg would have to be amputated six inches above the knee. Terry wanted to do something to give hope to people living with cancer and he decided to run across Canada to raise money for **cancer research.** After many months of training, during which he ran over 5,000 kilometers (3,000 miles), Terry dipped his artificial leg in the Atlantic Ocean on April 12, 1980 and began his **"Marathon of Hope."** He traveled courageously through six provinces and over 5,370 kilometers (3,330 miles) before being forced to retire near Thunder Bay, Ontario. The cancer had spread to Terry's lungs and he was flown home to British Columbia. Ten months later, in June 1981, Terry died at the age of 22. The country was in mourning.

An annual fundraising event was established in his memory and the first **Terry Fox Run,** held at more than 760 sites across Canada and around the world in 1981, raised C$3.5 million. By the year 2000, the total amount of money raised in Terry's name was close to C$270 million. Terry is a true Canadian hero and has become a symbol of hope and courage to people living with cancer and their families and friends.

Chateau Laurier Hotel), Jacques Cartier Park and Marina in Hull, and selected hotels. New in 2001, the Ottawa Riverboat Company and GrayLine Double Decker and Trolleybus Tours are offering a combined boat/bus sightseeing ticket. For C$30 (US$20) you can take a cruise on the *Sea Prince II* and take advantage of a three-day "hop on/hop off" bus pass. A free shuttle service is extended to guests of selected hotels in the city.

335 Cumberland St., Suite 200. ✆ **613/562-4888.** Tickets C$15 (US$10) adults, C$13 (US$9) seniors/students, C$7.50 (US$5) children 6–12, under 6 free, C$36.50 (US$24) family (max 2 adults and 2 children). Three to five departures daily in season from Ottawa dock at the foot of the Ottawa locks and from the Jacques Cartier Park marina in Hull; call for departure times.

Paul's Boat Lines   All ages. Paul's Boat Lines cruises the Ottawa River and the Rideau Canal. On the Ottawa River, the 150 passenger *Paula D* takes visitors on a 90-minute cruise, with spectacular views of the Parliament Buildings, Rideau Falls, and other sites. On the canal, you can glide along in one of three low profile tour boats for a 75-minute cruise. If you have young children (under 10 or so), then the Ottawa River cruise will be the better choice. There are two decks to walk around on and a small snack bar. The open design on the upper deck is perfect on a hot summer's day, as you can catch the cool breeze off the water. The canal boats have a single enclosed deck, and being low in the water the views are not as entertaining for youngsters.

219 Colonnade Rd. ✆ **613/225-6781** (Office), 613/235-8409 (Summer Dock). Tickets C$14 (US$9) adults, C$12 (US$8) seniors, C$10 (US$7) students, C$7 (US$4) children under 15, C$30 (US$20) family (Max 2 adults and 2 children). Four to seven departures daily in season from Ottawa dock at the foot of the Ottawa locks, from the Jacques Cartier Park marina in Hull, and from the Conference Centre on the Rideau Canal; call for departure times.

IN THE AIR

Hot Air Ballooning   **Preteens and up.** If you fancy floating in the sky at a leisurely pace with the city spread out below you and you're not afraid of heights, you might like a trip in a hot air balloon. For many people it's a once-in-a-lifetime experience and there are several companies in the Ottawa area, so go for it. There may be restrictions on the minimum age for passengers, so call and enquire before announcing the trip to everyone. If you decide against a trip yourselves, you can always go along to a launching and watch the balloons being prepared for flight and then watch the take-offs. Everyone from babies to grandparents will enjoy the sight of the huge, colorful silken spheres as they gracefully rise towards the sky. In the Ottawa area, the main operators are **High Time Balloon Co. Inc.,** ✆ **613/521-9921,** www.hightimeballoon.com, **Skyview Ballooning,** ✆ **613/724-7784,** www.skyviewballooning.com, **Sundance Balloons,** ✆ **613/247-8277,** and **Windborne Ballooning,** ✆ **613/739-7388.**

Private Small Aircraft   **All ages.** View the Ottawa area from the sky and have fun identifying the major landmarks on a flight with **Air Conquest,** 1 Crownhill St. ✆ **613/745-6747.** Twin-engine plane. Families welcome. Operates all year round from 8am to 9pm. Rates are C$35 (US$23) for adults, seniors, and children 10 and over. C$30 (US$20) children under 10. Sightseeing tours are available by seaplane with **Air Outaouais** which takes off from the Ottawa River in downtown Ottawa-Hull. Prices start at C$35 (US$23) per person depending on the tour. Air Outaouais operates from May to November, sunrise to sunset. Reservations required. Flights are accessible for **people with disabilities.** P.O. Box 442, Aylmer, QC. ✆ **819/568-2359.**

5 For Kids with Special Interests

Animals   To see farm animals at close range and perhaps get a chance to handle small ones or even help to milk a cow or shear a sheep, visit the **Agriculture Museum.** A tour of the **RCMP Musical Ride Centre** takes you right into the stables where you can pat the horses' noses and feed them carrots. At the **Museum of Nature,** most of the creatures are of the preserved variety, but they are extremely well displayed.

Creepy Crawlies   In the Creepy Critter Gallery in the **Museum of Nature,** there's only a pane of glass separating you from ants, cockroaches, worms, millipedes, leeches, snakes, spiders, and toads. At the **Ecomuseum** in Hull, there's an awesome collection of insects and other creeping and flying creatures, many of which are displayed at small-child height.

Dinosaurs   The **Museum of Nature** is the place to go to see real dinosaur skeletons. You can even climb up to a platform so that you can look them straight in the teeth.

Factory Tours   For budding engineers and mechanically inclined children, visit the Royal Canadian Mint to see how coins are made or travel to Smiths Falls, south of Ottawa for a free tour of the Hershey Chocolate Factory.

Fine Arts   Children with an interest in the visual arts will enjoy a trip to the **National Gallery.** This is also a good destination for kids who love to draw and paint.

Take Time for a Scenic Drive

For a leisurely picturesque drive, head east on Wellington Street past **Parliament Hill,** through Confederation Square. You'll pass the grand **Fairmont Chateau Laurier** on your left. Turn left at the lights (north) onto Sussex Drive. After passing the **American Embassy** on your left, glorious views open up across the islands.

Continue along Sussex Drive to St. Patrick Street, turning left into **Nepean Point.** Here you can share a fine view of the river with a statue of French explorer **Samuel de Champlain,** the first European to arrive in the region almost 400 years ago. Adjacent to Nepean Point is **Major's Hill Park,** where there are wonderful views of the canal locks, the Ottawa River, and the striking architecture of the **National Gallery.** Continuing northeast on Sussex Drive, crossing the Rideau River via Green Island. **Rideau Falls** are on your left. The road passes **24 Sussex Drive,** the **residence of the Prime Minister,** which is not open to the public. A little further on you'll find **Rideau Hall** also known as Government House, the Governor-General's residence. On the 88-acre grounds are scores of ceremonial trees planted by visiting dignitaries and heads of state, from Queen Victoria to John F. Kennedy, Richard Nixon, and Princess Diana. They're identified by name-plates at the base of the trees. In summer, a brief **Changing of the Guard** ceremony is held at noon at the main gate. Tours of the grounds and the interior public rooms are conducted daily in July and August and on weekends the rest of the year. For information, stop at the Visitor Centre (open daily 9:30am to 5:30pm) or call © **613/991-4422.**

Continuing, the drive becomes **Rockcliffe Parkway,** a beautiful route along the Ottawa River and through **Rockcliffe Park.** Watch for a right fork to Acacia Avenue, which leads to the **Rockeries,** planted with spring blooms. If you wish, continue along the Parkway to the **RCMP Musical Ride Centre** and the **Aviation Museum,** or retrace your route west towards downtown Ottawa.

First Nations   Many kids have a fascination with Native cultures and their ancestry. The **Canadian Museum of Civilization** has excellent exhibits on Native peoples and an impressive collection of giant totem poles. For a first hand experience and the opportunity to meet First Nations people at work and play, visit Victoria Island in the summer months to see the **Turtle Island** summer village with tipis, canoes, storytelling, and Native foods, or the annual **Odawa Spring Pow Wow,** held at Nepean Tent and Trailer Park in late May.

Flight   The obvious choice here is the **Canada Aviation Museum,** where kids can get close to dozens of real aircraft and sit in cockpit sections, fly a hang glider simulator, or go up for a ride in a vintage airplane. Visit the **Ottawa Airport**'s Observation deck and watch the big guys take off and land. The second weekend in September, beginning in 2002, enjoy the **National Capital Air Show.** And every Labour Day weekend (first weekend in September), there's the **Gatineau Hot Air Balloon Festival.**

Ghosts   Take kids with nerves of steel to visit the ghost of **Watson's Mill** in Manotick or the ghost that haunts the **Ottawa International Hostel** (the site of Canada's last public hanging in this former jail). Enjoy an evening of entertainment on the **Haunted Walk of Ottawa** or check out the gravestones in **Beechwood Cemetery,** the final resting place of many famous Canadians, including politicians, writers, poets, and 12 Hockey Hall of Fame members.

The Military   Visit the exhibits at the **Canadian War Museum** and the collection of artillery, weapons, and military vehicles at **Vimy House.**

Photography   Besides the displays of works by contemporary Canadian photographers, the **Canadian Museum of Contemporary Photography** runs family workshops on topics related to photography on Sunday afternoons.

The Postal Service   The **Postal Museum,** housed within the Canadian Museum of Civilization, traces the history of Canadian postal communications.

Rocks and Minerals   For those with an interest in rocks, minerals, fossils, meteorites, and ores, the small museum at **Logan Hall** is a good choice to spend an hour or two. The **Ecomuseum** in Hull and the **Museum of Nature** have excellent displays of rocks and minerals.

Science and Nature   For kids with a wide-ranging interest in science and nature, you'll get them in to the **Museum of Science and Technology** and the **Museum of Nature** easily enough, but good luck getting them to leave when it's time to go home. These museums are ideal for kids with a passion for these two subjects.

Trains   Train buffs will enjoy the locomotive collections at the **Museum of Science and Technology** and the **Smiths Falls Railway Museum.** If you want to really blow their whistle, take a trip on the **Hull-Chelsea-Wakefield Steam Train.**

7

For the Active Family

Ottawa is one of the greenest capital cities in the world. Beautifully groomed city parks are complemented by vast expanses of protected wilderness, and waterways flow to the north and through the center of the city.

Much of the credit for Ottawa's physical beauty goes to Jacques Gréber, a French urban planner. Following World War II, Prime Minister William Lyon Mackenzie King and the Federal District Commission (now the National Capital Commission) appointed Gréber to create a new layout for the city.

The National Capital Greenbelt, a swath of greenery that stretches around the city like an emerald necklace, can be largely attributed to Gréber's design. Stretching from Gatineau Park in Quebec across the Ottawa River, through Nepean in the west end, around the southern city limits, through Gloucester, and back up to the Ottawa River in the east, the Greenbelt encircles Canada's capital.

It's no accident that the logo, flag, and coat of arms created for the new City of Ottawa feature green and blue. The colors were chosen to represent the abundant green space and picturesque waterways and to reflect the connectedness of the natural environment and quality of life in Ottawa.

Ottawans appreciate the beauty of their surroundings, and you'll see hundreds of them cycling, walking, jogging, in-line skating, ice skating, and cross-country skiing to work or school or just getting outside in their leisure time. In fact, Ottawa residents have one of the highest participation rates in the country for golf, skiing, and cycling. With the expanse of waterways that meander around the city, boating, hanging out on the beach, and playing water sports are popular, as well.

Since Ottawa is a major urban center, there are also more citified ways to run, jump, and play. You can splash in a wave pool, scale a rock-climbing wall, or experience the thrill of high-tech arcade games. If you enjoy sports, you'll find plenty of places to play tennis or golf, go skiing, or swim. Many museums have organized activities for families on weekends and at peak vacation periods, so you'll always have an answer when your kids get into one of those "There's nothing to do!" moods.

 Maps for Active Families

To take full advantage of Ottawa's parks, pathways, and waterways, get hold of some specialized maps that clearly mark routes for cycling, walking, skating, or skiing. Some maps have suggested routes with information on the length and the level of difficulty. Good hunting grounds for maps are the **Capital Infocentre**, 90 Wellington St. (*© **800/465-1867*** or

613/239-5000); **Place Bell Books,** 175 Metcalfe St. (© **613/233-3821**), which specializes in maps, travel guides, and travel literature; and **A World of Maps,** 1235 Wellington St. (© **800/214-8524** or 613/724-6776), which carries topographic maps, nautical maps, and travel guides for the local region and the rest of the world. For maps of **Gatineau Park,** including highly detailed trail maps, visit the **Gatineau Park Visitor Centre,** 33 Scott Rd., Chelsea (© **800/465-1867** or 819/827-2020).

Here's a rundown of a few maps to get you started. **Explore the Recreational Pathways of Canada's Capital Region,** produced by the National Capital Commission, details pathways in **Gatineau Park** and other sites in Quebec, as well as pathways in Ottawa. There are 17 routes marked on the map, ranging from 1.5 kilometers (1 mile) to 31 kilometers (20 miles) in length. Descriptions of the terrain, level of difficulty, and points of interest are listed for each route. Five tours are highlighted. For the more adventurous, Environment Canada Parks Service provides a cycle touring map of the **Rideau Canal,** detailing routes along the 202-kilometer waterway between Ottawa and Kingston. One of the **Gatineau Park** maps available at the Gatineau Park Visitor Centre is a scale map that includes hiking trails, cycling paths, bridle paths, seasonal trails, and sections of the Trans Canada Trail. A new winter trail map for Gatineau Park includes contour lines, magnetic north, and exact drawings of ski trails, winter hiking trails, and snowshoe trails, with huts and shelters also marked. For trails in the **National Capital Greenbelt,** which encircles Ottawa from Kanata in the west, along the entire southern edge of the city, and around to Cumberland in the east, refer to the **Greenbelt All Seasons Trail Map.**

1 Green Ottawa

URBAN PARKS

Andrew Haydon Park   West of the downtown core, at the intersection of Acres Road and Carling Avenue, is this park on the southern banks of the Ottawa River. There are picnic sites with barbecues, walking paths, and a small artificial lake. The kids will enjoy splashing in the water sprinklers and jets, digging in the sand, and scrambling on the play structures, including a ship with rope ladders and swings. Refreshment pavilions and washrooms are on-site.

Brantwood Park   Turn east on Clegg Street off Main Street, and you'll soon come across Brantwood Park, on the west bank of the Rideau River. There's a wading pool and play structure. In winter, skaters can weave through a series of skating rinks joined by ice paths. For a delicious vegetarian snack or meal, visit the Green Door at 198 Main St. (see chapter 5, "Family-Friendly Dining," p. 82).

Brewer Park   Bordering the Rideau River and Bronson Avenue, Brewer Park is a good site for feeding waterfowl on the river, so bring along some crusts of bread. In the winter, a speed-skating oval is open to the public. There's a children's water park in the summer, with water sprays, jets, and slides. A specially designed tots' playground, a pool, an arena, baseball diamonds, picnic areas, and pathways along the river complete the scene.

Commissioner's Park   Situated along Dow's Lake, Commissioner's Park attracts thousands of visitors during the Canadian Tulip Festival with the largest tulip display in the region. An amazing 300,000 bulbs bloom in the park flowerbeds. Bring your camera and snap away.

Confederation Park   Major festivals are held in this downtown park at the intersection of Elgin Street and Laurier Avenue, including Winterlude and the Ottawa International Jazz Festival. There are memorials to Canadian history here, including a fountain that originally stood in Trafalgar Square in London and was dedicated to Colonel John By, the British engineer who supervised the building of the Rideau Canal. The colonel was a major influence in establishing Bytown, as Ottawa was formerly known.

Garden of the Provinces   Opposite the National Library and National Archives of Canada at the intersection of Wellington and Bay streets, the Garden of the Provinces commemorates the union of Canada's ten provinces and two territories. The display features two fountains and all the provincial arms and floral emblems.

Hog's Back Park   The parklands in this area surround the spectacular **Hog's Back Falls,** situated at the point where the Rideau Canal meets the Rideau River. They're named after rocks that are said to resemble the bristles on a hog's back. A refreshment pavilion, parking, and washroom facilities are available.

Major's Hill Park   Ottawa's oldest park, established in 1874, is tucked in behind the Fairmont Château Laurier. A statue of Colonel John By stands close to site of his house, which was destroyed by fire. This park offers outstanding views of the Parliament Buildings, the Rideau Canal, the Ottawa River, Hull, and the National Gallery. It's also a major site for many festivals and events, including the Tulip Festival. At the tip of the park, you'll find Nepean Point. You can share the view with a statue of Samuel de Champlain, who first explored the Ottawa River in 1613. The Astrolabe Theatre, a venue for summer concerts and events, is located here.

Mooney's Bay Park   South of Vincent Massey Park and Hog's Back Park along Riverside Drive, you'll find Mooney's Bay. There's a supervised, sandy swimming beach, a playground, shade trees, a refreshment pavilion, and public washrooms. A parking fee applies in the summer months.

New Edinburgh Park   On the east side of the Rideau River, south of Sussex Drive, New Edinburgh Park provides yet another peaceful refuge from the city within a few minutes' drive of downtown. Walking trails weave along the banks of the river, and because much of the park has been preserved in its natural state, there's an abundance of wildlife, including groundhogs, turtles, muskrats, butterflies, and blue herons. Bring binoculars and insect repellent. A children's playground will keep the kids occupied.

Fun Fact **A Sculptor not an Explorer**

The astrolabe (a 17th-century navigational instrument) held by the statue of Samuel de Champlain at Nepean Point was unwittingly placed upside down by sculptor Hamilton McCarthy. You can view the original astrolabe at the **Canadian Museum of Civilization.**

For the Active Family

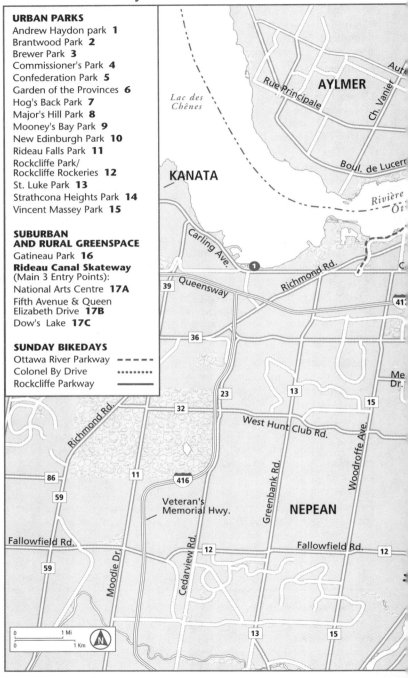

URBAN PARKS
Andrew Haydon park **1**
Brantwood Park **2**
Brewer Park **3**
Commissioner's Park **4**
Confederation Park **5**
Garden of the Provinces **6**
Hog's Back Park **7**
Major's Hill Park **8**
Mooney's Bay Park **9**
New Edinburgh Park **10**
Rideau Falls Park **11**
Rockcliffe Park/
Rockcliffe Rockeries **12**
St. Luke Park **13**
Strathcona Heights Park **14**
Vincent Massey Park **15**

**SUBURBAN
AND RURAL GREENSPACE**
Gatineau Park **16**
Rideau Canal Skateway
(Main 3 Entry Points):
National Arts Centre **17A**
Fifth Avenue & Queen
Elizabeth Drive **17B**
Dow's Lake **17C**

SUNDAY BIKEDAYS
Ottawa River Parkway -----
Colonel By Drive ·········
Rockcliffe Parkway ————

AYLMER

Rue Principale

Aut

Ch. Vanier

*Lac des
Chênes*

Boul. de Lucer

Rivière
Ôt

KANATA

Carling Ave.

Richmond Rd.

C

Queensway

39

41

36

Me
Dr.

23

13

15

32

West Hunt Club Rd.

Richmond Rd.

Woodroffe Ave.

86

11

Greenbank Rd.

59

416

Veteran's
Memorial Hwy.

NEPEAN

Fallowfield Rd.

Moodie Dr.

Cedarview Rd.

12

Fallowfield Rd.

12

59

0   1 Mi
0   1 Km

13

15

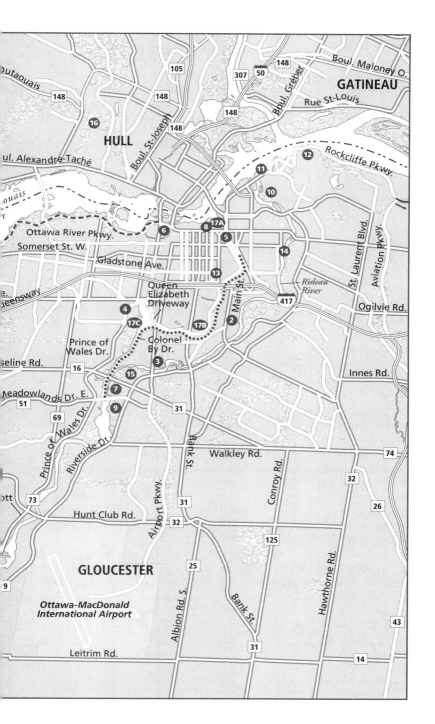

The Origin of Ottawa's Parkways & Pathways

In the 19th century, Ottawa's railways were an essential feature of the landscape. Vast networks of rail tracks crossed the city. Their existence, however, became a real challenge after World War II for the urban planners whose goal was to beautify Canada's capital while reclaiming and preserving the waterway shorelines. In 1950, work began on relocating the railway and converting old rail lines into Ottawa's parkways and pathways. Today, residents and visitors alike can enjoy the beautiful parks, pathways, and roadways of the Ottawa River shore, the Rideau Canal banks, and Dow's Lake. Most pathways are smooth asphalt on flat terrain, so they're terrific for the whole family.

Rideau Falls Park   Located just off Sussex Drive where the Rideau River empties into the Ottawa River, this park is beautifully landscaped. A footbridge spans the Rideau River and the 30-meter (98 ft.) falls are illuminated in the evening. **Canada and the World Pavilion,** which re-opened in 2001 as a permanent attraction, is located in the park.

Rockcliffe Park   Travel east along Sussex Drive just past the prime minister's residence to reach this pretty park, complete with a picnic site and stone shelter. You can take a scenic drive through the park and catch a glimpse of the grand residences in the area.

Rockcliffe Rockeries   Continue a little further east along Rockcliffe Parkway and you'll reach the Rockeries, with their gorgeous show of flowers from spring to fall.

St. Luke Park   At the intersection of Elgin Street and Gladstone Avenue, this park is a great place to hang out after a bout of shopping on Elgin. Sugar Mountain (candy heaven) and Pure Gelato (Italian ice cream), both guaranteed kid pleasers, are close by. There's a paddling pool, playground, and picnic tables.

Strathcona Park   On the south side of Laurier Avenue East, Stretching down to the banks of the Rideau River, beautiful Strathcona Park beckons. Relax on a bench under the huge shade trees and watch the royal swans lazily swim past on a sunny summer afternoon. Odyssey Theatre holds its outdoor summer performances here. There are paved walking paths for easy stroller pushing and an elegant water fountain. Visit the children's play area.

Vincent Massey Park   Located on Heron Road, west of Riverside Drive and just north of Hog's Back Park, Vincent Massey Park is a great place for family reunions and other large gatherings. Amenities include ball diamonds, horseshoe pits, a bandstand, picnic tables, fireplaces, a refreshment pavilion, playing fields, recreational pathways, drinking fountains, and public washrooms. A parking fee is charged from May to October.

Tips

Strathcona Park has a wonderful play area for children. The wading pool, playground, and castle ruins, complete with a slide and animal statuettes, are great fun to explore.

SUBURBAN & RURAL GREEN SPACE

Gatineau Park   This beautiful wilderness area, covering 361 square kilometers (141 sq. miles) in the Gatineau Hills, is under the care of the National Capital Commission. The south entrance to the park is located just across the Ottawa River in Hull, a few minutes' drive from downtown Ottawa. Hiking trails, cycling pathways, mountain-bike trails, cross-country ski trails, sandy beaches, and campgrounds are all located within the park. Your first stop should be the **Gatineau Park Visitor Centre,** at 33 Scott Rd. in Chelsea (*C* **800/465-1867** or 819/827-2020), open every day of the year. For more information on Gatineau Park, see chapter 10, "Exploring the Region."

The Greenbelt   The National Capital Greenbelt covers 200 square kilometers (125 sq. miles) of crescent-shaped land bordering Ottawa to the west, south, and east. A mix of forests, agricultural land, and natural areas, the Greenbelt has several sectors open to the public and accessible from major highways. Moose, beavers, chipmunks, foxes, raccoons, deer, pygmy shrews, rabbits, and squirrels all call this wilderness area home. For directions to specific sites, call the Capital Infocentre (*C* **800/465-1867** or 613/239-5000). Better yet, pick up a copy of the **Greenbelt All Seasons Trail Map,** available at the Infocentre opposite Parliament Hill. If you're venturing into the Greenbelt during bug season, protect yourself with insect repellent or use a bug jacket. Always respect the Greenbelt rules—place all litter in the waste bins provided in parking areas, keep your dog on a leash and pick up after it, and don't walk or snowshoe on cross-country ski tracks in winter.

The **Pine Grove Sector** is a large urban forest with a mixture of natural woods and plantations extending southeast from Hunt Club and Conroy roads. Along the wide, level trails are interpretive panels to help visitors identify more than 20 species of native trees and to explain the principles of modern forest management. **Stony Swamp Sector** has been designated a provincially significant wetland and contains over 700 species of plants and many types of animals. A recently constructed 5-kilometer (3 mile) section of the Trans Canada Trail runs through Stony Swamp, and the Rideau Trail also passes through this sector. In the summer months, the Sarsaparilla Trail in Stony Swamp is universally accessible. You can visit a restored pioneer homestead and working farm at the Log Farm in Stony Swamp (see chapter 6, "What Kids Like to See & Do").

The **Mer Bleue Conservation Area** on the southeastern edge of Ottawa is a unique ecological environment protected by international treaty. The area contains a large peat bog more than 5 meters (16 ft.) deep and a northern boreal forest, a type of forest that is typically found much farther north. If you visit on a cool morning in the spring or fall, you may be lucky enough to witness a bluish-tinged mist hanging over the bog, which gave the area its name (*mer bleue* is French for "blue sea"). There are several trails crossing the area, but the best one for kids and families is the Mer Bleue Interpretative Trail, an easy walk of just over 1 kilometer (0.66 mile) with a boardwalk and information panels. To reach the Interpretative Trail, follow Innes Road to Anderson Road, then go south to Borthwick Ridge Road and follow the signs. Elsewhere in the Greenbelt, during the winter you can go ice fishing on the Ottawa River, accessible from Parking Lot 1 at Shirley's Bay (Range Road north off Carling Avenue). For family tobogganing fun, try Bruce Pit (Parking Lot 12, Cedarview Road off Highway 416 at Hunt Club Road) or Conroy Pit (Parking Lot 15, south of Hunt Club Road on Conroy Road).

2 Playing Indoors

WHEN YOU WANT TO GET WET

Community Indoor Pools   For information on municipally owned and operated indoor pools, call ℂ **613/580-2400.**

Gloucester Splash Wave Pool   All ages. Easy to reach from downtown and the eastern end of Ottawa, Gloucester Splash Wave Pool is good, clean fun. A sloping entry to the wave pool makes playing in the waves almost as exciting for kids as being on a natural beach. There's also a 34-meter-high (112 ft.) water slide with its own landing pool, designed to reduce the risk of injury. A separate toddler pool with spray jets and toys keeps the little ones happy. There are plenty of deck chairs around the pool area, and a solarium is tucked to one side. During the summer, kids can play in a small outdoor playground, accessible from inside the building. There are water sprays and sprinklers, and a shallow stream, equipped with water wheels and dams that children can operate, winds its way around the play area. Family changing rooms are available. Bring your own towels and locks.

2040 Ogilvie Rd. ℂ 613/748-4222. Admission C$20 (US$13) family of 4. Take Trans Canada Hwy. 17 east from downtown for 5km (3 miles), exit at St. Laurent Blvd., and go north to Ogilvie Rd.

WHEN YOU WANT TO STAY DRY

Cosmic Adventures   Ages 0 to 12. If you've been blessed with a high-energy brood, head out to Cosmic Adventures and dare the little darlings to tire themselves out. One of Canada's largest indoor children's playgrounds, this 1,850-square meter (20,000 sq. ft.) playground has a four-level soft-play structure where kids can bounce, crawl, slide, climb, and swing. Features include tunnels, mazes, obstacle courses, ball pits, slides, and more. Structures are padded and there are no sharp corners. Children must wear socks at all times. There is a separate play area for toddlers where they can learn about colors, shapes, and sizes and improve their hand–eye coordination by playing with educational and developmental toys. In addition to the playground, there's a craft room, game room, theater, and restaurant. Cosmic Adventures is open daily from 9am to 8:30pm. The environment is smoke-free and the premises are wheelchair accessible. All children must be supervised by an adult aged 18 years or over. Call for admission rates.

1373 Ogilvie Rd. ℂ 613/742-8989. Take Trans Canada Hwy. 17 east from downtown for 5km (3 miles), exit at St. Laurent Blvd. and go north to Ogilvie Rd.

Cyberdome   Ages 5 & up. This high-tech play place is nicely situated in a major shopping mall. Do a little shopping, take the kids to Cyberdome for half an hour, do a little more shopping … you get the idea. You'll find lots of variety here. LaserForce laser tag is one of the games offered, with a choice of playing individually or in teams, and there are four other shoot-em-up games in the dark. The Power Tower is a 13.5-meter (45 ft.) climbing wall, which can be scaled by kids ages 5 and up. Climbers can choose from beginner, intermediate, or advanced paths up the wall and receive instruction from staff. Big and little kids will love racing on the downhill ski simulators, skateboard simulators, motorbikes, and Super GT racing cars. Play the latest arcade games and the old favorites like air hockey, or try out the multiplayer gaming stations. Climb into a personal motion simulator and fly a famous World War II airplane, or test-fly a new top-secret jet and experience computer-generated animation. Try out a stand-up virtual reality game, where you and a partner enter an alien metropolis and battle mean city streets to prevent an invasion of Earth.

1200 St. Laurent Blvd., St. Laurent Shopping Centre, Lower Level. ✆ 613/742-6540. Min. C$5 (US$3.30) game card. Take Trans Canada Hwy. 17 east from downtown for 5km (3 miles); exit at St. Laurent Blvd.

Gymboree Ages 0 to 5. Gymboree offers active play and music programs for infants and children under 5. The name of the game is parent participation. Each child must be accompanied by at least one adult at all classes (with the exception of "GymPairs," which allows two children under 5), and the adult must directly supervise the child at all times. Older siblings who are not enrolled cannot be brought to classes. Programs are generally 12 weeks in length, but there is a weekly PlayGym, designed as unstructured gym time, on Wednesdays from 2 to 4pm. Call for information on programs and fees. Regular classes are 45 minutes long. If you want to visit a complimentary preview class to see what all the fun is about, give them a call.

3825 Richmond Rd. ✆ 613/721-3400. PlayGym C$6.50 (US$4.30). Membership C$25 (US$17) one-time fee.

Midway Family Fun Park All ages. Located across the road from the Canada Science and Technology Museum, this fun park offers 2,200 square meters (24,000 sq. ft.) of noise and excitement for kids of all ages. Admission to the site is free, and you pay only for the rides and games you play. The family packages work out to be a little cheaper than buying all the tickets separately. There's a toddler play center just for little ones. Preschoolers and older will enjoy the nine-hole miniature golf course, set in a tropical landscape with waterfalls and flowers, as well as the large jungle gym with balls, tunnels, slides, tubes, and a bounce area. For family fun, try out the bowling lanes. There are even good old-fashioned bumper cars—eight mid-sized cars for drivers 1.1 meters (3 ft. 3 in.) tall and over. In addition, the midway has more than 100 arcade games, including skateboard and ski simulators, racing cars, pinball, air hockey, and foosball. Players who participate in skill games earn tickets that they can trade at the prize counter for items ranging from penny candies and small toys to bicycles and TVs.

2370 Lancaster Rd. ✆ 613/526-0343. Free general admission. Mini-golf C$2.75 (US$1.80), jungle gym C$5 (US$3), bumper cars C$2.75 (US$1.80), game tokens 25¢. Family packages available.

3 Sports & Games

BEACHES

Along the banks of the Ottawa River and the Rideau River, there are a number of beaches to cool off on a hot summer's day. Sandy shores abound, and there are usually washrooms, changing rooms, and snack bars nearby. Supervised swimming is available at Britannia Bay, Mooney's Bay, and Westboro beaches in the city of Ottawa. Water quality is checked regularly, and beaches may occasionally be closed for a brief period, usually after heavy rainfall. For water-quality updates and general information on beaches within the city, call ✆ 613/244-5678. You can get to **Britannia Bay,** on the Ottawa River, by following Richmond Road to Britannia Road or by traveling on the Ottawa River bike path. For **Mooney's Bay Park,** on the banks of the Rideau River, drive along Riverside Drive just north of Walkley Road, or take the Colonel By Drive bike path to Hog's Back, cross Meadowlands Drive, and take the path through the marina. You'll find **Westboro Beach** on the south shore of the Ottawa River, off the Ottawa River Parkway at Kitchissippi Lookout (west of the Champlain Bridge).

Just a short drive from the city you can visit **Baxter Conservation Area,** south of Kars on Dilworth Road (ⓒ **613/489-3592**), which has a beach on the Rideau River. The refreshing lakes of **Gatineau Park** (ⓒ **819/827-2020**) are open for public swimming from mid-June to early September. The park has five public beaches, located at Philippe, Meech, and La Pêche Lakes. Lifeguards are on duty daily from 10am to 6pm; swimming in the park is prohibited at other times. Swimming is also available in **Lac Beauchamp,** at **Parc du Lac Beauchamp,** 745 bd. Maloney, Gatineau, PQ (ⓒ **819/669-2548**).

BOATING

If you want to spend a lazy summer afternoon drifting around in a boat, visit Dow's Lake Pavilion, 1001 Queen Elizabeth Dr. (ⓒ **613/232-1001** general information, or 613/232-5278 marina). A fully operational marina at the pavilion site on Dow's Lake rents out paddle boats and canoes. Dow's Lake is an artificial lake that provides a quiet place for water recreation away from the main traffic in the Rideau Canal. If you cross the Ottawa River to Hull Marina, you can rent personal water craft, jet boats, fishing boats, and pontoon boats by the hour, day, or weekend at Location Moto Marine Outaouais, 71-B rue Jean Proulx, Hull, PQ (ⓒ **819/595-0909**). Boats are also available for rental at Gatineau Park. For boat rentals at Philippe Lake and Taylor Lake, call ⓒ **819/456-3555;** for La Pêche Lake, call ⓒ **819/456-3494.** If you like your outdoor activities wet 'n' wild, check out the white-water rafting adventure companies listed in chapter 10, "Exploring the Region."

BOWLING

On a rainy afternoon, you might like to spend an hour or two at a local bowling alley. Call ahead to book a lane; bowling leagues and children's birthday parties can take up a lot of lanes. The following bowling alleys have bumper bowling available for kids, which means the gutters are padded to prevent the ball from rolling into them. Everyone can knock down some pins and get on the scoreboard, even if their aim is a little off-kilter. When you call to book, ask for the lane to be set up with bumper pads if you have kids under 8, or thereabouts. Ask for five-pin bowling, since the ten-pin balls are too heavy for children to pick up and roll. And if you haven't been to a bowling alley since you were a kid yourself, you'll be glad to know that the scoring is computerized these days. **Kent Bowling Lanes** is opposite the bus terminal at 270 Catherine St. (ⓒ **613/232-0379**). **McArthur Lanes** is on the east side of the Rideau River at 175 McArthur Rd. (ⓒ **613/745-2117**). **West Park Bowling,** 1205 Wellington St. W. (ⓒ **613/728-0933**), has 14 computerized five-pin lanes and a family-style diner on the premises, **Fil's Diner,** open for breakfast, lunch, and dinner. In the south end of the city, **Merivale Bowling Centre,** 1916 Merivale Rd. (ⓒ **613/228-9190**), has 48 five-pin lanes.

CYCLING AND IN-LINE SKATING

Ottawa and its environs offer a comprehensive network of pathways and parkways where people can bike and in-line skate through beautiful natural scenery. In addition, there are designated bicycle lanes on a number of city streets. No wonder Ottawa has the highest per capita population of cyclists in Canada.

> **Fact** **A Cyclists' Dream Come True**
>
> Did you know that there are more than 370 kilometers (230 miles) of major bike routes and 273 kilometers (170 miles) of minor routes in the new City of Ottawa?

If you didn't bring your own equipment, **Rent-A-Bike,** at 1 Rideau St. (in the underground parking lot of the Fairmont Château Laurier) (✆ **613/241-4140**), has a professionally equipped workshop, bicycle store, and rental service. They have all kinds of bikes, including standard hybrid bikes designed for comfortable, leisurely touring, standard light-trail mountain bikes, on-road and off-road performance bikes, and on-road tandems. You can add a two-seat trailer for infants and toddlers or a one-seat trail-a-bike for 3- to 5-year-olds to your rental bike. In-line skates are also available. Daily bike rentals are C$23 to C$50 (US$15 to $33). Prices include taxes, a helmet, a lock, and a map. Self-guided bicycle tours and escorted tours (for groups of six or more) are available. **Cyco's,** at 5 Hawthorne Ave. (by the canal at Pretoria Bridge) (✆ **613/567-8180**), also rents out bicycles and in-line skates.

OCTranspo, Ottawa's public transit system, has installed **bike racks** on more than 150 buses—most buses on routes 2, 95, and 97 have racks. Each rack holds two bikes and is designed to make loading and unloading quick and easy. There's no cost to use the rack, other than regular bus fare. The program runs from spring through fall.

Use common sense when riding your bike or in-line skating, and be sure to follow the specific rules for cyclists. All cyclists under 18 must wear a **bicycle helmet.** Cyclists cannot ride on the sidewalk and must not exceed speeds of 20kmph (12.5 mph) per hour on multiuse pathways. Pass only when it is safe to do so, and use your bell or voice to let others know you're about to pass. Be considerate of other road or pathway users, and whether you're skating or cycling, always keep to the right.

If you're in the vicinity of the Rideau Centre and the ByWard Market, you can **park** your bike at a supervised facility. Located at Rideau and William streets, the facility operates daily 8:30am to 5:30pm, from Victoria Day until Labour Day weekend (third Saturday in May to first Monday in September). The maximum charge is C$2 (US$1.30).

For **maps** of the pathways and more information, head to the **Capital Infocentre,** opposite Parliament Hill at 90 Wellington St. (✆ **800/465-1867** or 613/239-5000).

> **Tips** **Park so You can Bike**
>
> If you're driving to the parkways to cycle, skate, or walk, here are a few good places to park.
> * For the **Rockcliffe Parkway,** park at the Aviation Museum.
> * For the **Ottawa River Parkway,** park at Lincoln Fields Shopping Centre, 2525 Carling Ave., or Kitchissippi Lookout off the Ottawa River Pkwy.
> * For the Rideau Canal, park along side streets in the Glebe.

Sunday Bikedays

In the summer, Sunday mornings present a real treat for lovers of the outdoors in Ottawa. No less than 65 kilometers (41 miles) of parkways in Ottawa and Gatineau Park are reserved exclusively for walking, running, cycling, in-line skating, and other non-motorized recreational activities. Motor traffic is banned. In Ottawa the motor-free period runs from 9am to 1pm. In Gatineau Park, there are 40 kilometers (25 miles) of hilly roadways to hike, bike, or skate from 6am to noon. **Sunday Bikedays** are sponsored by local radio stations and businesses. Many local organizations provide volunteers to supervise start and end points and crossings every Sunday morning during the event.

In Ottawa, there are three motor traffic–free areas for the event, all of which are fully accessible to people with disabilities. The **Ottawa River Parkway,** located on the south side of the Ottawa River just west of downtown, has a 9-kilometer (6 mile) stretch beginning at the Mill restaurant and continuing to Carling Avenue. If you drive to this section, park your vehicle at the Lincoln Fields Shopping Centre at Carling Avenue. Beginning at the Laurier Bridge, you can enjoy **Colonel By Drive** as it winds its way along the east side of the Rideau Canal to Hog's Back Bridge, a total distance of 8 kilometers (5 miles). Park your car on one of the side streets to access Colonel By Drive. **Rockcliffe Parkway** is another choice for the Sunday morning excursion. Just east of downtown, and running along the southern shore of the Ottawa River, is an 8-kilometer (5 mile) section between the Canada Aviation Museum and St. Joseph Boulevard. Parking is available at the Canada Aviation Museum.

For information about the Sunday Bikeday program, visit the **Capital Infocentre,** at 90 Wellington St. (✆ **800/465-1867** or 613/239-5000), or call the **Gatineau Park Visitor Centre** (✆ **819/827-2020**).

CROSS-COUNTRY SKIING

You're spoiled for choice for cross-country skiing in the Ottawa area. If you want to use the trails throughout the extensive **Greenbelt,** consult the **Greenbelt All Seasons Trail Map.** Or come to **Mooney's Bay Park,** 2960 Riverside Dr. (✆ **613/247-4883**) and ski on 5 kilometers (3 miles) of groomed and well-lit trails. Classic and skate skiing are available for a mere C$2 (US$1.30) per day or C$25 (US$17) for a season's pass. Across the Ottawa River in the city of **Gatineau,** you'll find **Parc Du Lac Beauchamp.** Winter activities in the park include outdoor ice skating and cross-country skiing. For information on Lac Beauchamp, call ✆ **819/243-4343.**

For the ultimate cross-country ski experience, visit **Gatineau Park.** The park has earned a reputation as one of the greatest ski-trail networks in North America for its remarkable 200 kilometers (125 miles) of trails, which are well maintained using the latest technology. The level of difficulty is marked on each trail, enabling skiers of all abilities to enjoy the meadows, valleys, and forests of the park. Both skiing styles are accommodated throughout the park, so you can glide along in classic Nordic fashion or burn up energy with the skate-skiing technique. There are eight heated shelters where you can stop to rest and refuel with a snack from your backpack. Gatineau Park ski patrollers are on watch to assist skiers in difficulty. When you arrive at the park, you can buy a day pass at each of the 16 parking lots, which give direct access to the ski trails, or at the **Gatineau Park Visitor Centre,** 33 Scott Rd., Chelsea, QC (© **819/827-2020**), open throughout the year, daily from 9am to 5pm. Weekday pass prices for cross-country ski trails are C$7 (US$4.50) for adults, C$4.50 (US$3) for seniors and youths, free for children 12 and under, C$18 (US$12) per family (2 adults and 3 teens). Weekend prices are C$8 (US$5) for adults, C$5 (US$3) for seniors and youths, and free for children 12 and under.

Always carry a map when in wilderness areas. When you arrive at the park, pick up the Gatineau Park official winter trail map from the visitor centre. The map costs C$5 (US$3) and is available on waterproof paper for C$10 (US$7). A new winter trail map has recently been produced through GIS technology, drawn to scale and including contour lines, magnetic north orientation, and exact representation of the trails. Depicted on the map are ski trails, winter hiking trails, snowshoe trails, huts, and shelters. Because skiing and weather conditions change frequently, Gatineau Park reviews and updates ski condition information three times daily.

FISHING

Fishing with a **license** is permitted in the **Gatineau Park** lakes (Philippe Lake, Meech Lake, and La Pêche Lake). **Mulvihill Lake,** near the Mackenzie King Estate, has a fishing jetty designed to accommodate wheelchairs. There are many classes of fishing license available, from a day to a year and longer. Ontario residents, other Canadian residents, and nonresidents all receive different licenses. **Access Ontario,** in the Rideau Centre (© **613/238-3630**), provides licenses, as well as a list of Ottawa-area merchants that sell them.

HIKING

Besides the pathways and trails through many of the city parks and the Greenbelt area, as discussed earlier in this chapter, you might wish to explore Gatineau Park, the Rideau Trail, and parts of the Trans Canada Trail, particularly if you're looking for more challenging, longer routes.

The **Rideau Trail** is a cleared and marked hiking trail, approximately 300 kilometers (185 miles) long, linking the city of Kingston, on the shores of Lake Ontario, with Ottawa. The trail path is indicated by orange triangular markers. To distinguish the two directions, Kingston-bound markers have yellow tips. The path crosses varied terrain, ranging from gentle agricultural land to the rugged Canadian Shield. The trail is designated for walking, cross-country skiing, and snowshoeing. You can pick up a guidebook with maps and a description of the trail from the **Rideau Trail Association,** P.O. Box 15, Kingston, ON K7L 4V6 (© **613/545-0823**). You'll also find the guidebook in major outdoor expedition stores in Ottawa, at the Scout Shop, 1345 Baseline Rd. and at A World of Maps, 1235 Wellington St. (see chapter 9, "Shopping with Your Kids," for details on these and other stores). Call the store of your choice before you make a special trip, as they may not always have the book on hand.

The **Trans Canada Trail** is a recreational trail currently under construction that will traverse Canada from coast to coast and cross every province and territory. In the Ottawa area, sections of the Trans Canada Trail can be found in **Gatineau Park, Hull,** the **National Capital Greenbelt,** and the **Ottawa River**

Parkway. The trail is signposted with trail markers featuring the Trans Canada Trail logo. For more information, call ✆ **800/465-3636** or visit www.tctrail.ca.

For information on hiking in **Gatineau Park,** see "Hull, Gatineau & the Outaouais Hills" in chapter 10, "Exploring the Region."

 The Trans Canada Trail

The **Trans Canada Trail,** currently under construction, is a recreational trail that will link Canada from coast to coast. At approximately 17,250 kilometers (10,700 miles) in length when completed, it will be the longest trail of its kind in the world.

Where practical, the trail is designated as a shared-use pathway with five core activities permitted: walking, cycling, horseback riding, cross-country skiing, and snowmobiling. Wherever possible, existing trails are used, provided they can accommodate these multiple uses. In addition, some provincial and federal park property, Crown land, abandoned railway lines, and rights-of-way on private land will become part of the trail.

The trail truly belongs to Canadians. Local organizations in communities across the country own, operate, and maintain their own segments, and more than 1.5 million volunteers are taking part in the project.

About half of the trail is already accessible, and it's expected that it will be substantially complete by late 2005. In some areas, it's virtually completed, but other sections still require a significant amount of work, so you won't find a final set of maps yet. Atlantic Canada's trail network is quite advanced, and this will be the first region to be mapped. In the fall of 2001, the Trans Canada Trail Foundation is scheduled to launch its first guidebook, focusing on Newfoundland, and in 2002, it will release a second guidebook covering the remaining Atlantic provinces.

In the Ottawa area, you'll find sections of the trail in **Gatineau Park, Hull,** the **National Capital Greenbelt,** and the **Ottawa River Parkway**—you can spot them by the trail markers with the Trans Canada Trail logo. For more information on the Trans Canada Trail, call ✆ **800/465-3636** or visit www.tctrail.ca.

ICE SKATING

The number one place to skate in the nation's capital is the world-famous Rideau Canal. If you visit Ottawa during the skating season, you must take everyone for a glide along the canal—it's an experience not to be missed. The **Rideau Canal Skateway** is the world's longest skating rink, offering almost 8 kilometers (5 miles) of continuous skating surface. The ice is usually ready in late December, and the season lasts until late February or early March. During the first three weekends in February, the Rideau Canal becomes the heart of **Winterlude,** Ottawa's winter festival. Skating is free. Heated shelters, skate and sled rentals, boot-check and skate-sharpening services, rest areas, food concessions, and toilets are located at various points along the Skateway. There are 35 access points along the canal for skating, so it's easy to get on the ice. To find out about ice conditions on the Rideau Canal, call the **Skateway Hotline** at ✆ **613/239-5234.**

For a special treat, visit the grounds of **Rideau Hall**, residence of the governor general, and skate on the historic outdoor rink built by Lord and Lady Dufferin in 1873. The rink is open to the public on weekends from noon to 5pm and reserved for organized groups on weekdays from noon to 8pm and weekends from 5 to 8pm. The rink opens in early January each year (weather permitting).

In **Brewer Park,** accessible from Hopewell Avenue near Bronson Avenue, there's a speed-skating oval that is open to the public. **Brantwood Park,** at Onslow Crescent between Elliot Avenue and Clegg Street, has a series of outdoor rinks connected by paths of ice so you can skate from one to another. Across the Ottawa River in the city of Gatineau, you'll find **Parc Du Lac Beauchamp.** Winter activities in the park include outdoor ice skating and cross-country skiing. For information on Lac Beauchamp call ℂ **819/243-4343.**

More than 70 outdoor skating rinks are scattered throughout the city. Pleasure skating, lessons, carnivals, and hockey are enthusiastically enjoyed at these sites. For the outdoor rink closest to you, and to find out the times of family pleasure skating at indoor arenas throughout the region, call the **Parks Seasonal Programs** at ℂ **613/244-5300,** ext. 3500.

 The Rideau Canal Skateway

- The Skateway is visited by more than one million skaters every year.
- Staff work around the clock to maintain the ice surface.
- Many residents use the Skateway to commute to work and school every day.
- The Skateway ice surface area is equivalent to 20 Olympic-size ice rinks.
- The average length of the skating season on the canal is 52 days.
- The shortest season was 30 days, and the longest was 90 days.
- A system of colored flags indicates the ice conditions: red = closed, yellow = fair to good, green = very good to excellent.

SWIMMING
You have a choice of riverbank beaches, municipal pools, and state-of-the-art wave pools. See "Beaches," earlier in this section, and "When You Want to Get Wet," earlier in this chapter.

TENNIS
If your kids are into tennis, the following courts are open to the public. Call ahead to book a court time. **Elmdale Tennis Club** is located close to downtown at 184 Holland Ave. ℂ **613/729-3644.** The **Ottawa New Edinburgh Club** provides affordable sporting facilities for its members and the community. Seven European-style, red clay courts are available. The club is located at 504 Rockcliffe Pkwy. ℂ **613/746-8540.** Public tennis courts can also be found at the **RA Centre,** 2451 Riverside Dr. ℂ **613/733-5100.** The **West Ottawa Tennis Club** is located in Brittania Park at the corner of Pinecrest Road and Carling Avenue (ℂ **613/828-7622**). During the summer season (May 1 to September 30), ten clay courts and three hard courts are open. The rest of the year, play is available on six clay courts. Instruction for all levels is available.

Tips Downtown Snowboarding

For loads of winter fun right in the city, visit **Carlington Snowpark,** at 941 Clyde Ave. 🕐 **613/729-9206.** Go tubing or snowboarding and get a comfortable ride back up the hill. There are 10 slides to choose from, with night illumination and machine grooming. Hourly passes are available.

---

4 Classes & Workshops

Children's classes and workshops are plentiful in the Ottawa area and are provided by the City of Ottawa and private businesses. Dance classes include African drum, ballet, baton, belly dancing, break dancing, creative movement, Highland dance, hip hop, jazz, step dancing, swing, and tap dancing. Music instruction is available for all kinds of instruments and for voice. Visual arts include carpentry, cartooning, drawing, jewelry making, painting, and pottery. Sports instruction and participation is available for just about any indoor or outdoor sport you can think of. In fact, there are so many activities offered for children that you could easily overschedule—a common complaint of parents these days. Our family limits our children's organized leisure activities and deliberately builds "free time" into our family schedule, but there are lots of families out there who just can't resist giving everything a try. Just make sure you strike a balance between stimulation and relaxation. Life should be enjoyed, not rushed through at a frantic pace.

If you're just visiting the city or you're looking for a drop-in activity, check out the museums around town. Most of them schedule workshops and children's programs on weekends and during school breaks, with themes related to the exhibits in their institutions. You and your kids will learn something new and have fun at the same time.

8

Entertainment for the
Whole Family

Ottawa enjoys a large federal arts presence and vibrant local culture. The lion's share of events takes place during the summer months, when the weather is warm and the number of visitors peaks. Whether your passion is theater, dance, music, film, spectator sports, or festivals, Canada's capital delivers.

FINDING OUT WHAT'S ON   For information about Ottawa's entertainment, pick up a copy of *Where,* a free monthly guide listing entertainment, shopping, and dining, available at hotels and stores in the city. Also keep an eye out for *Capital Parent,* a free monthly newspaper, *Ottawa Families,* a free bimonthly newspaper, *Ottawa City Magazine,* and *Ottawa Life* magazine. The *Ottawa Citizen* has a comprehensive Arts section on Fridays, with an emphasis on films; a special Going Out section on Saturdays, which lists upcoming live entertainment events; and a list of community activities for the coming week on the back page of Sunday's A section, with an emphasis on family events. For news and information about regional arts events and activities, drop in to **Arts Court,** 2 Daly Ave. (© **613/564-7240**), or call the **Council for the Arts in Ottawa (CAO)** (© **613/569-1387**).

GETTING TICKETS   Tickets to events at the **Corel Centre** and the **National Arts Centre** are sold at the on-site box offices or through **Ticketmaster** (Sportsline © **613/755-1166;** other events © **613/755-1111;** www.ticketmaster.ca). You can also visit the Ticketmaster box office at 112 Kent St. Monday to Friday from 9am to 5:30pm and Saturday from 9:30am to 1:30pm. Ticketmaster handles ticket sales for numerous venues. Also see the individual listings in this chapter.

SPECIAL EVENTS   Ottawa frequently hosts large sports and entertainment events, so check with the **Ottawa Tourism and Convention Authority** (www.tourottawa.org) or **National Capital Commission,** 40 Elgin St., Ottawa ON, K1P 1C7 (© **800/465-1867** or 613/239-5555; www.capcan.com) for special events scheduled during your visit. In February 2001, for example, the **Nokia Brier** Men's Curling Championship was held in Ottawa. In the summer of the same year, Ottawa played host to 3,000 athletes and artists from over 50 French-speaking nations who took part in the athletic and cultural competitions of the **IV Games of La Francophonie.**

1 The Big Venues

Centrepointe Theatre Featuring a unique blend of community and professional programming, the Centrepointe Theatre is home to the productions of many community groups, including the Nepean Choir, the Canadian Showcase Chorus, the Nepean All-City Jazz Band, Les Petits Ballets, the Nepean Concert Band, the Savoy Society, and the Orpheus Musical Theatre Society. Liona Boyd, Christopher Plummer, and Peter Ustinov have stood in the spotlight. Four spots are reserved for guests in wheelchairs on the orchestra level, and you can make special arrangements to accommodate larger groups. An audio-loop system for the hearing impaired is also available. To arrange for special seating, please specify your needs to the box-office attendant when purchasing tickets. Parking is free. Ben Franklin Place, 101 Centrepointe Dr. ℂ **613/727-6650.**

The Corel Centre This 18,500-seat multipurpose sports and entertainment complex, formerly known as the Palladium, opened its doors in January 1996. Home of the **Ottawa Senators** NHL team and the **Ottawa Rebel** lacrosse team, this complex hosts various sporting and entertainment events. Children under 2 do not require a ticket if they sit on the accompanying adult's lap. This rule may vary depending on the event, so check with the Corel Centre box office to confirm. Note that the view from Row A in every section may be obstructed for children owing to the placement of security bars. There are 170 seating spaces for people with disabilities on the Club and Main Concourse levels, as well as four elevators. If you require special seating, mention this when purchasing your tickets. There are more than 140 concession stands on the two public concourses, plus a Hard Rock Café, Marshy's Bar-B-Q and Grill, the Penalty Box Restaurant, and the Silver Seven Brew House. Official Ottawa Senators merchandise can be purchased at Sensations, located at Gate 1. **OC Transpo** (ℂ **613/741-4390**) provides direct bus service from Transitway stations across the city to all Senators games and most other events. Free parking is provided at five Park & Ride lots. The Corel Centre is a smoke-free building.

Landsdowne Park This large facility hosts hundreds of events annually, including trade and consumer shows, family entertainment, rock concerts, junior hockey tournaments, national and international athletic competitions, and the Central Canada Exhibition. A number of exhibition halls are on-site, as is the 10,000 seat **Civic Centre,** home of the Ontario Hockey League **Ottawa 67's.** 1015s Bank St. ℂ **613/580-2429** for general information; ℂ **613/232-6767** for information on the Ottawa 67's.

National Arts Centre Situated in the heart of the city, across from Confederation Square and Parliament Hill, the NAC is one of the largest performing arts complexes in Canada. Home to the internationally acclaimed 46-member National Arts Centre Orchestra, this center also stages a wide variety of performances on its four stages, including English and French theater, dance, music, and community programming. Children under 2 are admitted to children's shows at the lowest ticket price for that particular event, but they must sit on a parent's lap. For events other than children's shows, all patrons pay regular price. The NAC is fully accessible to guests with disabilities and provides special tickets for patrons in wheelchairs; all accessible seating can be booked through Ticketmaster (ℂ **613/755-1111**). Underground parking is available; entrances are located on Elgin Street (at the corner of Slater Street) and on Albert Street.

The largest of the four performing halls, **Southam Hall** hosts Broadway musicals, ballets, operas, musical acts, lectures, ceremonies, films, orchestral music, and other entertainment and corporate events. **Theatre Hall** is ideal for plays, musicals, seminars, conferences, films, chamber music, and other musical events, this stage also presents numerous Stratford Festival productions. Musicals such as Crazy for You have been showcased here. **Studio Hall** is a versatile venue has a capacity of 250 to 300, depending on the seating arrangement, and hosts performances, corporate seminars, and presentations. **The Fourth Stage** is a multipurpose performance space for community programming, including dance, music, storytelling, choral singing, and theater, the Fourth Stage can accommodate various stage configurations and seats up to 150. 53 Elgin St. ℂ 613/947-7000. For tickets visit the NAC box office or call Ticketmaster at ℂ **613/755-1111**.

Ottawa Congress Centre   This meeting facility hosts large-scale conventions and trade and consumer shows. The center includes the 600-square-meter (66,000 sq. ft.) Congress Hall and the Colonel By Salon, with floor-to-ceiling windows overlooking the Rideau Canal. Rooftop terraces also offer views of downtown Ottawa. Direct access to the Rideau Centre is provided. 55 Colonel By Dr. ℂ **613/563-1984**.

WordPerfect Theatre   For smaller events, the WordPerfect Theatre provides seating for 2,500 to 7,400 people. An automated retractable curtain system divides the arena in half. 1000 Palladium Dr. ℂ **613/599-0123**. For sports tickets call Ticketmaster Sportsline at ℂ **613/755-1166**; for other events call Ticketmaster at ℂ **613/755-1111**, or visit any Ticketmaster outlet or the Corel Centre box office (Gate 1).

2 Seasonal Events

Ottawa hosts numerous annual events, festivals, and celebrations. The city is often chosen to host special sports and arts events. Here's a selection of some annual festivals. Also see the calendar of events in chapter 2, "Planning a Family Trip to Ottawa."

Carnival of Cultures   Ottawa's international folkloric festival features music, song, and dance from around the world, held at the picturesque outdoor Astrolabe Theatre (by the National Gallery). Free for children under 12. Mid-June. ℂ **613/742-6553**.

Central Canada Exhibition   The Ex provides wholesome family entertainment at a great price, combining interactive theme exhibits, agricultural programs, performances, and a large midway with over 60 rides, including a roller coaster. Mid-August. ℂ **613/237-7222**.

Cisco Systems Bluesfest   Over 100 artists perform at Canada's biggest blues festival. Mid-July. ℂ **613/247-1188**.

CKCU Ottawa Folk Festival   This event celebrates Canada's rich folk tradition with music, dance, storytelling, and crafts. The main stage presents evening concerts by some of Canada`s finest acoustic musicians, and afternoon musical stages feature songwriting, Ottawa Valley fiddling and step-dancing, Celtic music, and vocal harmonics. A fun-filled family area offers crafts, activities, costumes, and children`s performers. Late August. ℂ **613/230-8234**.

Dragon Boat Festival   Watch the dragon boat racing on Mooney's Bay and be entertained by a variety of multicultural performances, visual displays, culinary arts, and other activities for the entire family. Free admission. Late June. *©* **613/238-7711.**

Festival 4–15　(Ottawa Festival of the Arts for Young Audiences). Formerly known as the Children's Festival, in 2001 this annual event received a new name as well as a new venue, the Canada Science and Technology Museum. The festival offers various children's activities, including arts and crafts, busker performances, and Canadian and international children's theater company productions. Early June. *©* **613/241-0999.**

Gatineau Hot Air Balloon Festival　Canada's largest balloon festival is held on Labour Day weekend. Around 150 hot-air balloons, plenty of shows and activities, fairground rides, and a dazzling fireworks display are some of the attractions. Early September. *©* **800/668-8383** or 819/243-2331.

Ottawa International Jazz Festival　Thousands enjoy listening to some of the world's best jazz musicians in intimate studio spaces and open-air venues throughout the downtown area. Mid-July. *©* **613/241-2633.**

The Ottawa Chamber Music Festival　North America's largest chamber music festival and one of Canada's most respected cultural events features the finest musicians from across Canada, the United States, and Europe. Some of the most beautiful churches in downtown Ottawa host 78 concerts over 2 weeks. July/August. *©* **800/267-8378** or 613/234-8008.

The Sparks Street Mall International Busker Festival　This is the second-largest busker festival in Canada. Jugglers, comedians, storytellers, fire-eaters, mimes, musicians, and magicians entertain from morning to night. Early August. *©* **613/230-0984.**

3 Theater

Many of Ottawa's theater offerings are geared toward adult audiences, although older children will enjoy selected productions. Some companies produce an annual family-friendly show.

Tips　**Start them early...**

For theater suitable for younger children check out the summer festivals, many of which offer children's entertainment.

NATIONAL ARTS CENTRE PRESENTATIONS

NAC English Theatre　The NAC English Theatre develops, produces, and presents an English-language theater program locally, as well as co-producing plays with theater companies in other Canadian centers. The season consists of a five-play Mainstage series; a three-play alternative Studio series; special presentations; family, youth, and education activities; and a new play development program. The plays that make up the season range from the classics to new Canadian works. The Family Theatre Series presents three plays in the studio on Saturday and Sunday afternoons in the winter and on Saturday evenings during the rest of the year. During the Christmas season, the NAC stages a special family holiday play, presenting *The Secret Garden* in 2000. **NAC French Theatre**

features a variety of French-language productions, including the Petits-Trots series for ages 4 and up and the Grands-Galops series for ages 7 and up. Performing at the NAC, 35 Elgin St. ✆ **613/947-7000**. For tickets visit the NAC box office or call Ticketmaster at ✆ **613/755-1111**. Ticket prices vary.

Opera Lyra Ottawa Ottawa's resident opera company performs in the NAC, staging three operas between September and April. Their holiday-season production, presented in cooperation with the University of Ottawa and performed at Taboret Hall, is suitable for all ages and features Sunday matinees. Past productions include *Hansel and Gretel* and *Cinderella*. Performing at the NAC, 35 Elgin St., and Taboret Hall, University of Ottawa, 550 Cumberland St. ✆ **613/233-9200**. For tickets call Ticketmaster at ✆ **613/755-1111**. Ticket prices vary.

LOCAL THEATER GROUPS

A Company of Fools Founded in 1990, the company's aim is to make Shakespeare entertaining and accessible. Initially, the troupe rehearsed and acted out Shakespearean scenes on the street. Audiences respond to their unique brand of high-energy performance, classical text, and modern slapstick. In 2001, the company performed at the Ottawa Fringe Festival and also presented "Shakespeare Under the Stars," featuring scenes, sonnets, and songs in various parks in the Ottawa region, beneath the night sky. Performing at various locations. ✆ **613/863-7529** booking hotline.

Dramamuse Since 1989, this resident theater company in the Canadian Museum of Civilization has been entertaining visitors. By performing short plays and playing colorful historical characters who mingle with visitors and interpret the museum exhibits, Dramamuse brings the museum to life for young and old. Performing at the Canadian Museum of Civilization, 100 Laurier St., Hull. ✆ **800/555-5621** or 819/776-7000.

Festival 4–15 Part of the Ottawa Festival of the Arts for Young Audiences, Festival 4–15 brings in theatre groups from around the world to entertain children in Ottawa during their summer festival (held at the Museum of Science and Technology in 2001, but the venue has not been confirmed yet for 2002 and beyond). For winter 2001, performances will be held in the theater at the Canadian Museum of Civilization. Call the information number for current information. Visit their website at www.ottawachildrensfestival.ca and sign up for free updates on their programming. Canada Science and Technology Museum, 1867 St. Laurent Blvd. ✆ **613/241-0999**. Canadian Museum of Civilization, 100 Laurier St., Hull, QC. ✆ **800/555-5621** or 819/776-7000.

Great Canadian Theatre Company The GCTC has provided bold, innovative, and thought-provoking theater to Ottawa audiences for more than a quarter of a century. Programming is predominantly aimed at adult audiences, but student tickets are available, so call ahead to find out about the suitability of a particular performance for family viewing. The season runs from September to March. Performing at 910 Gladstone Ave. ✆ **613/236-5196**. Tickets C$6–$23 (US$4–$15).

Odyssey Theatre This professional summer theater company is noted for its imaginative use of masks, dance-like movement, and original music. Its open-air productions are based on Italian Renaissance street theater, known as commedia dell'arte. Odyssey specializes in productions of classic comic texts and original works. For 5 weeks in late summer, they perform in Strathcona Park on the banks of the Rideau River, close to downtown Ottawa. For youth and family audiences, the troupe also stages one-hour versions of the summer production, with demonstrations and a question-and-answer period. Performing in Strathcona Park. Office at 2 Daly Ave. ✆ 613/232-8407.

Orpheus Musical Theatre Society   This company performs in three fully staged musical shows per season. Recent shows include *The Wizard of Oz, Man of La Mancha,* and *Anything Goes.* Performing at Centrepointe Theatre, 101 Centrepointe Dr. ✆ **613/727-6650**. Tickets C$12–$22 (US$8–$15).

Ottawa Little Theatre   Since 1913, this amateur community theater has been producing plays in Ottawa. The comfortable 510-seat auditorium was redesigned after the original building was destroyed by fire in 1970. The company stages eight productions, with one per month from September through May, as well as one popular and entertaining musical each year as part of the summer series. Productions range from comedies to dramas, mysteries, farces, and musicals, and include the works of William Shakespeare, Agatha Christie, and Neil Simon. Performing at 400 King Edward Ave. ✆ **613/233-8948**. Tickets C$12–$15 (US$8–$10).

Salamander Theatre for Young Audiences   Bringing theater to the schools, Salamander Theatre performs across Ontario and offers children and young adults a range of workshops, courses, and camps. Performing at various locations. Office at 2 Daly Ave. ✆ **613/569-5629**.

Savoy Society   The Savoy Society of Ottawa is an organization of people who share a common interest in performing the comic operas of Gilbert and Sullivan. The society staged its first production, *The Pirates of Penzance,* in 1976, and now presents one play annually, running seven public performances (including a Sunday matinee) plus a benefit performance. Performing at Centrepointe Theatre, 101 Centrepointe Dr. ✆ **613/727-6650**. Tickets C$10–$22 (US$7–$15).

The Tara Players   The Tara Players stage classic, modern, and contemporary dramas and comedies from and about Ireland and written by playwrights of Irish heritage. The plays are primarily for adult audiences, but some may be suitable for older children. Three productions are staged per season, from October to May. Performing at St. Patrick's Hall, 280 Gloucester St. ✆ **613/746-1410**. Tickets C$7–$10 (US$4–$7).

4 Dance

Anjali and Company   This troupe performs classical East Indian temple dances and presents innovative, contemporary choreography based on traditional forms. Recitals are performed against a backdrop of images of temples, goddesses, and remote corners of Bhutan and the Himalayas. Anjali (Anne-Marie Gaston), is a classically trained East Indian dancer, choreographer, teacher, lecturer, and photographer. Call for locations. ✆ **613/745-1368**.

Les Petits Ballets   Les Petits Ballets, a nonprofit organization, was founded in 1976 to develop youth ballet talent. Professional guest dancers and young local talent share the stage in full-length ballets, including *Coppelia* and *Cinderella.* Performances are held twice yearly. Performing at Centrepointe Theatre, 101 Centrepointe Dr. ✆ **613/727-6650** box office, or **613/596-5783** studio.

NAC Dance Productions   Throughout the year, the NAC hosts a variety of dance performances, ranging from classical ballet to contemporary dance. Guest dance companies include Les Grands Ballet Canadiens de Montreal, Toronto Dance Theatre, Iceland Dance Company, Ballet British Columbia, Brazilian

Dance Theater, National Ballet of Canada, and Royal Winnipeg Ballet. 35 Elgin St. ℂ **613/947-7000**. For tickets visit the box office or call Ticketmaster at ℂ **613/755-1111**. Ticket prices vary.

5 Music

Governor General's Summer Concerts   Six free outdoor concerts are held on the beautifully landscaped grounds of Rideau Hall, a national historic site and the official residence of Canada's governor general. Set up your lawn chairs, spread out the picnic blanket, and enjoy the sunshine. Most concerts are scheduled for late Sunday afternoons. Past performers include children's performers Sharon, Bram, and Friends, country musicians Farmer's Daughter, and East Coast fiddler Natalie MacMaster. Wheelchairs, washroom facilities, and picnic tables are available at Rideau Hall. Rideau Hall, 1 Sussex Dr. ℂ **800/465-6890** or 613/ 991-4422. www.gg.ca.

NAC Orchestra   Offering more than 100 performances a year, this vibrant, classical-size orchestra draws accolades at home and abroad. In 1998 Pinchas Zukerman became the fifth conductor to lead the orchestra. The NAC Orchestra performs two to three times a year with Opera Lyra Ottawa and frequently accompanies ballets, including regular performances in Ottawa by Canada's three major ballet companies—the National Ballet of Canada, the Royal Winnipeg Ballet, and Les Grands Ballet Canadiens. For family audiences, the **Pops Series** combines popular songs and light classical music in a series of six evening performances. **NACO Young Peoples Concerts** are directed to 7- to 11-year-olds and feature music, storytelling, animation, and audience participation; activities for young audiences also take place in the NAC foyer 1 hour before the show. Performing at the NAC, 35 Elgin St. ℂ **613/947-7000**. For tickets visit the box office or call Ticketmaster at ℂ **613/755-1111**.

Ottawa Chamber Music Society Concert Series   Some of Canada's most accomplished chamber music artists perform in downtown Ottawa churches from October to April. Performing at various locations. ℂ **613/234-8008**. Tickets C$10–$25 (US$7–$17).

Ottawa Symphony Orchestra   With 100 musicians, the Ottawa Symphony Orchestra is the National Capital Region's largest orchestra. A series of five concerts are held at the NAC from September to May, featuring the music of the 19th and early 20th centuries. Performing at the NAC, 35 Elgin St. ℂ **613/947-7000**. For tickets visit the box office or call Ticketmaster at ℂ **613/755-1111** or the OSO ticket office at ℂ **613/747-3104**. Tickets C$15–$45 (US$10–$30).

Ottawa Youth Orchestra and Ottawa Junior Youth Orchestra   These companies perform occasional concerts for the public in the city. For information contact the National Capital Music Academy ℂ **613/860-0378**.

Thirteen Strings   One of Canada's foremost chamber music ensembles, Thirteen Strings has an annual subscription series of six concerts at St. Andrew's Presbyterian Church in Ottawa and performs a wide range of music for strings from the 15th to the 20th centuries. Junior Thirteen Strings also performs an annual concert with the regular ensemble, following an intensive three days of coaching and rehearsals during which each junior player shares a stand with a member of the ensemble. Performing at St. Andrew's Presbyterian Church, 82 Kent St. ℂ **613/745-1142**. Tickets at the door C$22 (US$15) adults, C$5 (US$3) ages 18 and under.

6 Films

If you and your kids love the silver screen, you'll have plenty of choice in Ottawa. Experience the latest in cinematic technology at the **IMAX DOME** theater in the Canadian Museum of Civilization, cosy up at a budget family movie theater, or enjoy tiered seating and big sound at an urban monster megaplex.

HIGH-TECH CINEMA

IMAX DOME Theatre   This amazing theater at the Canadian Museum of Civilization is the only one of its kind in the world. The technology of IMAX plus a giant dome gives you the feeling of being wrapped in sights and sounds. At seven stories high, the IMAX screen is amazing enough, but the real adventure begins when the 23-meter (75 ft.) hemispheric dome moves into place overhead once the audience is seated. Not all films use the entire screening system. This theater is busy, so buy your tickets in advance and plan to arrive 20 minutes before show time—latecomers will not be admitted. All ages are admitted.

Canadian Museum of Civilization, 100 Laurier St., Hull ℂ 819/776-7010 for show times. For tickets visit the museum box office or call Ticketmaster at ℂ 613/755-1111. Tickets C$6–8 (US$4–5).

MAINSTREAM NEW RELEASES

The city is well serviced by large multiscreen movie theaters. For current listings and prices, check the ***Ottawa Citizen*** (Friday has the most comprehensive arts and entertainment coverage), or visit http://ottawa.film-can.com. If you wince at the cost of taking the family out to a movie these days, check cinemas for special offers. Full-price tickets run as high as C$12.50 (US$8.25), but if you shop around and go at off-peak periods, you may pay up to 50% less.

AMC 24 Kanata, at Highway 417 and Terry Fox Drive (ℂ 613/599-5500), offers C$6 (US$4) tickets every weekday for twilight shows (4–6pm). During regular-price periods, students with ID pay C$8 (US$5). **Rideau Centre Famous Players** is conveniently located at 50 Rideau St. in the Rideau Centre (ℂ 613/234-3712). **South Keys Cineplex Odeon,** 2214 Bank St. S. at Hunt Club Road (ℂ 613/736-1115), starts screening at around 10am daily, offering the greatest flexibility for families with young children. **World Exchange Plaza Cineplex Odeon,** 111 Albert St., 3rd Floor (ℂ 613/233-0209), is in the heart of downtown and screens matinees daily. **Coliseum 12 Famous Players,** in Ottawa's west end, is just north of Bayshore Shopping Centre at 3090 Carling Ave. (ℂ 613/596-1812). **Orleans Cinemas Cineplex Odeon,** 250 Centrum Blvd. in Place d'Orleans shopping complex (ℂ 613/834-0666), has a regular evening admission price of C$6.50 (US$4) and charges C$4.25 (US$2.80) on Tuesdays and for matinees. Children and seniors pay only C$4.25 (US$2.80) any time. **Silver City Gloucester Famous Players,** 2385 City Park Dr. (ℂ 613/749-3029), is situated in the big-box complex at the corner of Blair and Ogilvie roads.

REPERTORY CINEMAS

Bytowne Cinema   Ottawa's premiere independent cinema has been screening independent and foreign films in this large, locally owned and operated theater for over 50 years. Get real butter on your popcorn and settle down in the comfy chairs to enjoy the big screen and Dolby sound. Don't want to wait in line? Members can purchase vouchers, and anyone can buy same-day tickets for any show when the box office opens (half an hour before the first show). Two to four movies are screened every day, with the lineup changing every few days. 325 Rideau St. ☏ 613/789-FILM (613/789-3456). http://ottawa.film-can.com. Tickets C$5 (US$3) members, C$8 (US$5) nonmembers, C$4 (US$2.50) children and seniors.

Canadian Film Institute Cinema   The Canadian Film Institute presents a regular public program of contemporary, historical, and international cinema in the auditorium of the National Archives of Canada. There won't be many films to interest younger audiences, but if you have an interest or expertise in the art of cinematography, check out their calendar of events for a film to enjoy with your older children. All screenings at the National Archives Auditorium, 395 Wellington St. ☏ 613/232-6727. Tickets C$5 (US$3) members, seniors, and children 15 and under; C$8 (US$5) adult nonmembers; C$10 (US$7) annual membership.

Mayfair Theatre   Screening a mixture of recent releases and older films, the Mayfair changes its bill almost daily. An annual membership costs C$18 (US$12) and includes three free admissions. Thereafter, C$2 (US$1.30) is knocked off your admission price. Two films are run every night. 1074 Bank St. ☏ 613/730-3403. www.mayfair-movie.com. Tickets C$6 (US$4) members, C$8 (US$5) nonmembers, C$4.50 (US$3) children and seniors.

Ottawa Family Cinema   Also known as Westend Family Cinema, this nonprofit theater offers movies on the big screen with digital stereo sound, cartoons, and door prizes. A friendly, family atmosphere prevails, with special events and movie parties held throughout the season. Films include recent releases and older films that are suitable for family viewing. Snack bar items range from C$1 (US66¢). Recent screenings include the Beatles' *A Hard Day's Night* with prizes for the best '60s costume. 710 Broadview Ave. ☏ 613/722-8218. www.familycinema.org. Open Sat afternoons and every second Fri evening, Sept–May, except Christmas and Easter weekends. Tickets C$3–6 (US$2–4).

7 Puppet Shows

Rag and Bone Puppet Theatre   Established in 1978, this theater presents a repertoire of shows for school and family audiences locally and across Canada, including *The Nightingale, A Promise is a Promise, Felicity Falls, The Cow Show, The Story of Holly and Ivy, The Weaving of a Dream,* and *Macbeth.* The company has been awarded a Citation of Excellence in the Art of Puppetry from UNIMA, the international puppetry association. Most shows are less than an hour long. Performing at various locations. ☏ 613/824-5972. Ages 5 and up.

8 Story Hours

Chapters   This big-box bookstore has become a familiar name with Canadian shoppers over the past few years. With five locations to choose from in the Ottawa area, you're never far from their extensive selection of books, magazines, computer software, and music. The children's section is large, containing a reading area, CD-ROM station, and books for every age group. Story hours and family events vary, with some stores holding children's story times as often as twice daily, depending on demand. Call your nearest store for events and activities that the whole family will enjoy. 47 Rideau St. ☏ 613/241-0073; 2735 Iris St. ☏ 613/596-3003; 2210 Bank St. ☏ 613/521-9199; 2401 City Park Dr. ☏ 613/744-5175; and 400 Earl Grey Dr. ☏ 613/271-7553.

Collected Works   This independent store carries general fiction and non-fiction, with an emphasis on literary fiction and children's books. A drop-in children's story time is held on Mondays and Fridays between 10:30 and 11am. 1242 Wellington St. © **613/722-1265.**

Ottawa Public Library   Ottawa now has 33 library branches, with 17 offering programs for children, ranging from a weekly drop-in story time at smaller branches to crafts, puppet shows, bilingual readings, and mother-and-daughter book clubs at larger branches. Drop into any branch to pick up a current brochure, or visit the website at www.library.ottawa.on.ca. 120 Metcalfe St. (main branch). © **613/236-0301.**

9 Spectator Sports

Ottawa Lynx   Take me out to the ball game! For fun and affordable family entertainment, visit **JetForm Park,** where the Ottawa Lynx, Ottawa's Triple-A affiliate of the Montreal Expos, play 72 home games from April to September. JetForm Park, which opened in 1993, is a state-of-the-art building that combines the old-time ballpark experience with modern facilities and services. The stadium boasts an award-winning natural grass and clay field, comfortable seats, and excellent sightlines. The open-air stands hold 10,000 spectators, most of whom are families. Facilities include a picnic area, barbecue terrace, baby-changing stations in the women's washrooms, and parking for 800 cars. Since the team's inception in 1993, the Ottawa Lynx Baseball Club has set two attendance records in the league and has won the International League Championship. Jet-Form Park is close to Highway 417 (the Queensway), at the corner of Vanier Parkway and Coventry Road. Tickets are available at the park or by phone. 300 Coventry Rd. © **800-663-0985** or 613/747-LYNX (5969). Tickets C$6.50–$8.50 (US$4–$6); C$1 (US66¢) off for seniors and children 14 and under.

Ottawa Rebel   The popularity of lacrosse is on the rise and the Ottawa Rebel, playing at the **Corel Centre,** is one of nine National Lacrosse League franchises in northeastern North America. Come and watch the Ottawa Rebel take on the Toronto Rock, Washington Power, New York Saints, Philadelphia Wings, Rochester Knighthawks, Columbus Landsharks, Buffalo Bandits, and Albany Attack teams. The regular season runs from December to April. 1000 Palladium Dr. © **613/599-0123.** For tickets, visit any Ticketmaster outlet or the Corel Centre box office (Gate 1), or call Ticketmaster Sportsline at © **613/755-1166.** Tickets C$9 (US$6) and up.

Ottawa Senators   Experience all the excitement of true NHL action at the **Corel Centre,** home of the Ottawa Senators. Family and alcohol-free seating is at the west end of the arena, in sections 111 and 216 and in the Coca-Cola Family Fan Zone, sections 314, 315, and 316. Over 1,000 seats are available in the Family Fan Zone at the bargain price of C$19 (US$13). Note that because of the placement of security bars, the first row of each section may obstruct children's view of the ice. There are lots of concession stands, including the well-loved Ottawa **BeaverTails,** as well as **Pizza Pizza, Tim Hortons,** and **Nestlé.** A **Hard Rock Café** and other restaurants are also on-site for meals and snacks before or after the game. For all your Sens souvenirs, visit **Sensations,** the official merchandise outlet of the Ottawa Senators Hockey Club in the Corel Centre at Gate 1. 1000 Palladium Dr. © **613/599-0123.** For tickets, visit any Ticketmaster outlet or the Corel Centre box office (Gate 1), or call Ticketmaster Sportsline at © **613/755-1166.** Tickets C$19–$145 (US$13–$96).

Ottawa 67's   For up-close and personal OHL action, visit the **Civic Centre,** in Lansdowne Park, home of the **Ottawa 67's** since their inception in 1967. With a seating capacity exceeding 10,000 and 47 luxury suites, it is reputed to be one of the best homes in the Junior Hockey League. Free parking and family packages are available. 1015 Bank St. ✆ **613/232-6767.** Tickets C$11 (US$7) adults, C$7 (US$4.50) children.

University Sports Teams   Check out the variety of varsity sports at **Carleton University** (✆ **613/520-7400;** www.carleton.ca), including basketball, fencing, field hockey, golf, indoor hockey, rowing, rugby, skiing, soccer, swimming, and water polo. The **University of Ottawa** (✆ **613/562-5700;** www.geegees. uottawa.ca) also presents badminton, basketball, fencing, football, golf, hockey, rowing, rugby, soccer, skiing, volleyball, and water polo.

9

Shopping for the Whole Family

With a regional population topping 1.1 million, shopping facilities in Canada's National Capital Region are excellent. Whether you prefer dazzling, multistory, glass-and-steel malls, city streets lined with funky boutiques and cafes, or big-box discount stores, it's all here. Put on comfortable shoes, rev up your plastic, and get ready to shop 'til you drop.

HOURS   Most stores in the Ottawa area are open Monday through Saturday from 9:30 or 10am to 6pm, and many have extended hours one or more evenings a week. Sunday opening hours are from noon to 5pm, although some stores are closed. You should always call ahead.

TAXES   Sales taxes add a wallop to your shopping bill. The provincial retail sales tax in Ontario is 8% for most items—two exceptions are basic groceries and children's clothing, which are exempt. The federal goods and services tax (GST) is 7%. In general, nonresidents may apply for a tax refund (see "Fast Facts" in chapter 3, "Getting to Know Ottawa").

1 The Shopping Scene

GREAT SHOPPING AREAS

BANK STREET PROMENADE

You'll find 15 blocks of stores and services in this area, beginning at Wellington Street in the heart of downtown and stretching south to Gladstone Avenue. Around 500 businesses operate on this stretch of Bank Street, ranging from small, locally owned retailers, bargain stores, and souvenir shops to restaurants, bars, and cafes. Some of the shops are rather colorful. As the name suggests, the major banks established their first local offices on this street—in fact, the district is one of the city's oldest shopping areas.

BYWARD MARKET

More than 100 boutiques jostle for position with restaurants, pubs, services, and food retailers in the warren of side streets that make up the vibrant ByWard Market area, bordered by Sussex Drive, St. Patrick Street, King Edward Avenue, and Rideau Street. Head for this district to be entertained, excited, and delighted by what's on offer in the diverse collection of shops. The ByWard Market building, located on the original site where farmers and loggers met to carry out their business in the 1800s, was restored in 1998 and now houses gourmet food shops and the wares of local and regional artisans. Excellent quality local fruit, vegetables, flowers, and other farm products are available at stalls surrounding the market building.

DOWNTOWN RIDEAU

The stores and restaurants continue as you stroll from the ByWard Market toward the Rideau Centre, the major downtown shopping mall, so you won't notice that you've stepped into the shopping area known as Downtown Rideau. Bordered by the Rideau Canal, King Edward Avenue, George Street, and the MacKenzie King Bridge, this 23-block section of the city is promoted as the city's arts and theater district, with Arts Court, the National Arts Centre, and the Canadian Museum of Contemporary Photography in the vicinity, in addition to many national chain retailers and unique independent stores.

THE GLEBE

Further south on Bank Street, between the Queensway and the Rideau Canal, is a stretch of trendy, higher-end stores, services, and eateries serving the upscale middle-class neighborhood known as the Glebe. It's well worth spending a morning or afternoon strolling up one side of the street and down the other. If you begin at the north end, take a break near the canal before making your return journey. Brown's Inlet and Park are tucked 1 or 2 blocks west of Bank Street, north of Queen Elizabeth Drive. If you start at the canal end, take a break in Central Park, which straddles Bank Street in the vicinity of Powell and Clemow avenues. For winter strolling, take refuge in the atrium at Fifth Avenue Court, about midway down this section of Bank Street.

SPARKS STREET MALL

Canada's oldest permanent pedestrianized shopping street, Sparks Street Mall runs between Elgin and Lyon streets, 1 block south of Parliament Hill. Although it's busy during the working day because of the many office blocks that surround it, Sparks Street can seem deserted on evenings and weekends. In summer, restaurants set up patio tables and chairs and there's an annual busker festival (see "Seasonal Events," in chapter 8, "Entertainment for the Whole Family").

WELLINGTON STREET WEST

Not to be confused with Wellington Street in the downtown core, which runs in front of the Parliament Buildings, Wellington Street West is actually a continuation of Somerset Street West until you reach Island Park Drive, where it then changes name to Richmond Road. There's an interesting mix here, with fine-dining restaurants, neighborhood cafes, interior decorating retailers, and antique shops squeezed in beside the usual main street businesses.

WESTBORO VILLAGE

This traditional city neighborhood west of downtown has enjoyed a revitalization since the late 1990s. The addition of Richmond Road Mountain Equipment Co-op spurred retail growth in the west end of Westboro's commercial ribbon, and there is hope that the area will eventually link with Wellington Street West to form a shopping district much like the ByWard Market and the Glebe.

WHERE TO BROWSE THE BIG BOXES

Strategically placed clusters of big-box retailers have moved into the Ottawa area, as in other cities. Especially popular with consumers hunting for big-ticket items like electronics, furniture, and appliances, big boxes attract shoppers with their promise of lower prices and wide selection. Multiscreen movie theaters and popular chain restaurants are often located within the complex. The Centrum in Kanata (take the Terry Fox exit from the Queensway) and South Keys (Bank

Street north of Hunt Club Road) are two of the largest big-box sites. Bells Corners and Merivale Road in Nepean and Ogilvie Road in Gloucester are also worth a look.

MAJOR MALLS

Bayshore Shopping Centre   In Ottawa's west end, close to the Queensway, Bayshore Shopping Centre has three floors of shops and services, with the Bay and Zellers as the two anchor stores, plus Les Ailes de la Mode scheduled to open in 2001. With the exception of Please Mum (children's wear) on the first floor, most of the kid stuff is on the third floor, including Mrs. Tiggywinkles, the Disney Store, Gymboree, Jacob Jr., and Northern Getaway. The food court and Port Pizzazz Children's Playcentre are also on this level. At peak times, there can be quite a lineup for the main elevator, so try using those in the department stores. Families with small children will appreciate the zoned parking for new parents and expectant mothers, family washrooms, nursing rooms, free stroller rental, and highchairs and booster seats in the food court. Older kids will drool over the clothing in the Gap, Le Chateau, Roots, Stitches, and West 49. HMV, Sam the Record Man, and New York Fries are more places for kids over 11 to hang out and spend their allowance. The customer service center, on the first level near the Gap, offers car unlocking, battery boosting, and other services in addition to stroller, wheelchair, and walker rental. Regular shopping hours are Monday to Friday 9am to 9pm, Saturday 9am to 6pm, and Sunday noon to 5pm. Parking is free. ℂ **613/829-7491.**

Carlingwood Shopping Centre   On the corner of Carling and Woodroffe avenues, Carlingwood offers one-floor shopping, which is a boon if you're push-ing a stroller or have preschoolers in tow. Anchored by Sears and Loblaws, this mall has designated parking spots for parents, a children's play area, a nursing room, a baby-change room, a children's washroom, coat and parcel check, and free stroller and wheelchair rental. There are two kids' clothing stores, a mater-nity wear boutique, and a kids' shoe store. Older kids will enjoy playing with the giant chess set. If they're not chess players, take your older kids to Electronics Boutique, Fancy Sox, Levis 1850, Motionware Sports, or Sam the Record Man. Regular shopping hours are Monday to Friday 9:30am to 9pm, Saturday 9:30am to 6pm, and Sunday 10am to 5pm. Parking is free. ℂ **613/725-1546.**

Place D'Orléans   Follow Highway 174 east to the suburb of Orléans and you'll find this large mall just on the edge of the highway. Anchored by the Bay, the Bay Home Store, and Wal-Mart, Place d'Orléans offers two levels of shops and services, with half a dozen children's clothing stores, Mrs. Tiggy Winkle's toy shop, Kiddie Kobbler footwear, an indoor playground, and a playcare center run by the YMCA/YWCA. Kids' can join the Y's Kids Klub, which offers children's shows, make-and-take craft sessions, and free gifts. Preteens and young teens will enjoy fashion-forward Aldo and Transit for footwear; the Gap, Pantorama, Roots, Stitches, and West 49 for clothing; and HMV and Music World for the latest CDs. The guest services center is located right in the middle of the first floor beside the elevator. There is a nursing room on the main level, and stroller and wheelchair rental are free. Regular shopping hours are Monday to Saturday 9:30am to 9pm and Sunday 11am to 5pm. Parking is free. ℂ **613/824-9050.**

Rideau Centre   In the heart of downtown, with direct access from the Ottawa Congress Centre and the Westin Hotel, the Rideau Centre has over 200 stores, services, restaurants, and cinemas. Kid-oriented stores include Gap Kids,

Gymboree, the Disney Store, and Mrs. Tiggy Winkle's. For kids 11 and up, check out Aldo, Bikini Village, the Body Shop, HMV, Le Chateau, Claire's Boutique, Electronics Boutique, Fancy Sox, the Gap, Kernels Popcorn, Music World, Stitches, and Transit Shoes. Free stroller and wheelchair rental and a nursing room are available. Regular shopping hours are Monday, Tuesday, and Saturday 9:30am to 6pm, Wednesday to Friday 9:30am to 9pm, and Sunday noon to 5pm. ✆ **613/236-6565.**

St. Laurent Shopping Centre   Situated at the junction of the Queensway and St. Laurent Boulevard, this mall has an entertainment wing with a climbing wall and high-tech arcade zone. The Cyberdome has motion simulators, virtual reality games, air hockey, a batting cage, and laser tag. Guest services are located in the entertainment wing and include free stroller and wheelchair rental, parcel check, and car boosts. Nursing rooms, family washrooms, parking spots for expectant mothers and new parents, and highchairs in the food court are some of the family amenities in the mall. Anchor stores are the Bay, Sears, and Toys R Us. Half a dozen children's clothing stores and a Kiddie Kobbler will help you dress your child in style. Keep older kids from getting bored by browsing in Club Monaco, the Gap, Stitches, Thrifty's, HMV, International Musicland, Music World, Comics X-Cetra, Athlete's World/Nike, and Ottawa Sports Gallery. Regular shopping hours are Monday to Friday 9:30am to 9pm and Sunday 11am to 5pm. Parking is free. ✆ **613/745-6858.**

OTHERS   In the west end, bordered by the Queensway, Carling Avenue and Merivale Road **Westgate Shopping Centre** has a chocolate shop, kids' clothing stores, and a cinema complex. Downtown, several smaller, upscale indoor malls serve office workers and tourists alike. **L'Esplanade Laurier,** at the corner of Bank Street and Laurier Avenue, features women's fashions, gift shops, banking, and postal services. At the corner of Sparks and Bank streets, **240 Sparks Shopping Centre** has a large food court and is anchored by Holt Renfrew. **World Exchange Plaza,** at the corner of Metcalfe and Albert streets, combines movie theaters, boutiques, and a cafe.

2 Shopping A to Z

ART SUPPLIES

Artguise   This shop aims to meet the specialized needs of local artists and artisans with a wide selection of oils, alkyds, acrylics, water colors, brushes, papers, pencils, charcoal, sketch books, paint boxes, and solid oak studio easels. 590 Bank St. ✆ **613/238-3803.**

Loomis and Toles   You'll find fine art and framing supplies at reasonable prices, plus books, model figures, brushes, canvas, paper, drafting tables, easels, and lots more. Brand names include Pebeo, Winsor & Newton, Liquitex, and Staedtler.   499 Bank St. ✆ **613/238-3303.**

Wallack's   This store stocks fine art, graphics, and drafting supplies, including children's art supplies, airbrushes, books, writing instruments, papers, sculpture, and ready-made frames.   231 Bank St. ✆ **613/234-1800.** Also 603 Bank St. ✆ **613/238-8871,** and in Nepean and Hull.

BABY SHOP

Absolutely Diapers   Urban parents will find everything they need for their baby and some things they didn't know they needed here, expertly divided into categories so customers can speed through the store (change, feed, go, play, clean, and sleep). Originating in Toronto, there are now seven stores across the country. 862B Bank St. at Fifth Ave. © **888/447-2229** or 613/569-6661.

BOOKS

Benjamin Books   You'll find general fiction and nonfiction, and some children's books. Rideau Centre. © **613/241-0617.**

Bestsellers   Just as the name says, you'll find the most popular hardback and paperback books, plus videos, in this Carlingwood Shopping Centre chain store. 2121 Carling Ave. © **613/728-0689.**

Books on Beechwood   This independent store carries general fiction and nonfiction. The large children's section takes up about a quarter of the store. 35 Beechwood Ave. © **613/742-5030.**

Chapters   Dominating everything from big-box skylines to newspaper headlines, Chapters has become a familiar name with Canadian shoppers over the past few years. There are five locations to choose from in the Ottawa area, offering an extensive selection of books, magazines, computer software, and music. There's a good young adult section and a large children's section, with a reading area, a CD-ROM station, and books for every age group. Story hours and family events vary—call your nearest store to find out about events and activities for the whole family to enjoy. 47 Rideau St. © **613/241-0073**; 2735 Iris St. © **613/596-3003**; 2210 Bank St. © **613/521-9199**; 2401 City Park Dr. © **613/744-5175**; 400 Earl Grey Dr. © **613/271-7553.**

Coles   This well-established bookstore chain carries a variety of mainstream titles, including children's books. 2269 Riverside Dr. © **613/731-2444**; Place d'Orléans © **613/837-2312.**

Collected Works   This independent store stocks general fiction and nonfiction, with an emphasis on literary fiction and children's books. Drop-in children's story time is held Mondays and Fridays between 10:30 and 11am. 1242 Wellington St. © **613/722-1265.**

Librairie du Soleil   Come here for the most extensive selection of French-language books in Ottawa and the excellent children's section, with a wide variety of educational and story books for all ages. French/English dictionaries are available. 321 Dalhousie St. © **613/241-6999.**

Nicholas Hoare *Finds*   Specializing in British authors and publishers, this shop also offers a comprehensive children's section with child-size comfortable chairs for curling up in. The atmosphere is calm and the background music soothing. Floor-to-ceiling bookshelves line the walls, with elegant library ladders to allow access to the top shelves. Enjoy the selection of literature, popular fiction, art books, hardcover coffee table books, travel books, and cookbooks. 419 Sussex Dr. © **613/562-2665.**

Perfect Books   This independent bookseller of general fiction and nonfiction offers a small children's section. 258A Elgin St. © **613/231-6468.**

Place Bell Books   Specializing in travel books and maps, this bookstore has a hefty selection of titles on vacation destinations around the world. Local guide books and books featuring scenic photography of the Ottawa region are also on hand, as are general interest titles. In the Place Bell mall, entrance on Metcalfe St. 175 Metcalfe St. © **613/233-3821.**

Shirley Leishman Books   This independent store carries general fiction and nonfiction and French-as-a-second-language books. There's a large children's section at the back of the store with French translations of much loved Canadian children's author Robert Munsch. Westgate Shopping Centre. ✆ 613/722-8313.

Smithbooks   A large chain of bookstores primarily situated in malls, Smithbooks carries mainstream book titles in a variety of categories, including children's books for all ages. You can find Smithbooks at the following shopping centres: Bayshore, 240 Sparks, Carlingwood, Gloucester, Herongate, Merivale, Place d'Orléans, Rideau Centre, and St. Laurent.

CDs, TAPES & RECORDS

If you're looking for children's entertainers, you'll often find the best selection in independent toy stores. For preteens who have discovered boy bands, girl bands, and the rest of the bubblegum pop scene, try the following national chains in Ottawa:

HMV Canada   Located at the corner of Bank and Sparks streets and in a number of malls, including Bayshore Shopping Centre, Merivale Place, Place d'Orléans, Rideau Centre, and St. Laurent Shopping Centre.

Music World   Located at Billings Bridge Plaza, Merivale Mall different from Merivale Place), Rideau Centre, and St. Laurent Shopping Centre.

Sam the Record Man   Sam's, a mecca for music lovers, has branches at Bayshore Shopping Centre and Carlingwood Shopping Centre.

CHILDREN'S CLOTHING

Au Coin des Petits   Browse mainstream fashions for boys and girls up to young teens, including casual clothes, outerwear, dressy outfits, sleepwear, and underwear. St. Laurent Shopping Centre. ✆ 613/749-2426.

Club Monaco Boys & Girls   Simple monochromatic designs for the offspring of adult Club Monaco shoppers. Cool, urban, sophisticated. St. Laurent Shopping Centre. ✆ 613/745-0583.

Eclection   This small selection of locally made clothing for younger children is worth a look. 55 ByWard Market. ✆ 613/789-7288.

Gap Kids   Kids from grade 1 to high school and beyond want to be seen in Gap sweaters. Gap kid clothes are practical, the styles are fun, the colors are usually great, and they wash and wear well. Ottawa has two kid-dedicated stores plus two other locations with kids' sections (Bayshore Shopping Centre and Place d'Orléans). Rideau Centre ✆ 613/569-4110; St. Laurent Shopping Centre ✆ 613/746-8787.

Glebe Side Kids   If you don't want to dress your kids in the same stuff as your friends and neighbors, step into Glebe Side Kids for designer clothing in eye-catching colors and styles. You'll find casual and dressy clothing for boys and girls, and infants to teens. The quality is high and so is the price. 793 Bank St. ✆ 613/235-6552.

Gymboree   This store provides colorful, sturdy clothing and helpful staff, plus a play area at the back of the store. Prices can be on the high side, but they have frequent sales. The company also runs community play and music programs (see chapter 7, "For the Active Family"). Rideau Centre ✆ 613/565-3323; St. Laurent Shopping Centre ✆ 613/842-4716.

Jacob Jr.   This fashion-forward store sells clothing in scaled-down versions of adult styles, including separates and underwear for girls who just want to have fun. Bayshore Shopping Centre ✆ **613/828-2470**; St. Laurent Shopping Centre ✆ **613/746-7095.**

Kekos Children's Boutique   This is European kids' clothing, in sizes 1 to 16, with a good selection of special occasion clothing, including items for weddings, first communions, and bar mitzvahs. Westgate Shopping Centre. ✆ **613/798-0483.**

Kid's Cosy Cottons ⟨Value   Known best for their practical cotton basics in sizes from 3 months to adult, Kid's Cosy Cottons also makes clothes in polar fleece and microfibers. You'll find socks, pyjamas, and underwear, too, all Canadian made. 517 Sussex Dr. ✆ **800/267-2679** or 613/562-2679.

La Senza Girl   A spin-off of the lingerie mall chain, La Senza Girl has extremely girly childrens fashions. St. Laurent Shopping Centre. ✆ **613/741-3439.**

Laura Ashley Shops Ltd. ⟨Value   This excellent quality British clothing shop stocks dresses and separates for girls ages 2 to 9, with some lines co-ordinating with the adults line for an enchanting mother/daughter look. 136 Bank St. ✆ **613/238-4882.**

Northern Getaway   Younger school kids all seem to have something from Northern Getaway in their wardrobes. This is strongly themed clothing for boys (sports, wild animals, strong, dark colors) and girls (flowers, puppies, lilacs, and pinks). Kids like the clothes and the prices are middle-of-the-road. Sales come up often. Colors are coordinated so that separates for each season mix and match throughout the store. Bayshore Shopping Centre ✆ **613/829-0385**; Carlingwood Shopping Centre ✆ **613/722-6107**; Rideau Centre ✆ **613/569-2225**; Place d'Orléans ✆ **613/834-2377**; St. Laurent Shopping Centre ✆ **613/746-6150.**

Please Mum   Browse the bright, coordinated separates for active kids. St. Laurent Shopping Centre. ✆ **613/820-5145.**

Quintessence   This store offers a small selection of locally made clothing for younger children. 55 ByWard Market. ✆ **613/562-8350.**

Roots Canada Ltd.   Although Roots has been a well-known Canadian label for many years, their sponsorship of the Winter Olympics catapulted their coats, sweaters, and caps into the world spotlight. Demand has grown for their clothing line since that time, particularly in the States. This casual clothing, in infant to adult sizes, washes and wears well. There's a factory outlet location in the south end of the city; prices are slashed but the selection varies. 787 Bank St. ✆ **613/232-3790**; Bayshore Shopping Centre ✆ **613/820-4527**, Place d'Orléans ✆ **613/841-7164**; Rideau Centre ✆ **613/236-7760**; factory outlet 2210 Bank St. ✆ **613/736-9503.**

R.W.Kids ⟨Value   Ottawa's Osh Kosh store has perhaps Canada's best selection of Osh Kosh clothing. Most parents are familiar with Osh Kosh quality—kids just can't seem to wear it out and outfits still look good on the second or third child. The store is well laid out, with cascading hangers lining the walls so that styles and sizes are easy to find, and easy to navigate with a stroller. There's a playroom at the back and a rack of gently used Osh Kosh consignment clothing on display. A C$10 (US$7) annual membership entitles you to a 15% discount on all regular-price items. Hampton Park Plaza, Carling Ave. and Kirkwood Ave. ✆ **613/724-4576.**

West End Kids (*Finds*)   If you're tired of mall wear, head here for top-quality upscale clothing for infants to teens. Labels include Mexx, Columbia, Tommy Hilfiger, Deux Par Deux, and Fresh Produce. 373 Richmond Rd. **℃ 613/722-8947.**

Young Canada   These mainstream fashions for boys and girls up to young teens include casual clothes, outerwear, dressy outfits, sleepwear, and underwear. Place d'Orléans. **℃ 613/834-8645.**

CHILDREN'S FURNITURE & EQUIPMENT

Ikea (*Value*)   They advise you to wear comfortable shoes, and they mean it. This Swedish store has around 75 life-size rooms displaying their home furnishings, including playroom and bedroom furniture, storage units, bedding, and toys. Most furniture comes flat-packed and requires assembly at home. The fresh, young, urban image draws big crowds, especially on Saturdays. Free stroller rental, a baby-care room for feeding and changing, and a play area with ball room will make families happy. The on-site restaurant serves kids' meals. 2685 Iris St. **℃ 613/829-4530.**

Kidz   Located in the Leon's Furniture building, Kidz stocks children's furniture and accessories. 1718 Heron Rd. **℃ 613/737-0660.**

Linen Chest   A good selection of baby bedding, furniture, and accessories. 2685 Iris St., Pinecrest Shopping Centre. **℃ 613/721-9991.**

Sleepy Hollow   Furniture, strollers, cribs, linens, and bedroom sets. 2080 Walkley Rd. **℃ 613/733-4778.**

CHOCOLATES & SWEETS

Godiva Chocolatier Inc   Go ahead, indulge in top-quality chocolate confections. This shop is highly recommended for parents. Rideau Centre. **℃ 613/234-4470.**

Karen's Chocolates   You'll find lots of novelty chocolates for gifts—white chocolate ballet shoes, chocolate hockey skates, carpentry tools, and other unusual items. There's also ice cream, fudge, and a good selection of sugar-free chocolates. And don't forget those irresistible Beanie Babies and Beanie Kids. Westgate Shopping Centre. **℃ 613/729-9918.**

Laura Secord   This chocolatier has been a Canadian favorite for more than 85 years. The chocolates and truffles are quite delicious. Try the white chocolate almond bark and the butterscotch lollipops. Superkid ice cream is a favorite with my youngest. Santa and the Easter Bunny always stop at Laura Secord before visiting our house. 85 Bank St. **℃ 613/232-6830;** Billings Bridge Plaza **℃ 613/737-5695;** Rideau Centre **℃ 613/230-2576;** St. Laurent Shopping Centre **℃ 613/741-5040.**

Rocky Mountain Chocolate Factory   This BC-based company has lots of goodies—chocolate (of course!), cookies, fudge, candy apples, and other sweet treats. It's inside the market building at the south end. 55 ByWard Market. **℃ 613/241-1091.**

Sugar Mountain (*Finds*)   Kids love this place. Walls are lined with clear plastic bins at the right height for scooping the most outrageous colors and flavors of sugar-loaded confections into loot bags. Islands of boxed and wrapped candy and chocolates are dotted around the two-level store, and parents can be seen prowling here, searching for the sweets of their youth. Remember Thrills gum, black liquorice pipes, sherbet fountains, pink popcorn, and Curly Wurlys? They've all been spotted here. The selection changes frequently and there's often a good variety of British sweets. Get ready for a major sugar rush. 286 Elgin St. © 613/230-8886.

CHRISTMAS STORES

Christmas & Candles   This pretty gift store is worth a peek. 481 Sussex Dr. © 613/241-5476.

Christmas in the Capital Inc.   High-quality holiday ornaments and beautifully decorated trees fill the store. Children will love to look around, but hold onto those little hands and enforce the look-but-don't-touch rule. 231 Elgin St. © 613/231-4646.

The Christmas Shoppe on William   This attractively laid-out store has an excellent variety of ornament and decorations for the holiday season. I'll say it again—children will love the store, but keep them on a tight rein and remind them firmly to look with their eyes, not their hands. 71 William St. © 613/789-7171.

COMICS, GAMES & TRADING CARDS

The Comic Book Shoppe   Current and back issues of comic books, action figures, toys, posters, calendars, models, games, trading cards, videos, and a good selection of Japanimation will lure young collectors. 237 Bank St. © 613/594-3042; 1400 Clyde Ave. © 613-228-8386.

Entertainment Ink!   You'll find a wide selection of comics, plus action figures, posters, and games. Place d'Orléans. © 613/841-5531.

Fandom II   This store offers a good selection of role-playing games, figures, and books. 162 Laurier Ave. W. © 613/236-2972.

COMPUTERS, CAMERAS & ELECTRONICS

Compusmart   Shop for major brand names of computer hardware and software. Unit 18, 1547 Merivale Rd. © 613/727-0099.

The Focus Centre   Check out the new, used, and rental photographic equipment and supplies. There's also a large selection of digital cameras and accessories and a develop and print service. 254 Bank St. © 613/232-5368.

Ginn Photographic Co.   This store sells and rents new and used photographic equipment and supplies, plus darkroom equipment and supplies. There's also digital equipment and imaging service. 433 Bank St. © 613/567-4686.

Radio Shack   Offering the latest in home electronics, computers, and phones and lots of neat accessories, Radio Shack has almost a dozen locations in the city, so check out the Yellow Pages. 286 Bank St. © 613/238-6889; Rideau Centre, 1st floor © 613/563-1156 and 3rd floor © 613/241-2981.

DOLLS & DOLLHOUSES

Lilliput *(Finds*   A delightful collection of dollhouse furniture, fixtures, and accessories is beautifully displayed. Dollhouse kits in several styles are available, with some completed models on show. 9 Murray St. © 613/241-1183.

DRUGSTORES (24 HOURS)

Shoppers Drug Mart   Two locations are open 24 hours: 1460 Merivale Rd. at Baseline Rd. © 613/224-7270 and 2515 Bank St. at Hunt Club Rd. © 613/523-9999.

FLY FISHING

Brightwater Fly Fishing   Drop by Brightwater to pick up everything a fisherman (or junior fisherman) could ever want. Rentals and fly-tying instruction are available. Fishing is permitted in designated areas of Gatineau Park, but don't forget to purchase a provincial license (available in store) before casting your line. 336 Cumberland St. ℰ **613/241-6798**.

GIFT SHOPS

Abington's Animals   This store stocks lots of figurines and collectibles, plus Beanie Babies, Beanie Kids, and Harry Potter merchandise. St. Laurent Shopping Centre. ℰ **613/744-7094**.

Canada's Four Corners   Canadian fine crafts and quality Canadian souvenirs share space with a gallery of framed or matted prints. 93 Sparks St. ℰ **613/233-2322**.

Canadian Geographic Boutique   You'll find *Canadian Geographic Magazine,* Canadiana, clothes, books, and toys at this boutique. Rideau Centre. ℰ **800/267-0824** or 613/565-0479.

Canal Company   This 19th-century general store specializes in Canadian-made heritage gifts, goodies, souvenirs, and historical products. 89 Murray St. ℰ **613/244-5291**.

Inuit Artists' Shop   This nonprofit enterprise offers a wide range of Inuit art and worldwide shipping. 16 Clarence St. ℰ **613/241-9444**; 2081 Merivale Rd. ℰ **613/224-8189**.

Oh Yes Ottawa!   This terrific Canadian-made souvenir clothing is also sold at the airport. Rideau Centre. ℰ **613/569-7520**.

Ottawa Souvenirs and Gifts   Browse the selection of T-shirts, sweatshirts, mugs, plaques, spoons, and maple syrup products. Rideau Centre. ℰ **613/233-0468**.

The Snow Goose Limited   This Canadian arts and crafts shop specializes in Inuit and Native works in every price range. 83 Sparks St. ℰ **613/232-2213**.

HOBBY & CRAFT STORES

Dynamic Hobbies   Kids will love the radio-controlled model cars, airplanes, helicopters, and boats, on-site indoor and outdoor tracks, and the 45-meter (150 ft.) slot car track. 21 Concourse Gate, Unit 6. ℰ **613/225-9634**.

Hobby House Ltd   This store offers a wide variety of hobby supplies, including plastic model kits, model trains and accessories, military and aviation books, modeler's tools and supplies, rockets, kites, die-cast models, wooden ship kits, and puzzles. 80 Montreal Rd. ℰ **613/749-5245**.

Lewiscraft   Lots of materials and supplies for artistically inclined kids and grown-ups, plus knowledgeable and helpful staff. Rideau Centre. ℰ **613/230-7792**.

Michael's Arts and Crafts   Following the big-box challenge of trying to carry everything under one roof, Michael's has row upon row of shelves crammed with arts and crafts supplies for the home crafter and decorator, including kid-friendly supplies and seasonal stuff. Just keep everyone together in a group—if you get separated, you may be wandering up and down the aisles for quite some time before you meet up again. Classes, workshops, and kids' birthday parties are offered. 2210-F Bank St. ℰ **613/521-3717**; 2685 Iris St. ℰ **613/726-7211**.

The Sassy Bead Co. Kids of all ages love to browse the colorful jars, trays, and boxes filled with beads of every description. You and your daughter or granddaughter can sit at a table and create your own jewelry right in the shop. There's also a good selection of unique ready-made items. Workshops and kids' birthday parties are available. The Bank Street location carries a line of Sassy clothing. 757 Bank St. ℂ **613/567-7886**; 11 William St. ℂ **613/562-2812**.

MAPS/TRAVEL BOOK STORES

Place Bell Book Store Specializing in city, country, and worldwide maps, including Michelin, Rand McNally, British Ordinance Survey, and Canadian Topographical, this shop also offers a wide selection of travel guides and literature. 175 Metcalfe St. ℂ **613/233-3821**.

A World of Maps Situated where else but at the geographical centre of Ottawa, A World of Maps is both a retailer and mail-order company. It's a regional distributor for all Canadian government maps and charts produced by the Canada Map Office. Topographical, aeronautical, nautical, international, and world maps, atlases, globes, travel books, and other map-related items are available here. 1235 Wellington St. W. ℂ **800/214-8524** or 613/724-6776.

MARKETS

ByWard Farmer's Market (*Value*) The quality of the produce is outstanding at this thriving outdoor farmer's market, with about 200 vendors. In spring and early summer, flower stalls abound. Lots of family-oriented events are scheduled on weekends throughout the year. 55 ByWard Market Square. May–Oct daily 6am–6pm, Nov–Apr daily 9:30am–5:30pm.

Ottawa Organic Farmer's Market For fresh market produce grown without pesticides or other chemicals, head on down on a Saturday. The number of vendors varies from 8 to 17. Kingsway United Church, 630 Island Park Dr. Year-round Sat 10am–2pm.

Parkdale Farmer's Market This small open-air farmer's market, with 20 vendors on average, offers fresh, high-quality produce. Parkdale Ave. at Wellington St. Apr–Dec 24 daily 7am–6pm.

MUSEUM SHOPS

For descriptions of museum shops, see the individual listings in chapter 6, "What Kids Like to See & Do."

MUSICAL INSTRUMENTS

Ottawa Folklore Centre They repair, buy, sell, consign, trade, rent, and appraise just about any instrument you can think of, from guitars to amps, banjos, fiddles, Celtic harps, mandolins, recorders, folk flutes, hand drums, autoharps, accordions, and dulcimers. 1111 Bank St. ℂ **613/730-2887**.

Song Bird Music Dealing in new, used, and rental instruments, Song Bird Music has guitars, woodwinds, percussion, brass, keyboards, amps, and more. They outgrew their original store and had to open a second location across the street. 388 Gladstone Ave. ℂ **613/594-5323**.

OUTDOOR STORES

Bushtukah Great Outdoor Gear More than 1,100 square meters (12,000 sq. ft.) are stocked with tents, camping gear, sleeping bags, and other assorted outdoor equipment. 203 Richmond Rd. ℂ **613/792-1170**.

The Expedition Shoppe   In the outdoor shopper's corner of Ottawa, along with Bushtukah, Mountain Equipment, and Trailhead, this store sells clothing and outdoor equipment for travel, hiking, and camping, as well as guide books and maps. 369 Richmond Rd. ✆ **613/722-0166**; 43 York St. ✆ **613/241-8397.**

Irving Rivers   If you like the great outdoors, hike over to this outdoor emporium, stuffed with rain gear, camping clothing, travel appliances, backpacks, heavy-duty footwear and everything else for a back-to-nature vacation. 24 ByWard Market St. ✆ **613/241-1415.**

Mountain Equipment Co-op   The quintessential Canadian outdoor gear shop. Whether you're camping, climbing, snowshoeing or just want a cool bag or jacket, this is the place. As it's a co-op, there's a one-time lifetime membership fee of C$5 (US$3.30). 366 Richmond Rd. ✆ **613/729-2700.**

The Scout Shop Camping Centre   You can't miss the huge totem pole on the front lawn. Housed in the Scouts Canada Headquarters building, the Scout Shop has lots of practical, neat, and useful camping accessories, plus books, Scout uniforms, and small toys. 1345 Baseline Rd. ✆ **613/224-0139.**

Trailhead   Another outdoor adventure and hiking store, conveniently situated close to most of the others above, and not far from the bridge to Gatineau Park. Come here for canoes, kayaks, skis, snowshoes, travel clothing, and accessories. 1960 Scott St. ✆ **613/722-4229.**

PARTY SUPPLIES

The Papery *Finds*   This store sells unusual, delicate, pretty, and funky things made of paper—cards, wrapping paper, ribbons, invitations, stationery, journals, albums, and pens. During the holiday season, check out their selection of Christmas crackers and exquisite table-top angels. 850 Bank St. ✆ **613/230-1313.**

Party City   With balloons, decorations, plastic and paper tableware, cake-decorating products, invitations, and more, this is the perfect place to plan birthdays, baby showers, and other special events. 1595 Merivale Rd. ✆ **613/727-7480**; 2280 City Park Dr. ✆ **613/746-4712.**

Penguin's Palace Party Center   Come here for licensed kids' party supplies, Hallowe'en supplies and costumes, baby-shower supplies, balloons, decorations, and theme-party supplies. 105–2446 Bank St. ✆ **613/738-2898.**

SCIENCE & NATURE

Birder's Corner   Everything for the care and feeding of wild birds is sold here, from bird baths to feeders, seed, videos, nature books, and nature- and environment-themed educational toys. 2 Beechwood Ave. ✆ **613/741-0945.**

Wild Birds Unlimited   Serving birds and their admirers in the south end of the city, this franchised store stocks supplies and equipment for the care and feeding of wild birds. 1500 Bank St. ✆ **613/828-2849.**

Wizards and Lizards   Upstairs at Mrs. Tiggy Winkle's in the Glebe, you'll find toys in the science and nature vein, as well as helpful and friendly staff. 809 Bank St. ✆ **613/234-3836.**

SHOES

Kiddie Kobbler   For casual and dress shoes, boots, sandals, slippers, and dance shoes for your child, visit one of four Ottawa mall locations. Carlingwood Shopping Centre ✆ **613/722-5565**; Place d'Orléans ✆ **613/834-8876**; Rideau Centre ✆ **613/560-5311**; St. Laurent Shopping Centre ✆ **613/746-6411.**

SPORTS EQUIPMENT & CLOTHING

Cyco's   Specializing in rental and sales of in-line skates, bikes, and clothing and accessories for both sports, this store also sells used sports equipment. 5 Hawthorne Ave. (beside Rideau Canal) ℂ 613/567-8180; 780 Baseline Rd. ℂ 613/226-7277.

En equilibre   Come here for snowboards, skateboards, wakeboards, clothing, shoes, and accessories. 1071 Bank St. ℂ 613/730-8266.

Figure 8 Boutique Ltd   Whether you're skating in competitions or just gliding along the canal, Figure 8 has a skate for you. They offer new, used, and rental skates, as well as expert sharpening and skate mounting and hockey-skate blade replacement. 1408 Bank St. ℂ 613/731-4007.

Fresh Air Experience   This is the store for bicycles (mountain, hybrid, road, and children's), cross-country skis, and specialty clothing. 1291 Wellington St. W. ℂ 613/729-3002.

Kunstadt Sports   These ski, bike, snowboard, tennis, and hockey specialists offer equipment, clothing, and service. 1583 Bank St. ℂ 613/260-0696; 462 Hazeldean Rd. ℂ 613/831-2059.

Ritchie's Sports-Fan Apparel Shop   Sports fans will love the wide selection of licensed souvenirs, caps, and jerseys for all the major sports—hockey, baseball, football, basketball, and soccer. 134 Sparks St. ℂ 613/232-6278.

Running Room Canada   Come here for footwear and apparel for running, walking, swimming, and fitness. 911 Bank St. ℂ 613/233-5617; 160 Slater St. ℂ 613/233-5165; 1568 Merivale Rd. ℂ 613/228-3100.

Sensations   If you're looking for Sens gear this is the place to go. The official merchandise outlet of the Ottawa Senators Hockey Club is located in the Corel Centre at Gate 1 and is stocked with hats, jerseys, jackets, pucks, sweaters, shirts, T-shirts, and sticks. Corel Centre, 1000 Palladium Dr. ℂ 888/688-7367 or 613/599-0333.

Tommy & Lefebvre   One of the city's best-known sporting goods retailers, in business since 1958, Tommy & Lefebvre has an extensive selection of goods for adults and children. 464 Bank St., 2206 Carling Ave., and locations in Orléans and Gatineau. ℂ 888/888-7547.

THEME STORES

The Disney Store   All kinds of products, ranging from videos to dress-up costumes, baby and preschool clothing, beach towels, and stuffed Disney character toys, will thrill your little ones. You can even buy passes to Disney theme parks here. Staff love children, and the customer service is good. Rideau Centre ℂ 613/569-5500; Bayshore Shopping Centre ℂ 613/721-4155.

Hard Rock Café   This retail outlet in the restaurant sells souvenir Hard Rock Café merchandise featuring their logo, including T-shirts, caps, jackets, and pins. 73 York St. ℂ 613/241-2442.

TOYS

Ikea *(Value*   In addition to home furnishings especially for younger family members, Ikea has a great selection of European-style toys, including puppets, dollhouses, musical instruments, bean bags, and china tea sets. Of course, they have lots of toy storage, cushions, tables, and chairs, too. See "Children's Furniture," earlier in this chapter.

Lost Marbles   Grown-ups and kids alike will find this store fascinating. Where else would you find a plush moray eel, a build-your-own set of shark's jaws, a table with human legs, or 16 different kinds of dice? 315 Richmond Rd. ℭ 613/722-1469.

Mrs. Tiggy Winkle's   This store stocks a wide variety of educational and high-quality toys and games for infants to teens. It's a great place to browse. There's a two-floor emporium in the Glebe and several mall locations. 809 Bank St. ℭ 613/ 234-3836; Bayshore Shopping Centre ℭ 613/721-0549; Place d'Orléans ℭ 613/834-8988; Rideau Centre ℭ 613/230-8081.

Playvalue Toys   This is a full-line dealer for Little Tikes, Step 2, Brio, Play-mobil, Lego, and other quality toys. 1501 Carling Ave. ℭ 613/722-0175.

Scholar's Choice Retail Store   This store carries educational and high-quality toys for infants and up, as well as elementary teachers' resources. 2635 Alta Vista Dr. ℭ 613/260-8444; Carlingwood Shopping Centre ℭ 613/729-5665.

Toys R Us   This big-box retailer has a large selection of mainstream toys and other products for children. If they've seen it on TV, this is the place to get it. 1683 Merivale Rd. ℭ 613/228-8697; 1200 St. Laurent Blvd. ℭ 613-749-8697.

TRAVEL AGENCY

Let's Take the Kids Travel Agency   Yep, it's just what it says—a travel agency specializing in family travel to worldwide destinations. Don't leave home without picking up some brochures, resources, and advice for traveling with your children. The agency is tucked inside an office building and is accessible from Elgin or Metcalfe streets. 160 Elgin St. ℭ 613/594-5633.

VIDEOS

Two major video stores in the Ottawa area are **Blockbuster Video** and **Rogers Video,** both with more than a dozen locations. DVD and VHS movies, and games are available for sale and rental. Rental requires a membership.

10

Exploring the Region

As if there wasn't enough to do in Ottawa itself, if you travel around the area surrounding Canada's capital you'll find yourself planning an entire vacation of scenic drives, picturesque towns and villages, summer and winter sports, and museum visits. Leisure activities and tourist attractions in eastern Ontario and western Quebec could fill another book, but in this chapter I've highlighted some of the best daytrips to destinations around Ottawa that you can reach within an hour or so by car.

1 Hull, Gatineau & the Outaouais Hills

VISITOR INFORMATION

To obtain information for visitors to Quebec, visit the **Association touristique de l'Outaouais,** 103 Laurier St., Hull, PQ J8X 3V8 (*©* **800/265-7822** or 819/778-2222; fax 819/778-7758; www.western-quebec-tourism.org). The office is open mid-June to Labour Day (first Monday in September) Monday to Friday 8:30am to 8pm, Saturday to Sunday 9am to 6pm. The rest of the year, it's open Monday to Friday 8:30am to 5pm, weekends 9am to 4pm. The building is wheelchair accessible and there is free parking on the west side. The easiest way to reach the tourist office from Ottawa is to walk or drive across the Alexandra Bridge, which leads off Sussex Drive just east of the Parliament Buildings and west of the National Gallery. You'll see the office facing you as you come to the end of the bridge.

HULL

Hull was established in the early 1800s by Philemon Wright, an American Loyalist who shrewdly exploited the area's rich natural resources, primarily the forests of red and white pine. The forestry industry brought lumber camps and wood-processing factories to the region and attracted new residents—lumbermen, rafters, farmers, tradespeople, and merchants. Today, the pulp-and-paper mills of the Outaouais region still play an important role in the economy, with the federal government and the service industry as other major employers.

WHERE TO EAT

Hull is renowned for its excellent French cuisine. The many fine dining restaurants to be found there are not places to feed babies, toddlers, or fidgeters, but if you love to indulge in gourmet food and your children are older and well behaved or you can snag a baby-sitter, venture out to one of the following restaurants, or ask staff at your hotel or a visitors center to suggest one. Reservations are recommended to avoid disappointment. **Café Henry Burger** has been preparing fine cuisine in elegant surroundings for its patrons since 1922. It's located across from the Museum of Civilization, at 69 rue Laurier (*©* **819/777-5646**). **Café Jean Sebastian Bar** has a more casual atmosphere, serving mussels,

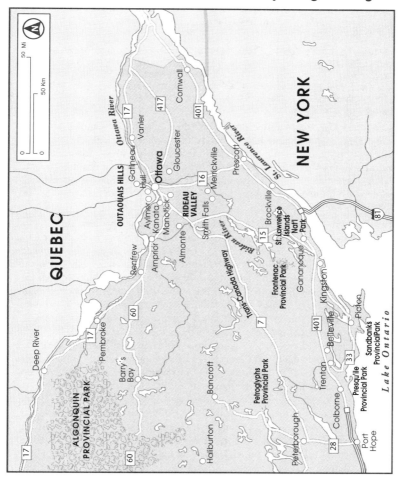

cassoulet, and filet mignon from its location at 49 rue St-Jacques (☎ **819/771-2934**). For dishes featuring local, seasonal produce, visit **Le Tartuffe,** at 133 rue Notre Dame (☎ **819/776-6424**). Housed in an old railway station, **Laurier sur Montcalm** is a small restaurant with a delicious menu. You'll find it at 199 rue Montcalm (☎ **819/775-5030**).

TO SEE & DO IN HULL

Canadian Museum of Civilization   The striking architecture of the Canadian Museum of Civilization simply cannot be missed as you gaze across the Ottawa River toward Hull. A short walk from Ottawa across the Alexandra Bridge will take you there, but you can also take a cab or drive if the weather is wicked. To explore the museum thoroughly, you need a full day, particularly if you want to spend time in the Children's Museum and the Postal Museum, which are in the same building (there's no extra charge for these attractions), and take in an IMAX film (you *do* need separate tickets for the IMAX). For detailed information on the Museum of Civilization, see chapter 6, "What Kids Like to See & Do," p. 98.

100 Laurier St., Hull, PQ. © 800/555-5621 or 819/776-7000. Admission C$8 (US$5) adults, C$6 (US$4) students, C$7 (US$4.50) seniors, C$4 (US$2.50) children 2–12, C$20 (US$13) family (max. 5 members). Sun half-price. Additional fee for IMAX theater. May 1–Thanksgiving (second Mon in Oct) daily 9am–6pm, Thurs until 9pm; July 1–Labour Day (first Mon in Sept) also open Fri until 9pm; Thanksgiving–Apr 30 Tues–Sun 9am–5pm, Thurs until 9pm. IMAX screenings do not always correspond with museum hours and extended evening hours do not apply to the Children's Museum.

Canadian Children's Museum   Inside the Canadian Museum of Civilization, there's a unique place for children to play and explore. Included with the admission price to the main exhibits, the Children's Museum is a trip around the world—kids can tour the pyramids of Egypt, listen to African drum beats, and take a ride on an Indian tour bus through the exciting exhibits, all kid-size and all designed for maximum interaction. See chapter 6, "What Kids Like to See & Do," for more details.

Ecomuseum (ECOMUSÉE)   Don't be fooled by the apparent size of this museum, housed in a quaint historic building. Good things come in small packages, and this museum is a fine place to spend a couple of hours. There's a little bit of everything in here. A huge sphere representing the planet Earth greets you as you wind your way down a curved pathway to the main exhibits, which trace the origins of life on Earth up to the arrival of modern humans. There are lots of authentic fossils on display, which fascinate many kids. Interactive exhibits demonstrate the formation of continents, volcanoes, earthquakes, and magnetic fields. If you've ever wondered what an earthquake feels like, step into the high-tech simulator and experience two quakes—the larger one reaches 7.0 on the Richter scale. More than 5,000 insect specimens are displayed in the Insectarium and along the sides of the main corridor. Don't worry, they don't crawl or creep around. There are spiders, beetles, moths, butterflies, and stick insects to marvel over, in myriad colors, forms, and sizes. Kids aged 4 to 6 (aka dinosaur crazy) will love the life-size replica of a Styracosaurus, a dinosaur that once roamed the Canadian prairies more than 65 million years ago. In the main lobby is a small souvenir shop where kids can choose knick knacks with insect motifs. There's a good selection of rocks and minerals, many at kid-friendly prices. My daughter enjoyed choosing five small polished stones from a large goldfish bowl for the grand sum of C$2 (US$1.50). Take a few minutes to watch the water clock in operation before you go. Free parking is available in the lot across the street.

170 Montcalm St., Hull, PQ. © 819/595-7790. Admission C$5 (US$3) ages 16 and over, C$4 (US$2.50) students, seniors, and children 6 and over, C$13 (US$9) family (max. 4 members), free for children 5 and under. May 1–early Sept daily 10am–6pm; early Sept–Apr 30 Tues–Sun 10am–4pm.

PARKS

On the shore of the Ottawa River next to the Canadian Museum of Civilization, **Jacques-Cartier Park** has beautiful pathways for strolling or cycling. The small stone house at the western end of the park was built by Philemon Wright, the founder of Hull, in the late 1830s. At the opposite end of the park, you'll find an information booth, La Maison du Vélo, where you can obtain information on recreational pathways in the Outaouais region. Jacques-Cartier Park offers spectacular views of the Ottawa skyline and hosts Winterlude activities, as well as a fireworks display on Canada Day. **Lake Leamy Ecological Park** is bordered by

Lake Leamy, the Gatineau River, and the Ottawa River. Vehicular access is via boulevard Fournier. The park offers a supervised beach, a refreshment pavilion, washrooms, and picnic tables. The Casino de Hull is on the opposite shore of Lake Leamy. For park information, call ✆ **819/239-5000.** If you want to walk in the steps of history, seek out the Indian Portage Trail at Little Chaudière Rapids in **Brébeuf Park.** To reach the park, take boulevard Alexandre-Taché, turn left onto rue Coalier, opposite the south entrance to Gatineau Park, then continue to Brébeuf Park. At the eastern end of the park, where the trail continues beside the river, is the old portage route that was used by First Nations peoples, fur traders, and explorers. A statue of Saint Jean de Brébeuf memorializes this 17th-century French missionary. Look for the rock steps used by the voyageurs when they transported their goods and equipment by land to circumvent the rapids.

Hull–Chelsea–Wakefield Steam Train   For a great day out, take the family for a trip on an authentic steam train, one of the last steam trains in operation in Canada. Traveling along one of the most scenic rail routes in eastern Canada, a 1907 steam locomotive will take you on a 64-kilometer (40 mile) journey along the banks of the Gatineau River bordering Gatineau Park. The nine air-conditioned coaches, built in the 1940s, can accommodate 528 passengers. One car is accessible for passengers with disabilities, but if you require seating in this coach, you should say so when you book your tickets. There are two washrooms in each coach, and the train has a snack bar and souvenir shop on board. The round trip is 5 hours long—the journey is 1½ hours in each direction, and there's a 2-hour stopover in the pretty village of Wakefield. While you're in Wakefield, you can watch the locomotive turn around for the return journey on the only manually operated turntable in Canada. There are boutiques and restaurants in Wakefield to help you pass the time until you hop back on the train, or you might take one of the guided tours of Wakefield or the steam train.

Tips

Ask one of the train engineers if your kids can climb up into the locomotive cabin while the train is in the station.

During the journey, you'll be entertained by strolling minstrels and bilingual tour guides, who will share stories and music surrounding the region's history and the steam locomotive's colorful past. There are many special events, including Mother's Day brunch, Sunday brunch, Fall Foliage Tours, Sunset Dinner Trains, and Family Packages featuring accommodations, museum admissions, and sightseeing tours in addition to the steam train excursion.

165 Deveault St., Hull, PQ. ✆ **800/871-7246** or 819/778-7246. Return ticket prices starting from C$29 (US$19) adults, C$26 (US$17) seniors, C$25 (US$16) students, C$14 (US$9) children, C$74 (US$49) family of 2 adults and 2 children. Price varies according to season and package. Reservations required. May–Oct on various days.

GATINEAU

The city of **Gatineau,** across from Hull on the Gatineau River, was created in 1975 with the merger of seven smaller communities. With a population over 100,000, Gatineau is now the largest city in the Outaouais region. Gatineau's

Municipal Arts Centre features entertainment throughout the year. Every year on Labour Day weekend, the **Gatineau Hot Air Balloon Festival** draws large crowds. Rue Jacques-Cartier has numerous sidewalk cafes that offer a great view of Ottawa and the Ottawa River. **Lac-Beauchamp Park** is a large urban park where you can swim, picnic, canoe, bike, skate, and cross-country ski. For park information call ℭ **819/669-2548.**

For more information on the city of Gatineau, call ℭ 800/668-8383 or 819/243-2345, or contact the **Association touristique de l'Outaouais,** 103 Laurier St., Hull, PQ ℭ 800/265-7822 or 819/778-2222.

AYLMER

The town of Aylmer lies to the west of Hull. A cycle path follows the shores of the Ottawa River and there is a large family beach. For information on outdoor activities in Aylmer, contact the **Association touristique de l'Outaouais,** 103 Laurier St., Hull, PQ ℭ **800/265-7822** or 819/778-2222.

GATINEAU PARK

Just a short drive from downtown Ottawa lies a beautifully preserved wilderness park. Within the 361 square kilometers (141 sq. miles) of Gatineau Park, there are 200 kilometers (125 miles) of cross-country ski trails and 175 kilometers (115 miles) of hiking and biking trails. The park's landscape is carved from the Canadian Shield, and the exposed rocks, dating back to the Precambrian Era, are among the oldest exposed rocks on earth. More than 50 glacial lakes are scattered throughout the park. The forested areas consist mainly of maple and oak; spruce, white pine, and eastern hemlock cover only about 3% of the park's land. The large number of rare plant and animal species has stimulated many scientific research projects. Gatineau Park is open year-round and has something to offer in every season. Vehicle access fees are in effect in certain areas of the park during the peak summer period of mid-June to early September. Your first stop should be the **Visitor Centre,** at 33 Scott Rd., Chelsea, PQ (ℭ **800/465-1867** or 819/827-2020), open every day of the year. It's a great source for all kinds of park maps and information on special events and festivals. The knowledgeable and friendly staff are available to answer questions and help you to plan your visit.

Mackenzie King Estate The estate of William Lyon Mackenzie King, Canada's longest-serving prime minister, lies in the midst of Gatineau Park and was bequeathed to the Canadian people upon his death in 1950. You can visit the restored cottages on the property and stroll through the gardens, which include formal flower beds, a hidden rock garden, and a collection of picturesque ruins. The estate screens short films describing the life and times of Mackenzie King, and guides are on hand to answer questions. There is a tearoom on the premises serving light refreshments. The estate is open mid-May to mid-October, weekdays 11am to 5pm, weekends and holidays 10am to 6pm. For more information call ℭ **819/827-2020.**

WILDLIFE Lakes in the park are home to 40 species of **fish,** including trout, yellow perch, pike, and bass, which are all popular sport-fishing catches. Around 2,000 **white-tailed deer** also live in the park. They are most likely to be observed feeding in early morning or late afternoon, close to La Pêche Lake and Philippe Lake, or in open fields and alongside roads. In the far northwest corner of the park live one or two **timber wolf** packs. You are unlikely to see them as they avoid contact with humans, but you might be lucky enough to hear them howl. A wolf pack howls in a drawn-out, harmonious chorus, which is distinguishable from the short, high-pitched bark of a **coyote** pack.

When you're on the trails, have the kids keep an eye out for **bear** tracks on muddy sections of the trail and around beaver ponds. If you're unfamiliar with animal tracks, drop into the Visitor Centre before your hike and ask the staff for information. Kids love to play at being a tracker. They can also watch for claw marks on the trunks of trees—bears love to climb.

Along the Gatineau Parkway, there are numerous **beaver** ponds, where you can observe these busy, furry creatures in action, especially at dawn and dusk. Other wildlife that make the park their home include the **bobcat, Canada lynx, wolverine, mink,** and **otter.** If you enjoy bird-watching, you're in for a treat. The waterways, fields, forests, wetlands, and rocky escarpments provide vital food and shelter for around 230 species of **birds.** A brochure listing dozens of species and hints for when and where to observe the park's feathered friends is available from the Visitor Centre. **Grass snakes, turtles, frogs, toads, bull frogs, tree frogs, salamanders,** and **newts** are also native park inhabitants.

Tips **What should I do if I meet a bear?**

The bear population in Gatineau Park is estimated at around 200. If you happen to see a bear on a trail, make loud noises and keep your distance. Never try to feed a bear or approach it, as you may make the bear feel threatened. Keep well away from a mother and her cubs, and never position yourself between them. Never try to outrun, outswim, or outclimb a bear, since the animal may interpret your actions as a sign of weakness.

CAMPING   Gatineau Park has three campgrounds, each offering a different outdoors experience. **Philippe Lake** is the largest campground, with 246 wooded campsites. Sandy beaches, a convenience store, and plenty of water taps and washrooms contribute to a comfortable family vacation. If you don't mind fewer modern conveniences in exchange for being a little closer to the wilderness, try **Taylor Lake,** which offers rustic tent camping with only 33 sites, all close to the lake. If you want still more of a back-to-nature adventure, **La Pêche Lake** has canoe-in camping available at 35 individual in a dozen wooded areas around the lake. For all three sites, call © **819/456-3016** or fax © 819/456-3134 to make campsite reservations. To arrange boat and mountain-bike rentals for Philippe Lake and Taylor Lake, call © **819/456-3555.** To rent a boat for La Pêche Lake, call © **819/456-3494.** Note that alcholic beverages are not allowed in the campgrounds or elsewhere in the park. Pets are not allowed in campgrounds, picnic areas, or on beaches, although dogs on a leash are permitted on hiking trails.

CYCLING/MOUNTAIN BIKING   Grab a map at the Visitor Centre to help you plan your route on the network of trails and paved bikeways in the park. The length and variety of mountain-bike trails are excellent. Trails are open from May 15 to November 30. The sport is restricted to designated trails to protect the natural environment; you may not use cross-country ski trails for winter biking. Mountain bikes are available for rental. Contact the Visitor Centre for more information.

Tips **Tough Bike Trails**

Because of its topography, the park's network of bike paths requires cyclists to be in good physical condition and experienced in cycling on challenging terrain. If you have young children, you will find the relatively flat and smooth surface of the bikeways in Ottawa easier and more enjoyable for a family cycling excursion. You might also consider cycling in the park on Sunday mornings in the summer, when the main roadways are closed to motorized traffic.

HIKING   There are 175 kilometers (115 miles) of hiking trails in the park, including around 90 kilometers (56 miles) of shared-use trails (walkers and mountain bikers), with the remainder set aside exclusively for hiking. Some of the shorter trails feature interpretation panels and are suitable for wheelchair and stroller access. If you are considering hiking one of the longer trails, make sure you and your family are sufficiently prepared, with appropriate clothing, food, water, and sturdy, comfortable footwear. The Gatineau Visitor's Centre has an excellent map available (1:25,000 scale) for C$5 (US$3); it is strongly recommended for hikers and mountain bikers.

If you enter the park at the south entrance, off boulevard Alexandre-Taché in Hull, the first short trail you'll find is **Des Fées Lake,** a 1.5-kilometer (1 mile) trail around a small lake; the trail should take about an hour to walk. A little further along the Gatineau Parkway, **Hickory Trail** is a short trail, just under 1 kilometer (0.5 mile) long, which takes about 20 minutes to walk. The trail has been designed so you can comfortably push a stroller or wheelchair along the route, and a picnic area and interpretive panels provide diversion along the pathway.

As you drive deeper into the park, you'll pass **Pink Lake.** This site is exceptionally beautiful in the fall, when the many deciduous trees turn to red, orange, and yellow against a background of dark green firs. Pink Lake (it's green, by the way, not pink) is unusual because it is one of only a dozen or so meromictic lakes in Canada. Because there is no circulation between the different layers of water, the lake harbors prehistoric bacteria, 10,000-year-old sedimentary deposits, and saltwater fish that have adapted to fresh water. There is a 2.5-kilometer (1.7 mile) trail around the lake, which takes around an hour and a half to walk.

Fun Fact **Is it squishy on the bottom?**

A "meromictic" lake is an unusual body of water where there is no circulation between the different layers of water. It typically has a green colour and is home to saltwater fish that have adapted to freshwater conditions. There are often sedimentary deposits dating back 10,000 years and prehistoric bacteria in its depths.

If you're looking for panoramic vistas, try one of the trails leading to the top of the **Eardley Escarpment.** A steep 2-kilometer (1.25 mile) path called **King Mountain Trail** rewards hikers with a wonderful view of the Ottawa Valley.

Further into the park, the **Champlain Trail,** 1.3 kilometers (0.9 mile) long, has interpretive panels explaining how the site has evolved since the time of the last glaciers. From the **Champlain Lookout,** the valley view sweeps majestically for miles. To reach the picturesque **Luskville Falls Trail,** travel west on boulevard Alexandre-Taché past the main south entrance to Gatineau Park, and continue west on Highway 148 to Luskville. Follow signs for Luskville Falls, where you'll find a parking lot and picnic site. The 5-kilometer (3 mile) trail leads to the top of the Eardley Escarpment, where you will have a great view of the Ottawa Valley.

SWIMMING   There are five public beaches with lifeguard supervision within the park, located at Philippe, Meech, and La Pêche lakes. The beaches are open 10am to 6pm daily from mid-June to early September. Swimming is prohibited in the beach areas outside these times, and at all times elsewhere in the park.

WINTER IN THE PARK   Outdoor families don't hibernate in the winter, and Gatineau Park has lots to offer them. An extensive network of cross-country ski trails and special trails for hiking, snowshoeing, and kick-sledding will keep you and your kids active and outside. For downhill skiing and snowboarding, Camp Fortune ski resort is right in the park. Lessons and equipment rental are available. See "Family Adventures," later in this chapter. For more information, contact **Camp Fortune** at ✆ **819/827-1717.**

SPECIAL EVENTS IN GATINEAU PARK

Other events may be scheduled in addition to the ones listed above, and dates may change from year to year. For more information, contact the **Gatineau Park Visitor Centre,** 33 Scott Rd., Chelsea, PQ ✆ **819/827-2020.**

January

The park celebrates winter with a weekend ski festival, including ski lesssons for beginners and activities for the whole family.

February

The annual Keskinada Loppet has a cross-country ski event for every member of the family—there's even a 2-kilometer (1.25 mile) mini-Keski for children under 12.

March

A spring celebration on the second Sunday of the month marks the end of winter.

May

The Mackenzie King Estate opens for the summer season.

The Canadian Tulip Festival is celebrated at Mackenzie King Estate.

Sunday Bikedays begin for the season.

July

Canada Day celebrations take place at Mackenzie King Estate.

The Mackenzie King Estate hosts the Flower Festival.

September

Mackenzie King Estate celebrates Labour Day weekend with festivities.

September/October

Fall Rhapsody, a celebration of nature's autumn colors, takes place in the park.

October

Thanksgiving weekend activities are held at Mackenzie King Estate.

2 The Rideau Valley

The Rideau Valley lies southwest of Ottawa, following the path of the **Rideau Canal.** The canal is actually a continuous chain of beautiful lakes, rivers, and canal cuts, stretching a distance of 202 kilometers (125 miles) between Ottawa and Kingston, and often described as the most scenic waterway in North America. The Rideau Canal waterway has been designated a national historic site and is one of nine historic canals in Canada. Parks Canada has the responsibility of preserving and maintaining the canal's natural and historic features and providing a safe waterway for boats to navigate. You can explore the region by boat; drive along the **Heritage Route,** which will take you through the towns and villages along the waterway; or hike a portion of the **Rideau Trail,** a cleared and marked footpath about 300 kilometers (185 miles) long that meanders between Ottawa and Kingston.

RIDEAU CANAL AND LOCKS

The canal and locks that link the lakes and rivers of the Rideau Valley were constructed between 1826 and 1832 to provide a safe route for the military between Montreal and Kingston in the wake of the War of 1812. Colonel By, the British engineer in charge of the project, had the foresight to build the locks and canal large enough to permit commercial traffic to access the system, rather than building the canal solely for military use. As things turned out, the inhabitants of North America decided to live peaceably. The canal became a main transportation and trade route, and communities along the canal grew and thrived. With the introduction of railroads in the mid-19th century, the commercial traffic subsided and the canal gradually became a tourist destination owing to its beauty and tranquility. The locks have operated continuously since they first opened.

MANOTICK

Manotick is a quiet village about 24 kilometers (15 miles) south of Ottawa on the banks of the Rideau River. The original settlement grew around a water-powered grist mill, now known as **Watson's Mill,** on the west side of the river. The village expanded around the original buildings, which date from the mid-1800s, and now includes residences on Long Island, a 3.5-kilometer (2 mile) long island in the river, and an area on the east side of the river. **Dickinson Square,** in the heart of the village, is a good spot for strolling and visiting local shops. Wander across the dam and take the kids to feed the ducks on the millpond. **Watson's Mill** is open to visitors in the summer. Every second Sunday afternoon from June to October, the mill swings into operation, grinding wheat to make flour. You can wander through the five-story historic stone

Rideau Canal Numbers

- Number of locks in the main channel   45
- Number of lockstations   24
- Length of canal (Ottawa–Kingston)   202km (125 miles)
- Length of man-made canal cuts   19km (12 miles)
- Minimum available water depth   1.5m (5 ft.)
- Size of locks   41m (134 ft.) by 10m (33 ft.)
- Travel time, one-way   3 to 5 days

building or take a guided tour. Call 𝓒 **613/692-2500** for information on opening hours and tour times. To get to Manotick from Ottawa, take Riverside Drive south to the village. To reach the mill, cross the bridge to the west bank of the river.

(*Fun Fact* **The Haunted Mill**

Watson's Mill is reputedly haunted. Ghostly sightings have been reported of a tall, fair-haired young woman, believed to be the wife of Joseph Currier, one of the original mill owners. During a visit to the mill in 1861, the young bride's long skirts were accidentally caught in a revolving turbine shaft. She was thrown against a nearby support pillar and died instantly.

MERRICKVILLE

The picturesque village of Merrickville is a popular tourist destination, especially in the summer months when the streets are decorated with flowers. The community was chosen as Ontario's most beautiful village in 1996 and as Canada's most beautiful village in 1998. Many professional artists make their home in the vicinity of Merrickville, and their wares, ranging from paintings to leather crafts, wood carvings, blown glass, pottery, and other creations, are available in boutiques and shops in the village. The village, founded in 1793 by William Merrick, was originally a large industrial center on the Rideau with a number of woolen mills, sawmills, and grist mills. The original blockhouse, overlooking the locks, is now a small museum. Several cafes and restaurants are dotted about the village. Just west of the village is the **Rideau National Migratory Bird Sanctuary.** To reach Merrickville, continue south along the scenic route beside the Rideau River and past Manotick. If you travel along the west bank of the river on County Road 13, you'll pass **Baxter Conservation Area,** where you can stop for a picnic, stroll, or swim. Continue on County Road 13 to County Road 5. Turn left toward Becketts Landing, passing **Rideau River Provincial Park** on your left, another pleasant spot to stretch and enjoy the outdoors. Just after the park, the road changes to County Road 2 and takes you straight to Merrickville. For a more direct, faster route from Ottawa, use Highway 416 south (exit 42 or 43).

SMITHS FALLS

The town of Smiths Falls, established in the mid-1800s, was built around the heart of the Rideau Canal. There are three small museums in the town that chronicle the history of the canal, the railroads, and the pioneers who settled in this district. Check opening hours before visiting, since two of them are open by appointment only during the winter months. There's one other attraction that your kids will not let you drive by—the **Hershey Chocolate Factory.** To reach Smiths Falls, take County Road 43 west from Merrickville (exit 43 on Hwy. 416). An alternative route from Ottawa is to take the 417 west to Highway 7 west, then take Highway 15 south to Smiths Falls.

Heritage House Museum   Adjacent to the Rideau Canal, Old Slys Lockstation, and a Victorian landscaped picnic area, this house has been restored to the time of Confederation. Seven period rooms are featured, reflecting the lifestyle of a wealthy millowner. Special programs, tours, and events are scheduled throughout the year. There's an annual strawberry social, Victorian tea served on Thursday afternoons in July and August, and Christmas celebrations in the winter.

Old Slys Rd. (off Hwy 43), Smiths Falls, ON. ℂ **613/283-8560**. Call for admission fee. Jan 2–Apr 30 Mon–Fri 11am–4:30pm; May 1–Dec 21 daily 11am–4:30pm.

Hershey Canada Chocolate Factory Tour   Kids of all ages will love this free tour of the Hershey plant. My youngest never tires of taking family and friends to watch thousands of chocolate bars take shape right before her eyes. The tour is actually a self-guided walk along an enclosed gallery with windows looking down to the factory floor. You can see huge vats of melted chocolate being stirred, chocolate molds traveling along conveyor belts to be filled with chocolate, individual bars being wrapped and packed for shipping, and boxes moving along the conveyor belt around the factory. At the end of the tour, where else do you end up but in the middle of a store selling Hershey products. We buy a small treat for each child when we make the trip. You may snag a bargain, but be prepared to elbow your way past customers with bulging bags of calories as they line up at the cash registers. You can shop at the store without taking the tour, if you wish. The factory is easy to find by road, since it's well signposted once you reach the town of Smiths Falls.

Hershey Canada Inc., 1 Hershey Dr., Smiths Falls, ON. ℂ **613/283-3300**. Free admission. Mon–Sat 9am–6pm, Sun 10am–4pm. Closed on some holidays, so call before you go.

Rideau Canal Museum   This museum has many hands-on displays for visitors to explore. You can operate a working lock model or test your skill as a canal skipper as you maneuver a model boat. Climb up to the lookout to get a bird's-eye view of the Rideau Canal and Smiths Falls. Lots of artifacts and historical displays share five floors with high-tech touch-screen computers and laserdisc mini-theaters.

34 Beckwith St. S., Smiths Falls, ON. ℂ **613/284-0505**. Call for admission fee. Mid-June–Labour Day (first Mon in Sept) daily 10am–6pm; spring and fall Tues–Sun 10am–5pm; winter by appointment.

Smiths Falls Railway Museum   Railroad buffs will enjoy a visit to this museum, which has a collection of railway artifacts, including express train and passenger train memorabilia, archives, track tools, and old photographs and prints. Kids will love the full-size locomotives, passenger coaches, and cabooses.

90 William St., Smiths Falls, ON. ℂ **613/283-5696**. Call for admission fee. May–Oct daily 10am–4:30pm; Sept–April by appointment.

3 Family Adventures

DOWN THE HILLS

Within a short drive of Ottawa are many ski centers that will thrill downhill skiers and snowboarders. Elevation at the ski hills near Ottawa ranges from 106 to 381 meters (350 to 1,250 ft.). The facilities and runs are compact compared to those in major resort destinations like Mont Tremblant and Mont Ste-Anne, but they have the advantage of being close by. Equipment rental, lessons, daycare for under 5s, children's ski areas, snowboard parks for teenagers, and challenging runs for mom and dad—it's all here on a small scale and you can be home in time for supper.

Calabogie Peaks   Reputed to have the highest vertical in Ontario, the resort offers 22 runs and a snowboard terrain park. Ice skating is available at the resort, and cross-country skiing, ice fishing, snowshoeing, and snowmobiling facilities are nearby. In the summer, you can swim, fish, canoe, windsurf, play tennis or beach volleyball, go mountain biking, or just lie on the beach. To get to Calabogie Peaks, travel on Highway 417 (the Queensway) west. Approximately 8 kilometers (5 miles) past Arnprior, turn left onto Calabogie Road and continue to Calabogie Peaks Resort.

Calabogie Rd., near Arnprior, ON. ✆ **800/669-4861** or 613/752-2720. www.calabogie.com.

Camp Fortune   Only about a 15-minute drive from downtown Ottawa in the heart of Gatineau Park, Camp Fortune has 17 runs, a snowboard park, a designated children's area, and several quad lifts. A new kids' park opened during the 2000/2001 winter season with a handle tow for little snowbunnies. The kids' park has a mini half-pipe and rollers so kids can learn skiing and boarding in a fun but safe environment. The supervised park is open on weekends and holidays. Renovations were recently made to one of Camp Fortune's main lodges. You can book a single ski lesson at Camp Fortune or join a program lasting several days or weeks. Family nights are held on Saturdays from 5pm onwards with a special offer of two-for-one ticket and ski rentals. Mountain biking is offered in summer. To get to Camp Fortune, take Highway 5 north to exit 12, signposted CHEMIN OLD CHELSEA. Travel west on Meech Lake Road and turn left into Camp Fortune.

300 chemin Dunlop, Chelsea, PQ. ✆ **888/283-1717** or 819/827-1717. www.campfortune.com.

Edelweiss   Edelweiss made a number of improvements prior to the 2000/2001 ski season. They renovated the main lodge and added a new cafeteria with a great mountain view and twice the seating capacity of the old refreshment area. They also installed a new magic carpet lift for children, purchased a fleet of new snow-making guns, and created a new snowboard park to take advantage of the mountain's natural terrain. A ski bus runs on weekends and holidays, leaving from three locations in Ottawa (outside Tommy & Lefebvre sports stores). On Saturday nights from 6pm to closing, a two-for-one deal is available on all categories of lift tickets. There's also a special family package, which in 2000/2001 offered full-day lift tickets for two adults and two children ages 6 to 12 for C$70 (US$46).

To get to Edelweiss, take Highway 5 north to Route 105 toward Wakefield. Take Route 366 east (chemin Edelweiss) to the ski hill. It's about a half-hour drive from Ottawa.

540 chemin Edelweiss, Wakefield, PQ. ✆ **819/459-2328**. www.edelweissvalley.com.

Le Grand Splash Water Park   In Edelweiss Valley, Quebec, you can also swoosh down the hills in the summer months. This family water park features five water slides, a children's pool, a lounge pool, and an enormous 50-foot hot tub. Picnic areas and tennis courts are also on-site. Follow Highway 5 north to Highway 105 north and exit on Highway 366 east.

Edelweiss Valley, PQ. ✆ **819/459-3551**.

Mont Cascades   This resort offers plenty of activities in winter and summer. There are 6 lifts and 15 runs, with illuminated night skiing on 11 of those. Lessons and equipment rental are available. The six-slide **water park** has something for everyone. There's an area for kids under 121 centimeters (4 ft.) tall, with water sprays, a small slide, and a wading pool. For older and braver kids, there's a tunnel slide, a six-story drop slide, and larger slides that several people can slip down together in a raft. When it's time to eat, visit the restaurant or bring your own lunch and munch on a picnic table in the shade. To get to Mont Cascades from Ottawa, take the Macdonald-Cartier Bridge to Hull, then take Highway 50 east. Take the first exit, which is boulevard Archambault. Turn right onto Highway 307. Turn left on chemin Mont Cascades, and proceed 7 kilometers (4.3 miles) to Mont Cascades. It's about half an hour's drive from Ottawa.

448 chemin Mont-Cascades, Cantley, QC © **888/282-2722** or 819/827-0301. www.moncascades.ca.

Mont Ste-Marie   This resort has the highest vertical in the Outaouais region at more than 1,200 feet. Two peaks and two high-speed chairlifts give beginners and experienced skiers a choice of 24 runs in total. One of the longest beginner trails in western Quebec, snowboard parks, a huge half-pipe, and a permanent bordercross course will provide the kids with plenty of thrills. Rentals and lessons are available. To reach Mont Ste-Marie, take Highway 5 north through Hull and join Highway 105 north. Stay on 105 until you see the signs for Mont Ste-Marie, a driving time of about 1 hour from Ottawa. A ski bus operates from Ottawa, leaving from Lansdowne Park on Saturday and Sunday mornings all season.

76 chemin de la Montagne, RR#1. Lac Ste-Marie, PQ. © **800/567-1256** or 819/467-5200. www. montstemarie.com.

Mount Pakenham   West of Ottawa, Mount Pakenham offers downhill and cross-country skiing, snowboarding, and snowtubing. Pakenham is equipped with 7 lifts and 10 alpine runs. There's a snowboard and terrain park, and night skiing is available. Family lesson packages are offered, so the whole family can learn a new sport or improve their technique together. To get to Mount Pakenham, take the Queensway (Hwy. 417) west past Kanata. The road will reduce to two lanes and become Highway 17. Turn left on Road 20 across a stone bridge, and turn left at the stop sign onto Road 29/Highway 15. Drive through the village of Pakenham. Turn right on McWatty Road to a T-junction. Turn right to Mount Pakenham. It's approximately 25 minutes' drive from the Corel Centre exit on Highway 417.

Pakenham, ON. © **800/665-7105** or 613/624-5290. www.mountpakenham.com.

Ski Vorlage   This resort offers a choice of 15 runs for family skiing and boarding, with 12 illuminated for night skiing. Bring along your skates (there's no charge to use the rink) or try snowtubing. Our family loves tubing—in fact, we prefer it to old-fashioned tobogganing, but that might have something to do with the fact that you get towed back up the hill on your tube instead of struggling up the slope on foot while lugging a toboggan behind you. Tubing tickets are C$10 (US$7) per person for two hours or C$14 (US$9) for four hours. If you're buying a lift ticket for skiing or snowboarding, tubing tickets are just C$5 (US$3). A few words of advice: Two hours of tubing on a chilly winter's day will be plenty. You get very little exercise when tubing and therefore get cold quickly. It's also not recommended for children under 4. But it's loads of fun. A new child-care center opened in the 2000/2001 season to provide day care for tots too small to ski. Vorlage is about 25 minutes from Ottawa by car. Follow Highway 5 north to Highway 105 north and turn right into Wakefield. Turn onto Burnside Road and follow the signs to Vorlage.

65 Burnside Rd., Wakefield, PQ. © **877/867-5243** or 819/459-2301. www.skivorlage.com.

OUT OF THE SKY

Great Canadian Bungee   Try to picture a majestic limestone quarry with 60-meter (200 ft.) high sides, surrounding a spring-fed lagoon of deepest aqua blue. Now, imagine your loved ones jumping off a platform suspended above the water, attached by a bungee cord. You either love the idea or you hate it, but it's certainly an unusual spectacle. If you don't want to take part in the madness, come to enjoy the barbecue and picnic facilities, play and swim at the supervised beach area, rent a paddle boat or kayak, and be entertained by all those crazy dudes who are willing to pay up to C$100 (US$66) for the biggest adrenaline rush of all time. Note that there are no age restrictions, but jumpers must weigh at least 36 kilograms (80 lb.). Recently another thrill ride was introduced at the site—the RIPRIDE. It's a 310-meter (1,015 ft.) cable slide that accelerates as you travel along its length, reaching a top speed of 100kmph (62 mph). You can ride tandem on the slide if the combined weight is between 36 and 127 kilograms (80 and 280 lb.). Life will never be the same again.

Morrison's Quarry, Wakefield, PQ. ✆ **819/459-3714**. infoweb.magi.com/~bungee/.

ALONG THE RIVER

The Ottawa River, one of the most popular white-water rafting and kayaking rivers in Canada, has everything for the white-water enthusiast—dozens of islands, rapids, waterfalls, sandy beaches, and dramatic rock formations. It's even said the water is warm (I can't confirm or deny that, but you're welcome to tackle the white water and find out for yourself). An hour or two northwest of Ottawa, a number of white-water tour operators have established businesses that allow novices and families to enjoy running the rapids just as much as experienced extreme-sports participants.

Esprit Rafting   Offering day trips and longer-stay outdoor adventure packages, Esprit Rafting operates on the Ottawa River about 90 kilometers (60 miles) from Ottawa; the company can arrange transportation between Ottawa and the rafting site. Esprit offers a white-water experience for the whole family. In the morning, the family (children must be 7 or older) rafts together with the assistance of an experienced guide. In the afternoon, children under 12 take part in supervised shore activities while parents and children over 12 take a more adventurous trip over the rapids. The day trip meets at a rendevous point along the highway. Get directions when you call to make your reservation.

✆ **800/596-7238** or **819/683-3641**. www.espritrafting.com.

Madawaska Kanu Center   The Madawaska River Family Float Trip is a 2-hour ride along a 5-kilometer (3 mile) stretch of the Madawaska River near Algonquin Park. This is such a gentle ride that children age 2 and over are accepted on the raft. The trips run Monday to Thursday, departing hourly from 10am to 2pm. No daycare or refreshments are provided at this site. Reservations are required.

P.O. Box 635, Barry's Bay, ON K0J 1B0. ✆ **613/756-3620**. www.owl-mkc.ca.

Owl Rafting   Owl Rafting operates on the Ottawa River near Forester's Falls, between Renfrew and Pembroke off Highway 17. They offer a half-day family float trip that takes you over 6 kilometers (3.7 miles) along the river, through white water and calm pools. They return you to base on a gentle cruising raft (with chairs and a barbecue lunch on board). Passengers must weigh a minimum of 22 kilograms (50 lb.) and be at least 8 years old. Day care is available at the base for any child under the age of 12, at a cost of C$18 (US$12) per child. Trips run on weekdays, and lifejackets and helmets are provided. Wetsuits are available at extra cost. No paddling is required—just hold on and enjoy riding waves up to 1 meter (3 ft.) in height. Reservations are required.

P.O. Box 29, Forester's Falls, ON K0J 1V0. ✆ **613/646-2263**. www.owl-mkc.ca.

River Run Rafting and Paddle Center River Run, just a 90-minute drive northwest of Ottawa, is a 137-acre riverfront resort on the Ottawa River. They offer a half-day family rafting trip on a gentle route over the rapids, and everyone on board gets involved—you get to paddle on this one. There's also a complete range of outdoor recreational activities at the resort, including horseback riding, camping, and splat ball. Family packages with overnight accommodation can be arranged.

P.O. Box 179, Beachburg, ON K0J 1C0. ✆ 800/267-8504 or 613/646-2501. www.riverrunners.com.

Wilderness Tours Wilderness Tours is a 650-acre resort and adventure destination on the banks of the Ottawa River. Family raft trips are geared toward families with children between the ages of 7 and 12. Raft trips are 4 to 6 hours long and include professional guides and a post-trip video and barbecue. They run a popular family program, which combines a gentle rafting day trip with a second day on the river in sportyaks or voyageur canoes. The package includes meals, scenic camping or cabin rental, use of the resort facilities, and a supervised children's program in the evenings.

P.O. Box 89, Beachburg, ON K0J 1C0. ✆ 800/267-9166 or 613/646-2291. www.wildernesstours.com.

UNDER THE GROUND

When you've explored air, land, and water, what do you do next? Go underground, of course.

Diefenbunker Cold War Museum Visit an underground bunker built during the period of the Cold War and designed to shelter the Canadian government in the event of nuclear attack. This is a rare opportunity to glimpse a somber and alarming period of recent world history, when precautions were taken against the possible threat of nuclear war. The huge four-story bunker, buried deep under a farmer's field, is designed to house more than 500 people and enough supplies for a month in the event of nuclear war. The guided walking tour takes about 1½ hours. Many of the guides used to work in the Diefenbunker before it was decommissioned in 1994. During the tour you will see the blast tunnel and massive blast doors, the CBC radio studio, the Bank of Canada vault that was designed to hold Canada's gold reserves, the War Cabinet room, the decontamination unit, a detailed model of the bunker, a 1-megaton hydrogen "practice bomb," a reconstruction of a family fall-out shelter, and lots more. To get to the Diefenbunker from Ottawa, follow Highway 417 (the Queensway) west, take the Carp–Stittsville exit, and bear right onto Carp Road. Travel about 8 kilometers (5 miles) into the village of Carp. Watch for signs on the left indicating the entrance to the Diefenbunker.

3911 Carp Rd., Carp, ON. ✆ 800/409-1965 or 613/839-0007. Admission C$12 (US$8) adults, C$10 (US$7) seniors and students, C$5 (US$3) children 6–15, free for children 5 and under. Guided tours begin in summer daily at 11am, noon, 1pm, 2pm, and 3pm; in fall, winter, and spring weekdays at 2pm and weekends at 1pm and 2pm.

LaFleche Caves Visit the white marble caverns at LaFleche Caves and explore the large network of domes, rooms, and tunnels that were carved into the rock by the pressure from water and ice during the last Ice Age. The general tour is suitable for all ages and takes about an hour. More adventurous souls can follow an experienced guide on a 3-hour tour of narrow spaces and galleries. The temperature inside the caves remains steady all year-round between 3°C and 7°C (37°F to 45°F). Wear sturdy walking shoes and warm clothing. Guides will provide you with hard hats and headlamps for both tours, as well as with the extra equipment needed for the caving adventure tour. Above ground, enjoy the skating rink, snowshoe trails, and slides in winter and picnic areas and nature trails in summer. Reservations are required for cave tours. To reach LaFleche Caves, take Highway 50 north through Hull, exit on Highway 307 north, and travel to Val-des-Monts. It's about a half-hour drive from Ottawa.

Route 307, Val-des-Monts, PQ. © **877/457-4033** or 819/457-4033. Admission C$12 (US$8) adults, C$8 (US$5) ages 13–18, C$6 (US$4) children 12 and under, C$30 (US$20) family (max. 2 adults and 2 children). Caving Adventure C$45 (US$30) per person. Open year round.

Index

See also Accommodations and Restaurant indexes, below.

GENERAL INDEX

Aboriginal village, 114
Accommodations, 46–64. *See also*
  Accommodations Index
    airport, 63–64
    babysitting, 42
    bed and breakfasts, 7, 47, 53–56, 58,
      59, 60
    camping, 47
    downtown, 48–59
    east, 61–62
    Glebe, 59–61
    hostels, 7, 58–59
    maps, 54–55
    nonsmoking, 47
    nonsmoking rooms, 47
    rack rates, 47
    room rates, 48
    south central, 59–61
    west, 62–63
Afternoon tea, 4
Agricultural museum, 4, 19, 21,
  101–103
Air show, 22
Air travel complaints, 41
Air travel, 26–28
Airport, 41
American Express, 41
Amphibus (water/land tour), 114, 116
Andrew Haydon Park, 122
Animals, farm, 118
Animation festival, 22
Anjali and Company (dance), 142
Arboretum, 101
Area codes, 41
Art supplies, 151

Art Walk (walking tour), 116
ATM networks, 15
ATMs, 41–42
Auto shows, 18, 20
Aviation museum, 4, 105
Aylmer, 166

Baby goods, 151–52
Babysitting, 42
Bank Street Promenade, 148
Baseball, 18–19, 146
Bayshore Shopping Centre, 150
Beaches, 129–30. *See also* Lakes
Beads, 6
Bed and breakfasts, 7, 47, 53–56, 58,
  59, 60
Bicycling. *See* Cycling
Big box stores, 149–50
Billings Estate Museum, 111–12
Bird sanctuary, 171
Birdwatching equipment, 6
Blues festival, 21, 139
Boat show, 18
Boat tours, 2–3, 98
Boating, 130. *See also* Rafting
Bookstores, 4–5, 145, 146, 152
Bowling, 130
Brantwood Park, 122
Brewer Park, 122
Bungee jumping, 174–75
Bus travel, 28–29, 38
Buses
    city, 37
    double decker, 114
    information about public transit, 45
Business hours, 42

Busker festival, 21–22, 140
Bytown Days, 22
Bytown Museum, 112
Bytowne Cinema, 144–45
ByWard Farmer's Market, 3, 6,
   112–13, 148
ByWard Market Auto Classic, 20

Calabogie Peaks, 172–73
Calendar of events, at agriculture
   museum, 102–103
Camera stores, 156
Camp Fortune, 173
Camping gear, 6
Camping shows, 18
Camping, 47
   in Gatineau Park, 167
Canada Agriculture Museum & Central
   Experimental Farms, 101–103
Canada and the World Pavilion,
   107–108
Canada Aviation Museum, 4, 105
Canada Dance Festival, 20
Canada Day Celebrations, 2, 20, 49,
   169
Canada Music Week, 23
Canada Science & Technology
   Museum, 103–104
Canadian Agriculture Museum, 4, 19,
   21
Canadian Children's Museum, 3, 4,
   93–94, 98, 99, 100, 164
Canadian Film Institute Cinema, 145
Canadian Museum of Civilization, 3, 4,
   98–101, 163–64
Canadian Museum of Contemporary
   Photography, 108
Canadian Museum of Nature, 94–95,
   120
Canadian Postal Museum, 98, 100, 108
Canadian Ski Marathon, 18
Canadian Ski Museum, 108
Canadian Tulip Festival, 3–4, 19
Canadian Virtual War Memorial, 109
Canadian War Museum, 109

Capital Classic Show Jumping
   Tournament, 21
Capital Double Decker and Trolley
   Tours, 114
Car travel, 29
Carlingwood Shopping Centre, 150
Carnival of Cultures, 20, 139
Cars
   classic, 19, 20
   renting, 39–40
Caves, 176–77
CDs, 153
Central Canada Exhibition, 21, 139
Centrepointe Theatre, 138
Chamber music festival, 140
Chamber music, 21, 143
Changing of the Guard, 20, 92
Chapters (bookstore), 145, 152
Children's Hospital of Eastern Ontario
   Teddy Bear Picnic, 21
Children's museum, 3, 4, 93–94, 98,
   99, 100, 164
Chocolate factory, 171, 172
Chocolates, 155–56
Christmas carolling, 23
Christmas Lights Across Canada, 23
Christmas stores, 156
Cinemas. See Films
Cisco Systems Bluesfest, 21, 139
CKCU Ottawa Folk Festival, 21, 139
Classes for children, 136
Classic cars, 19, 20
Climate, 17
Clothing stores, 5, 153–55
Coffee shops, 78
Collected Works (bookstore), 146
Comic books, 156
Commissioner's Park, 3, 123
Company of Fools, A, 141
Computer stores, 156
Concerts. See Music events
Confederation Park, 123
Consulates, 43
Conventions, 139
Corel Centre, The, 138
Cosmic Adventures, 128

Cottage show, 18
Craft stores, 6, 157–58
Credit cards, 15–16
Currency, 14–16
Currency exchange, 42
Currency Museum of the Bank of
    Canada, 109–10
Customs regulations, 13–14
Cyberdome, 128–29
Cycling, 40–41, 130–31, 167–68

Dance events, 20, 142–43
Day trips from Ottawa, 162–77
Dentists, 42
Diapers, 151–52
Diefenbunker Cold War Museum, 176
Dining. See Restaurants; Restaurants
    Index
Dinosaurs, 118
Directory assistance, 42
Disabilities, travelers with, 26, 38, 99,
    118
Disability services, 42
Disney paraphernalia, 6
Doctors, 42
Dollhouses, 5, 156
Dolls, 156
Double decker buses, 114
Dow's Lake, 3, 97, 130
Dragon Boat Festival, 20, 139–40
Dramamuse, 141
Driving rules, 40
Drugstores, 42, 156
Dry cleaning, 43

Eastern Ontario maps, 163
Ecomuseum, 164
Edelweiss, 173
Electricity, 43
Electronics stores, 156
Embassies, 43
Emergencies, 43, 44
Entry requirements to Canada, 13–14
Esprit Rafting, 175
Eyeglasses, 43

Fairs, 19, 21, 22, 139
Fall Home Show, 22
Fall Rhapsody, 22
Farmer's markets, 3, 6
Festival 4–15 (Ottawa Festival of the
    Arts for Young Audiences), 19, 140,
    141
Festival Franco-Ontarien, 20
Films, 144–45. See also IMAX theaters
Fireworks, 2
First Nations
    events, 19, 114
    history, 119
Fishing equipment, 5, 157
Fishing, 5–6, 133
Folk festival, 139
Folk music, 21
Fox, Terry, 116, 117
Francophone events, 20
Free activities, 4
Furniture stores, 155

Galleries, 110–11, 118
Games, 6
Games stores, 156
Garden of the Provinces, 123
Garden Party at Rideau Hall, 20
Gardens, 3, 19, 101, 123, 126
Gatineau Hot Air Balloon Festival, 22,
    140
Gatineau, 165–66
Gatineau Park, 4, 127
    camping, 167
    cycling, 167–68
    Fall Rhapsody, 22
    fishing in, 5–6
    hiking, 168–69
    in winter, 169
    Mackenzie King Estate, 166
    mountain biking, 167–68
    special events, 169
    swimming, 169
    wildlife, 166–67
Geological Survey of Canada, 110
Ghosts, 120

Gift stores, 157
Glebe, The, 149
Gloucester Fair, 19
Gloucester Splash Wave Pool, 128
Goods and Services Tax. *See* GST
Government, in Canada, 87–88
Governor General's New Year's Day
    Levee, 17
Governor General's Summer Concerts,
    143
Grayline Sightseeing Tours, 115
Great Canada Theatre Company, 141
Great Canadian Bungee, 174–75
Great Pumpkin Weigh-Off, 22
Greek Summer Festival, 21
Greenbelt, The, 127
GST, 45, 66, 148
Gymboree, 129

Haunted mill, 171
Health concerns, 24–25
Help Santa Toy Parade, 23
Helping Other People Everywhere
    (HOPE), 21
Heritage attractions, 111–14
Heritage House Museum, 171–72
Hershey Canada Chocolate Factory
    Tour, 172
Hiking, 4, 133–34, 168–69
History of Ottawa, 10–11
Hobbies (stores), 157–58
Hockey, 22, 138, 146, 147
Hog's Back Park, 123
Holidays, 17
Home show, 18, 22
Hospitals, 43
Hostels, 7, 58–59
Hot air balloon festival, 22, 140
Hot air ballooning, 118
Hotels. *See* Accommodations;
    Accommodations Index
Hull area, 162–65
Hull
    parks, 164–65
    steam train, 165

Hull-Chelsea-Wakefield Steam Train,
    165

Ice cream, 9, 69, 75, 77, 81
Ice skating. *See* Skating
Ice-cream making, 21
IMAX theaters, 3, 4, 98, 99, 100–101,
    144
Information about events, 137
In-line skating, 130–31
Insects museum, 118
International Student Animation
    Festival of Ottawa, 22
International Youth Orchestra
    Festival, 21
Internet access, 43
Italian Week, 20
Itineraries
    ages 6 to 8, 85
    ages 8 to 10, 85–86
    preschoolers, 84–85
    preteens, 86

Jazz festival, 21, 140

Keskinada Loppet, 18
Kids Help Phone, 43
Kiwanis Music Festival, 18

Lacrosse, 23, 138, 146
LaFleche Caves, 176–77
Lakes, 3, 97, 130, 166, 167, 168
Landsdowne Park, 138
Laundry, 43
Laurier House, 113
Layout of Ottawa, 32–33
Le Grand Splash Water Park, 173
Les Petits Ballets, 143
Libraries, 43
Library of Parliament, 88
Liquor, 43–44
Little Italy, 36
Locks, 97–98

Logan Hall, Geological Survey of Canada, 110

Mackenzie King Estate, 166
Madawasa Kanu Center, 175
Magazines, 44
Mail, 44
Major's Hill Park, 123
Malls, 150–51
Manotick 170–71
Map stores, 6, 158
Map
    accommodations, 54–55
    attractions for kids, 90–91
    of Eastern Ontario, 163
    of parks, 124–25
    purchasing, 44
    of restaurant locations, 72–73
    sources for, 121–22
    specialty stores, 158
Markets, 112–13, 158. *See also*
    ByWard Farmer's Market; Farmer's
    markets
Mayfair Theatre, 145
Medical concerns, 24–25
Medical services, 42
Members of Parliament, 44
Merrickville, 171
Midway Family Fun Park, 129
Military history, 120
Models, 6
Mont Cascades, 173–74
Mont Ste-Marie, 174
Mooney's Bay Park, 123
Mother's Day Celebration, 19
Mount Pakenham, 174
Mountain biking, 167–68
Movies. *See* Films
Museum of Canadian Scouting, 110
Museum of Nature, 4
Museum shops, 158
Museums, 3, 4, 19, 21, 93–95, 98–105,
    107–12, 118, 120, 158, 163–64,
    171–72, 176

Music events, 18, 20, 21, 23, 139, 140,
    141, 142, 143
Musical instruments, 158
Musical Ride, 4

NAC Dance Productions, 142–43
NAC English Theatre, 140
NAC French Theatre, 140–41
NAC Orchestra, 143
National Arts Centre, 138–39, 140–41
National Capital Air Show, 22
National Capital Dragon Boat
    Festival, 20
National Capital Greenbelt, 127
National Capital Race Weekend, 19
National Gallery of Canada, 110–11
National Library of Canada, 111
Nature museum, 94–95, 120
Nature stores, 159
Neighborhoods
    ByWard Market & Downtown, 33
    Downtown, west of canal, 36
    Glebe, 36–37
    Little Italy, 36
    map, 34–35
    Somerset Heights, 36
    Somerset Village, 36
    Sussex Drive, 33–36
    Westboro Village, 36
Nepean Museum, 111
New Edinburgh Park, 123
New Year's Day, 17
Newspapers, 44

Oakroads (sightseeing tour), 115
Odawa Spring Pow Wow, 19
Odyssey Theatre, 141–42
Opera Lyra Ottawa, 141
Orient Express Rickshaws, 115
Orpheus Musical Theatre Society,
    142
Ottawa 67's, 22, 147
Ottawa Boat, Sportsmen's & Cottage
    Show, 18

Ottawa Chamber Music Festival, 21, 140

Ottawa Chamber Music Society Concert Series, 143

Ottawa Congress Centre, 139

Ottawa Family Cinema, 145

Ottawa Festival of the Arts for Young Audiences. *See* Festival 4–15

Ottawa International Animation Festival, 22

Ottawa International Jazz Festival, 21, 140

Ottawa Little Theatre, 142

Ottawa Lynx, 18, 146

Ottawa Paddlesport & Outdoor Adventure Show, 18

Ottawa Public Library, 146

Ottawa Rebel, 23, 146

Ottawa River, 2–3, 97

Ottawa Riverboat Company, 116–17

Ottawa Senators, 22, 146

Ottawa Spring Home Show, 18

Ottawa Spring RV and Camping Show, 18

Ottawa Symphony Orchestra, 143

Ottawa Walks (walking tour), 116

Ottawa-Hull International Auto Show, 18

Outdoor gear, 158–59

Owl Rafting, 175

Parades, 23

Parking, 40, 46–47

Parks, 3, 4, 5, 6, 22, 122–27, 138, 166–69

Parliament Buildings, 3, 88

Parliament Hill, 87–93

   Centre Block, 88

   Changing of the Guard, 92

   East Block, 88

   events, 19, 20

   Library of Parliament, 88

   Peace Tower, 3, 88

   self-guided walking tour, 116

   Sound and Light on the Hill, 92

Party supplies, 159

Path of Heroes (walking tour), 116

Paul's Boat Lines, 117

Peace Tower, 3, 88

Photography museum, 108

Photography workshops, 120

Pizza, 10, 68, 70

Place D'Orléans, 150

Playgrounds, indoor, 128–29

Police, 44

Pool safety, 47, 52

Pools

   community, 128

   in hotels, 47, 52

Post offices, 44

Postage, 44

Postal museum, 3, 98, 100, 108

Postal service, 120

Public transportation, 26, 37–41, 45

Pumpkin-growing contest, 22

Puppet shows, 145

Racing, 19

Rack rates, 47

Radio, 44

Rafting, 175–76

Rag and Bone Puppet Theatre, 145

Rail travel, 28

Railway museum, 172

Rates, rack, 47

RCMP Musical Ride, 19

   centre, 4

   stables, 106–107

Records, 153

Restaurants

   afternoon tea, 71

   American, 71–74

   Asian, 80

   bagels, 78, 79

   bakery style, 75, 76, 78

   bistro, 70–71

   chains, 70

   Chinese, 80

   coffee shops, 78

   crepes, 75

deli, 69
desserts, 76
diner, 69, 70
fusion, 66, 68
ice cream, 69, 75, 77, 81
Indian, 68, 74
Italian, 74–75, 77–78, 81
maps, 72–73
Mediterranean, 67–68
pancakes, 75
pizza, 10, 68, 70
seafood, 70, 71, 77
takeout, 69, 75, 78, 79, 81
Tex-Mex, 70, 81
tipping, 45, 66
vegetarian, 76, 82
Vietnamese, 80
Rickshaws, 115
Rideau Canal Museum, 172
Rideau Canal Skateway, 134–35
Rideau Canal, 96, 170
skating, 2, 134–35
Rideau Centre, 150–51
Rideau Falls Park, 126
Rideau Falls, 96
Rideau Hall, 20, 113–14
garden party, 20
teddy bear picnic, 21
Rideau Locks, 170
Rideau River, 96
Rideau Valley, 170–72
River Run Rafting and Paddle Center, 176
Rock hounding, 120
Rockcliffe Park, 126
Rockcliffe Rockeries, 126
Room rates, 48
Royal Canadian Mint, 104
Royal Canadian Mounted Police, 106.
 See also RCMP

Safety concerns, 24–25, 44
Safety in hotel pools, 47, 52
St. Laurent Shopping Centre, 151
St. Luke Park, 126

Salamander Theatre for Young Audiences, 142
Santa Claus Parade, 23
Savoy Society, 142
Science museum, 120
Scouting museum, 110
Seasonal events, 17–23, 139–40
Sheep Shearing Festival, 19
Shoe stores, 159
Shopping
areas, 148–49
art supplies, 151
baby goods, 151–52
big box stores, 149–50
birdwatching equipment, 6
bookstores, 4–5, 152
cameras, 156
CDs, 153
children's clothing, 5, 153–55
chocolates, 155–56
Christmas stores, 156
clothes, 5, 153–55
comic books, 156
computers, 156
crafts, 6, 157–58
Disney paraphernalia, 6
dollhouses, 5, 156
dolls, 5, 156
drugstores, 156
electronics, 156
fishing equipment, 5, 157
furniture, 155
games, 156
gift stores, 157
hobbies, 157–58
malls, 150–51
maps, 6, 158
markets, 158
models, 6
at museums, 158
musical instruments, 158
nature stores, 159
outdoor gear, 6, 158–59
party supplies, 159
records, 53
shoes, 159

sports equipment, 160
tapes, 153
theme stores, 160
toys, 5, 160–61
trading cards, 156
videos, 161
Show jumping, 21
Sightseeing. See Tours
Skating, 2, 134–35
Ski and Snowboard Show, 22
Ski museum, 108
Ski Vorlage, 174
Skiing, 18, 132–33, 172–74
Smiths Falls Railway Museum, 172
Smiths Falls, 171–72
Snowboarding, 22, 136, 172–74
Sound and Light on the Hill, 92
Sparks Street Mall International
    Busker Festival, 21–22, 140
Sparks Street Mall, 149
Sports. See also Baseball; Hockey;
    Lacrosse; Skiing; Snowboarding
        spectator, 146–47
Sports equipment stores, 160
Sports equipment show, 22
Sportsmen's show, 18
Steam train, 165
Story telling, 145–46
Strathcona Park, 126
Supreme Court of Canada, 111
Swimming, 129–30, 135, 169. See also
    Pools

Tapes, 153
Tara Players, The, 142
Taxes, 44–45
    on meals, 66
    on purchases, 148
Taxis, 38
Teddy bear picnic, 21
Telephones, 45
Tennis, 135
Theaters, 138–42, 145
Theme stores, 160
Thirteen Strings (chamber music), 143

Tickets, for events, 137
Tipping, 45, 66
Tour buses, 38–39
Tours
    air, 118
    boat, 2–3, 98
    bus, 114
    chocolate factory, 172
    double decker, 114
    driving, self-guided, 119
    factory, 118
    of Parliament Hill, 89–89
    self-guided, 89
    trolley, 114
    walking, guided, 115–16
    walking, self-guided, 116
    water, 116–17
Toy stores, 5, 160–61
Toys, 6
Trade shows, 139
Trading cards, 156
Train museums, 120
Train travel, 28
    light rail, 37–38
Trains, steam, 165
Trans Canada Trail, 134
Travel agencies, 161
Travel insurance, 25
Travel
    by air, 29
    by bus, 29
    by car, 29, 39
    with kids, 29
    by rail, 29
Traveler's checks, 15
Tulip festival, 3–4, 19
Turtle Island Aboriginal Village, 114

Underground bunker, 176
Unisong (concerts), 20
University sports teams, 147

Vegetarian restaurants, 76, 82
Video stores, 161
Vincent Massey Park, 126

Visitor information, 12–13, 31–32
Volleyball tournament, 21

Walking tours, 115–16
War memorial, 109
War museum, 109
Water activities, 128, 129–30
Water parks, 173
Waterways, 96–98
Watson's Mill, 170, 171
Wave pool, 128
Weather forecasts, 45
Weather, 17

Websites
    for travel planning, 27
    virtual war memorial, 109
Wellington Street West, 149
Westboro Village, 149
White-water rafting, 175–76
Wilderness Tours, 176
Wildlife, Gatineau Park, 166–67
Wind Odyssey: Sound and Light on
    Parliament Hill, 19
Winter activities, 18, 22, 132–36, 169,
    172–74
Winterlude, 18
WordPerfect Theatre, 139
Workshops for children, 120, 136

ACCOMMODATIONS

Adam's Airport Inn, 64
Albert at Bay Suite Hotel, 49
Aristocrat Suite Hotel, 49
Arosa Suites Hotel, 53
Auberge "The King Edward" B&B, 58
Best Luxury Hotel, 6
Best Western Barons Hotel, 8, 62
Best Western Macies Hotel, 62–63
Best Western Victoria Park Suites, 7, 49–50
Blue Spruces B&B, 59–60
By-the-Way B&B, 60
Capital Hill Hotel & Suites, 52
Carleton University Tour and Conference Centre, 60–61
Cartier Place and Towers Suite Hotels, 7–8, 50
Chimo Hotel, 61
Comfort Inn East, 61
Crowne Plaza Ottawa, 50

Delta Ottawa Hotel and Suites, 48
Embassy Hotel and Suites, 58
Fairmont Chateau Laurier, 4, 6–7, 56
Hampton Inn, 8, 61–62
Les Suites Hotel Ottawa, 57
Lord Elgin Hotel, 50
Marriott Residence Inn Ottawa, 7, 51
Mid-Towne Heritage B&B, 7, 53
Minto Place Suite Hotel, 8, 51–52
Natural Choice/4Nature B&B, 53–54
Novotel Ottawa, 57
Ottawa International Hostel, 7, 58
Quality Hotel Ottawa Downtown, 58
Ramada Hotel & Suites Ottawa, 53
Rose on Colonel By, A, 60
Sheraton Ottawa Hotel, 52
Southway Inn, The, 63–64
Travelodge Hotel Ottawa West, 63
WelcomINNS, 62
Westin Ottawa, 7, 57

RESTAURANTS

BeaverTails, 75
Black Tomato, 10, 70–71
Bravo Bravo, 67–68
Café Colonnade, 10, 68
Canal Ritz, 10, 77–78
Cow's Ottawa, 75
Creperie, The, 75
Dunn's Famous Delicatessen, 69
Elgin Street Diner, 4, 69
Fettucine's, 69
Fish Market, The, 10, 71
Flippers, 77
French Baker, The/Le Boulanger
   Français, 9, 75–76
Green Door, The, 82
Hard Rock Café, 71–74
Haveli, 74
Kettleman's Bagels, 8, 78
L'Amuse Gueule, 9, 78
La Roma, 81
Le Moulin de Provence, 9, 76
Lone Star Cafe, The, 81–82
Luciano's, 9, 81
Mamma Grazzi's Kitchen, 9, 74
Marchélino, 9, 76
New Mee Fung, 8, 80
Oh So Good Desserts Café, 76
Oregano's Pasta Market, 74–75
Ottawa Bagelshop & Deli, 79
Parma Ravioli, 79
Pasticceria Gelateria Italiani Ltd., 81
Peace Garden Cafe, 76
Piccolo Grande, 77
Pure Gelato, 9, 69
Roses Café, The, 68
Savana Café, 68
Shanghai Restaurant, 80
Wild Oat Bakery and Natural Foods,
   78
Yangtze, 80
Zoe's, 4, 71

Canada for the whole family!

Frommer's®
W I T H   K I D S

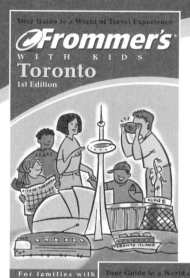

Your Guide to a World of Travel Experience

Frommer's®
W I T H   K I D S
Toronto
1st Edition

For families with

Your Guide to a World of Travel Experience

Frommer's®
W I T H   K I D S
Vancouver
1st Edition

with kids of all ages

Your Guide to a World of Travel Experience

Frommer's®
W I T H   K I D S
Ottawa
1st Edition

For families with kids of all ages

FROMMER'S® COMPLETE TRAVEL GUIDES

Alaska
Amsterdam
Argentina & Chile
Arizona
Atlanta
Australia
Austria
Bahamas
Barcelona, Madrid & Seville
Beijing
Belgium, Holland &
  Luxembourg
Bermuda
Boston
British Columbia & the
  Canadian Rockies
Budapest & the Best of Hungary
California
Canada
Cancún, Cozumel & the
  Yucatán
Cape Cod, Nantucket &
  Martha's Vineyard
Caribbean
Caribbean Cruises & Ports
  of Call
Caribbean Ports of Call
Carolinas & Georgia
Chicago
China
Colorado
Costa Rica
Denmark
Denver, Boulder & Colorado
  Springs
England
Europe

European Cruises & Ports of Call
Florida
France
Germany
Greece
Greek Islands
Hawaii
Hong Kong
Honolulu, Waikiki & Oahu
Ireland
Israel
Italy
Jamaica
Japan
Las Vegas
London
Los Angeles
Maryland & Delaware
Maui
Mexico
Montana & Wyoming
Montréal & Québec City
Munich & the Bavarian Alps
Nashville & Memphis
Nepal
New England
New Mexico
New Orleans
New York City
New Zealand
Nova Scotia, New Brunswick &
  Prince Edward Island
Oregon
Paris
Philadelphia & the Amish
  Country
Portugal

Prague & the Best of the Czech
  Republic
Provence & the Riviera
Puerto Rico
Rome
San Antonio & Austin
San Diego
San Francisco
Santa Fe, Taos & Albuquerque
Scandinavia
Scotland
Seattle & Portland
Shanghai
Singapore & Malaysia
South Africa
Southeast Asia
South Florida
South Pacific
Spain
Sweden
Switzerland
Texas
Thailand
Tokyo
Toronto
Tuscany & Umbria
USA
Utah
Vancouver & Victoria
Vermont, New Hampshire
  & Maine
Vienna & the Danube Valley
Virgin Islands
Virginia
Walt Disney World & Orlando
Washington, D.C.
Washington State

FROMMER'S® DOLLAR-A-DAY GUIDES

Australia from $50 a Day
California from $70 a Day
Caribbean from $70 a Day
England from $70 a Day
Europe from $70 a Day

Florida from $70 a Day
Hawaii from $70 a Day
Ireland from $60 a Day
Italy from $70 a Day
London from $85 a Day

New York from $80 a Day
Paris from $80 a Day
San Francisco from $60 a Day
Washington, D.C.,
  from $70 a Day

FROMMER'S® PORTABLE GUIDES

Acapulco, Ixtapa &
  Zihuatanejo
Alaska Cruises & Ports
  of Call
Amsterdam
Australia's Great Barrier Reef
Bahamas
Baja & Los Cabos
Berlin
Boston
California Wine Country
Charleston & Savannah
Chicago

Dublin
Hawaii: The Big Island
Hong Kong
Houston
Las Vegas
London
Los Angeles
Maine Coast
Maui
Miami
New Orleans
New York City
Paris

Phoenix & Scottsdale
Portland
Puerto Rico
Puerto Vallarta, Manzanillo &
  Guadalajara
San Diego
San Francisco
Seattle
Sydney
Tampa & St. Petersburg
Vancouver
Venice
Washington, D.C.

FROMMER'S® NATIONAL PARK GUIDES

Family Vacations in the
  National Parks
Grand Canyon

National Parks of the American
  West
Rocky Mountain
Yellowstone & Grand Teton

Yosemite & Sequoia/
  Kings Canyon
Zion & Bryce Canyon

FROMMER'S® MEMORABLE WALKS

Chicago
London

New York
Paris

San Francisco
Washington, D.C.

FROMMER'S® GREAT OUTDOOR GUIDES

Arizona & New Mexico
New England

Northern California
Southern California & Baja

Southern New England
Vermont & New Hampshire

FROMMER'S® BORN TO SHOP GUIDES

Born to Shop: France
Born to Shop: Hong Kong,
    Shanghai & Beijing

Born to Shop: Italy
Born to Shop: London

Born to Shop: New York
Born to Shop: Paris

FROMMER'S® IRREVERENT GUIDES

Amsterdam
Boston
Chicago
Las Vegas
London

Los Angeles
Manhattan
New Orleans
Paris
San Francisco

Seattle & Portland
Vancouver
Walt Disney World
Washington, D.C.

FROMMER'S® BEST-LOVED DRIVING TOURS

America
Britain
California
Florida

France
Germany
Ireland
Italy

New England
Scotland
Spain
Western Europe

THE UNOFFICIAL GUIDES®

Bed & Breakfasts in California
Bed & Breakfasts in
    New England
Bed & Breakfasts in the North-
    west
Bed & Breakfasts in Southeast
Beyond Disney
Branson, Missouri
California with Kids
Chicago
Cruises
Disneyland
Florida with Kids

Golf Vacations in the
    Eastern U.S.
The Great Smoky &
    Blue Ridge Mountains
Inside Disney
Hawaii
Las Vegas
London
Mid-Atlantic with Kids
Mini Las Vegas
Mini-Mickey
New England with Kids

New Orleans
New York City
Paris
San Francisco
Skiing in the West
Southeast with Kids
Walt Disney World
Walt Disney World for
    Grown-ups
Walt Disney World for Kids
Washington, D.C.
World's Best Diving Vacations

SPECIAL-INTEREST TITLES

Frommer's Britain's Best Bed & Breakfasts and
    Country Inns
Frommer's France's Best Bed & Breakfasts and
    Country Inns
Frommer's Italy's Best Bed & Breakfasts and
    Country Inns
Frommer's Caribbean Hideaways
Frommer's Adventure Guide to Australia &
    New Zealand
Frommer's Adventure Guide to Central America
Frommer's Adventure Guide to India & Pakistan
Frommer's Adventure Guide to South America
Frommer's Adventure Guide to Southeast Asia
Frommer's Adventure Guide to Southern Africa
Frommer's Gay & Lesbian Europe
Frommer's Exploring America by RV
Hanging Out in England

Hanging Out in Europe
Hanging Out in France
Hanging Out in Ireland
Hanging Out in Italy
Hanging Out in Spain
Israel Past & Present
Frommer's The Moon
Frommer's New York City with Kids
The New York Times' Guide to Unforgettable
    Weekends
Places Rated Almanac
Retirement Places Rated
Frommer's Road Atlas Britain
Frommer's Road Atlas Europe
Frommer's Washington, D.C., with Kids
Frommer's What the Airlines Never Tell You